Built on the Foundation
of the Apostles and Prophets

Sola Scriptura in Context

"Built on the Foundation of the Apostles and Prophets"

Sola Scriptura in Context

Westfield House International Symposium

15–18 August 2012

Editor: Tapani Simojoki

The Evangelical Lutheran Church of England
North European Luther Academy

Published in 2013
by The Evangelical Lutheran Church of England
28 Huntingdon Road
Cambridge
CB3 0HH
United Kingdom

www.westfieldhouse.org.uk

Cover Illustration: Kimmo Pälikkö

ISBN-10: 0-902388-06-1
ISBN-13: 978-0-902388-06-2

Contents

List of Contributors

THE REV. JOHN BOMBARO, PhD
Pastor, Lutheran Church—Missouri Synod, USA; lecturer in theology and religious studies at the University of San Diego

ADAM FRANCISCO, DPhil
Associate Professor of History and Political Thought, Concordia University Irvine, California, USA

THE REV. BORIS GUNJEVIĆ, PhD
Pastor, Evangelical Church in the Republic of Croatia

DANIEL JOHANSSON, PhD
Lecturer, Lutheran School of Theology, Gothenburg

THE REV. JEFFREY J. KLOHA, PhD
Associate Professor of Exegetical Theology, Concordia Seminary, St. Louis, USA

THE REV. JONATHAN MUMME, Drs.
Tutor in Theology and Church History, Westfield House, Cambridge, UK

THE REV. JOSEPH RANDRIANASOLO, PhD
Professor of Systematic Theology, Lutheran Graduate School of Theology at Ivory-Avaratra, Fianarantsoa, and Rector of the Lutheran Institute of Management and Entrepreneurship, Madagascar

THE REV. PROF. DAVID P. SCAER, ThD
Professor of Systematic and Biblical Theology, Concordia Theological Seminary, Fort Wayne, Indiana, USA

THE REV. ANSSI SIMOJOKI, ThD
Pastor, Evangelical Lutheran Mission Diocese, Finland

THE REV. TAPANI SIMOJOKI, STM
Pastor, The Evangelical Lutheran Church of England, UK

REV. MARTTI VAAHTORANTA, ThD
Pastor, Evangelical Lutheran Mission Diocese, Finland

THE REV. ARMIN WENZ, ThD
Pastor, Independent Evangelical Lutheran Church (SELK), Germany

Preface

In August 2007, Westfield House, the House of Theological Studies of the Evangelical Lutheran Church of England (ELCE), received a very generous grant from the Marvin M. Schwan Charitable Foundation, which enabled it to hold the inaugural Westfield House International Symposium. A small group of invited delegates from four continents gathered together to tell of their churches and to hear of one another's churches, to pray and hear God's word together, and to study matters relating to ecclesiology. That Symposium was well received by the participants and turned out to be fruitful in fostering new relationships within the Lutheran world.

Apart from study, one clear intention of the Westfield House Symposium was to cut across historic dividing lines and barriers amongst Lutherans. This intention grew out of a conviction that many of these dividing lines emerged in a world that is increasingly vanishing. We no longer live in a world where membership in a particular church body is an accurate predictor of the theological position of a person. Historically 'liberal' churches frequently have within them minority groups that are staunchly 'confessional', and *vice versa*. As such, it is of greater importance than ever that like-minded people—in this case, specifically, confessional Lutherans—find one another wherever they can be found in order to build up the body of Christ together, walking together into an unknown future.

In August 2012, the second Westfield House International Symposium gathered in Cambridge. This time, the Symposium was held as a free conference in conjunction with the North European Luther Academy (NELA). As a result, of the 50 participants, both clergy and laity, roughly a half came from the Nordic countries of Finland, Sweden, Norway and Denmark. The remainder represented Canada, USA, Japan, South Africa, Madagascar, Tanzania, Russia, Estonia, Latvia, Croatia, Germany and the United Kingdom. Owing to insuperable challenges created by representatives of the UK Foreign and Commonwealth Office, invited guests from the Democratic Republic of Congo, Congo–Brazzaville and Rwanda were unable to board their flights. Again, the participants represented churches from the Lutheran World Federation, the International Lutheran Council or, in some cases, both. Some held the highest offices of their churches, some were leaders of seminaries, others were individual clergymen, yet others interested laymen and women.

Having been well-received, the basic structure of the first Symposium was replicated. Each day began and closed with a liturgical prayer service with a homily. There were six main papers, each of which was followed by a prepared response. The time allocated to these prepared presentations was matched by time given to open discussion. In addition to these papers, representatives of several Lutheran seminaries and organisations introduced their institutions. The final event was a panel discussion of four church leaders (an archbishop, a bishop, a chairman and a dean—a delicious picture of the freedom in ecclesiastical customs that is so important to churches of the Augsburg Confession!). And, naturally, plenty of time was devoted to eating and drinking, which are essential not only for refreshment but also for what is nowadays called 'networking', and for theological rumination. Indeed, it has been said that what happens over cups of coffee is of greater value than what takes place in the lecture theatre— at most, only a slight exaggeration.

What is gathered in the following pages are the main papers presented at the Symposium, together with the prepared responses. It was intended originally to prepare a summary of the discussion following each paper, since each discussion was extremely fruitful in bringing clarity, critique and further elaboration and development to what was presented. This was truly a symposium, not merely a conference. Unfortunately, the resources to do that were not available, and the decision was made not to delay publication any further. Likewise, the homilies had to be omitted for the same reason, together with the panel discussion. Should there be sufficient demand, perhaps a future edition may fill in this regrettable lacuna.

In the absence of this material, I should add a few comments about some of the discussion that did take place. First, some of the discussion was remarkably free of controversy. Both Dr. Kloha and Dr. Francisco were blessed with respondents who were largely in agreement with them, and with an audience that was almost exclusively appreciative of their contribution. In the case of Dr. Scaer's and Dr. Simojoki's presentations, their respondents posed some critical questions, which were answered in the discussion that followed, apparently to the satisfaction of all parties. Likewise, Dr. Wenz faced some robust criticism as well as appreciation from his respondent, some of which was based more on what was he had left unsaid rather than what he proposed. The discussion gave him the opportunity to respond to these questions.

Finally, owing to a number of factors beyond the control of the organisers, there was no prepared response to Dr. Bombaro's presenation. This was unfortunate, since this paper elicited a stronger reaction than anything else at the entire Symposium. Above all, a concern was expressed that Dr. Bombaro was verging dangerously close to Gospel reductionism—a charge he categorically denies. Some of the notes in the printed version presented in this volume reflect the lively discussion that followed the presentation. Again, it may be possible to give an outline of this discussion in a future edition.

The papers presented in this volume appear in the form that their authors have submitted them. Orthography and punctuation have been made consistent with British standards. The style of references has likewise been standardised as far as possible. Whatever inconsistencies do remain is the responsibility of the undersigned. Naturally, the views presented are those of the authors.

In many ways, Cambridge is at the centre of the Lutheran world, on the Western edge of Europe, roughly equidistant from Western Asia, East Africa and North America. This fact alone made it both natural and possible to draw together participants from three of the four corners of the round earth. However, such an enterprise is only possible in practice if sufficient financial resources are available. Many of the participants came from churches that are impoverished. The ELCE itself would not be able to subsidise travel to enable the Symposium to take place in the intended form, and therefore to fulfil its unique rôle. The organisers are therefore profoundly grateful to the Board of the Marvin M. Schwan Foundation for their generous support of the second Westfield House International Symposium, without which it could never have taken place.

Above all, thanks are due to Almighty God for His faithful care of His holy Church. It is my prayer that this volume, and the Symposium out of which it has sprung, may serve to strengthen God's people and bring glory to His holy name.

Michaelmas 2013
Tapani Simojoki

Part I

Was ist das? The Nature and Basis of Biblical Hermeneutics

Chapter 1

Was ist das? The Nature and Basis of Biblical Hermeneutics

Rev. Dr. Jeffrey Kloha

As I expound [the Psalter], I do not want anyone to suppose that I shall accomplish what none of the most holy and learned theologians have ever accomplished before, namely, to understand and teach the correct meaning of the Psalter in all particulars. It is enough to have understood some of the psalms, and those only in part. The Spirit reserves much for Himself, so that we may always remain His pupils. There is much that He reveals only to lure us on, much that He gives only to stir us up. And, as Augustine has put it surely if no human being has ever spoken in such a way that everyone understood him in all particulars, how much more is it true that the Holy Spirit alone has an understanding of all His own words! Therefore I must openly admit that I do not know whether I have the accurate interpretation of the psalms or not, though I do not doubt that the one I set forth is an orthodox one.[1]

By 1519, when Luther began his lectures on the Psalms in Wittenberg, he had abandoned the fourfold-sense approach to the Scriptures. Here he expounds the

---

[1] Martin Luther, Preface to *Operationes in Psalmos* [1519] in *Luther's Works*, vol. 14 (ed. Jaroslav Pelikan and Daniel E. Poellot; St. Louis: Concordia Publishing House, 1958), 284--85.

"literal sense" (p. 285). Yet he admits that he cannot claim to have "completely un-derstood even a single psalm" (p. 285). Perhaps even less confidently he continues:

> I have now come to the conclusion that as long as someone else's inter-pretation is pious, one should not reject it unless he wants his own to be rejected in turn, according to "the law of the fang". One falls short in some ways, another in more ways. I see some things that blessed Au-gustine did not see; on the other hand, I know that others will see many things that I do not see. What recourse do we have but to be of mutual help to one another and to forgive those who fall, since we ourselves have already fallen or are about to fall?[2]

Although Luther is writing prior to the Enlightenment, Modernism, and Post-Modernism, he recognizes his limitations and the tentativeness of his interpretation, indeed the inability to do anything except express what he is able at that moment. Similar thoughts are expressed in his preface to the 1519 Galatians commentary, concerning which he says:

> A slight thing it is indeed. It is not so much a commentary as a testi-mony of my faith in Christ, lest perhaps I have run in vain and have not adequately grasped Paul's meaning (Gal 2:2). For here, because it is God's affair and surely of the utmost importance, I am eager to be in-structed by any child. I, too, would certainly have preferred to wait for the commentaries promised long ago by Erasmus, a man pre-eminent in theology and impervious to envy. But since he is postponing this (God grant it may not be for long), the situation which you see forces me to come before the public. I know that I am a child and unlearned, but in spite of this (so bold I may be) I am devoted to Christian piety and instruction.[3]

For Luther, his exposition will have value not because it is *the* correct interpreta-tion—for others will surpass his—but because he is "devoted to Christian piety and instruction" . If he, the reader, is properly formed, then he will be able to read faith-fully, if not perfectly.

---

[2] *Ibid.*, 285

[3] Martin Luther, *Lectures on Galatians*, trans. Richard Jungkuntz, in *Luther's Works*, vol. 27 (ed. Jaroslav Pelikan and Walter A Hanson; St. Louis: Concordia Publishing House, 1964), 159–60.

1 Definition of Theological Hermeneutics

Was ist das? The phrase is almost untranslatable into English. I wonder if its traditional rendering, "what does this mean" is no longer satisfactory. When most
people hear this phrase, I fear that they hear "meaning" and think of some kind of
abstract, cognitive truth that is floating around somewhere. But in Luther's catechism, "meaning" is not abstract and cognitive. When I first glanced the title I was
to consider for this conference I thought that it I was to consider *"Was ist dasein?"*
and panic set in that I would have to try to sort out Heidegger.[4] But the catechism does not encourage speculation on existence or awareness. Rather, when given
a credal, biblical statement, the "meaning" is that we *do* something, and *do not do*
other things. "Thou shalt not kill" does not invite speculation as to the meaning of
the word "kill" and then decide how to "apply" the abstract notion of killing. "What
does this mean?" Simply to fear and love of God so that we do not hurt nor harm
our neighbour in his body, but help and befriend him in every bodily need.

Notice that there is a "theology" inherent in these explanations. Luther's "theology" does not begin with an assertion that the Bible is God's Word, and as such
must simply be obeyed as a divine command that reveals inscrutable, divine will.
Rather, he explains the Scriptures as part of a narrative: Christ has come, Christ has
risen, Christ will come again; and by Christ's Word in which he continues to speak
and the sacraments in which he works, his Spirit has laid claim to me and given me
new life. The new life is imperfect in this age, but is nevertheless anticipatory of and,
in some ways, participatory in the age to come. The Scriptures, including the commandments (such as "Thou shalt not kill" form us to live in a certain way. There is
a goal, a *telos*, to the Scriptures. It is God's goal. "Theological Hermeneutics" seeks
to frame our hearing of the Scriptures so that God's work is accomplished in and
among us.

If God is at work, though, why do different "meanings" result from the same
text? Individualized interpretation is a relatively new phenomenon in the life of
the church. Prior to the Reformation, there was no "Bible"—66 books, under one
cover, easily (or at all) accessible to the average person. Before Wycliffe and Luther
and Tyndale and dozens of other individuals whose names are not so well known put
their lives at risk, the Scriptures were unavailable to the vast majority of the Baptised.
Partly this was the result of economics and technology—a hand-copied biblical manuscript was fabulously expensive, and even Gutenberg's Bible (in Latin, remember)

---

[4]See Umberto Eco, *Kant and the Platypus: Essays on Language and Cognition* (trans. Alistair
McEwen; San Diego: Harcourt, 1997), 11, 28–30.

cost about the same as a house in the nice part of town. As great a hindrance was that most people could not read at all. There was no public education system and the church did not have schools for the laity. To hear from God, one had to trust what his representative, be it pope, council, bishop, priest, or friar, said on his behalf. This could be good, or it could be very bad, depending on how faithful all those popes and councils were. By the early 16th century, the teaching far to often did not match up with the Scripture's message. There was more preaching of indulgences than of Gospel; in fact, Gutenberg himself made far more money printing indulgences than he did printing Bibles.

But the great flow of history that came together in the early 16th century led to the rise of technologies that could cheaply produce printed books, a middle-class that could afford Bibles and education, and a desire to make God's Word available, as Erasmus described it, to every ploughboy and weaver at her loom. So Luther took up his lexica and grammar books and translated into German; Tyndale, inspired by Luther, produced the New Testament and parts of the Old Testament in English before e was tracked down and murdered. What we take for granted today—the ability to read the Bible for ourselves, individually and privately, sitting at our tables or in our reading chair or in our study—has been a part of the life of the church for only about 20 percent of the church's history since the outpouring of the Spirit at Pentecost.

So now everyone can read the Bible. Is this good? Our instinctive answer is, of course, yes! Print Bibles by the millions. Put them in hotel rooms. Give them away to visitors to a worship service. Pass them out at county fairs. Get the word out as far and as wide as possible—on brochures, coffee mugs, web pages, billboards, everywhere.

Or, perhaps not. Take a look at this billboard, which appeared along American highways in the Spring of 2012:

You cannot not respond viscerally, revoltingly, automatically to that billboard. One writer offered this explanation for the problem:

The problem with this is that the sign shows what is lacking in the complaints by village atheists. First, there is something we call "biblical hermeneutics", which is the art and science of biblical interpretation. Do atheists really want to take the time to understand and learn about how to interpret the Bible? Probably not. If atheists truly care about understanding biblical passages, they should take the time to learn some of the basics of hermeneutics. Otherwise, signs like these make them look like they just want to present a distortion of the Christian faith which is not backed up by proper research.

I think I understand how this writer is attempting resolve the "problem"—learn the "rules", and you won' make these kinds of mistakes. Such "solutions", however, leave several problems unresolved. First, the Bible does not come with any "rules". There is no book called "hermeneutics" standing after Malachi or Revelation from which we can cite chapter and verse to find the "rules" for reading properly. Consequently, all the "rules" are made up. We made them up; we inherited them from people like Irenaeus and Origen and Augustine and Tychonius and Flacius and Voelz. Many are helpful, of course, many have stood the test of time, but others are not. They are all the result of the trial-and-error (at times it seems, mostly error) of thousands upon thousands of readers over thousands of years.

Second, I would like us to use more care when we use terms like "hermeneutics". "Hermeneutics" is not "advanced rules" for interpretation. Hermeneutics is not the equivalent of a great big, bloated, Microsoft Windows -sized program that uses all

7

the rules and all the if-then statements to crunch a biblical text and spit out the right "interpretation" on your screen. A standard resource in biblical studies provides a helpful definition of "hermeneutics":

> "Hermeneutics" denotes critical reflection upon processes of interpre-
> tation and understanding, especially the interpretation of biblical texts
> or texts that originate from within other cultures. However, this may
> include all kinds of communicative processes, from signs and visual art
> to institutions and literary phenomena.[5]

Similarly, Voelz maintains this distinction between "exegesis" and "hermeneut-ics": "The actual interpretation of the Scriptures is called exegesis. The study of the principles of interpretation, the theory which stands behind the actual perform-ance of exegesis, is hermeneutics." The reason that study of hermeneutics is neces-sary, he notes, is because the diversity of interpretations are caused by the conscious or unconscious decisions made by the *interpreter* about how to approach the text. This includes assumptions about matters which will be widely agreed upon (such as grammatical matters), others will be less widely shared, such as linguistic theory, understanding of the historical nature and setting of a text, view of revelation, the person and work of Jesus Christ, one's own relationship to the text, and "view of the world at large, including the possibility of understanding".[6] The problem of under-standing, specifically how we come to "understand" what a text "means", is the focus of this essay.

Key in all this is that all readers/hearers of a text have a hermeneutic, whether they acknowledge it or not. In fact, I have found that those who presume that they operate without hermeneutics produce more mischief with the text than those who are forthright about their approaches and agendas. The last item listed by Voelz is the most significant: what is our view of the "possibility of understanding" How do we come to know something to be true, and not merely the construct of our own situatedness? The basic hermeneutical task is to account for the reader—why does the reader come up with the meaning that he or she does, and is it a faithful mean-ing? Exegesis is studying the text, hermeneutics is studying the reader. Both are necessary. But given the multiplicity of interpretation and the fact that most read-ers of the Scriptures, frankly, seem rather poor readers of the text, it essential that

---

[5] 'Hermeneutics' in *Dictionary for Theological Interpretation of the Bible* (ed. K. J. Vanhoozer; SPCK/Baker Academic, 2005), 283.

[6] J. Voelz, *What Does This Mean? Principles of Biblical Interpretation in the Post-Modern World* (Concordia Scholarship Today; St. Louis: CPH,) 13–15.

we look at readers and how they create meaning, not merely learn "rules". For the "rules", after all, are only that which the reader—back to the reader again—chooses to apply in his act of reading.

Let's return to this billboard and ask some hermeneutical questions—What does this mean? Why did *we* respond the way that we did when we saw that billboard?

First, we live in the 21st century and the intended audience of the billboard is an American. We have had, collectively, horrific experiences with the word "slave". When we hear the word "slave" we think of the American experience, the war fought 150 years ago, the Emancipation Proclamation, the Thirteenth Amendment to the U. S. Constitution, whips, abuse, chains. Slavery is a blight on our national history. The billboard, of course, primes us to think of exactly that when it places a troubling image of this conception of "slave" next to the passage. So when the average American drives by this billboard and sees "slaves, obey your masters", we cannot help but read the passage as antiquated at best and at worst as an agent of oppression and evil. Of course, this is exactly what the purchasers of the billboard want you to think about "the Bible". But the problem is not the text; it is the reader, who has been shaped and formed to react in this visceral, automatic way to that image and that word. In other words, slapping four words and that image on a billboard— which is viewed at highway speed, no less—does not allow for the kind of reflection that would lead to the obvious conclusion that 19th century American chattel slavery cannot be the same thing as slavery in a first-century, Græco-Roman context.

The same goes for "obey". If you were told by a police officer to "obey" the speed limit", or by your parents that you had to obey their curfew rules, you probably would not react in revulsion or horror (granted, teenagers might). But put the word "obey" next to our American notion of "slave" and, again, next to that image, and our automatic reaction will be negative. It becomes an intolerable word.

And again, "master". "Master" as a noun has for the most part fallen out of common American usage. Probably because of its connection to slavery. So our immediate reaction to that word, as with "slaves" and "obey", is to think of the American form of slavery, and again we respond negatively to the passage on the billboard.

Notice, I have not yet discussed what the text "means", or the "rules", only how most Americans will read the text. This is hermeneutics, and such practices enable us to understand that our reading may not be consistent with God's purposes in giving the text. Hermeneutics exposes the problem: That you and I are reading the text, and you and I have been shaped and formed to read it in a certain way because of our education, our cultural environment, the kinds of books we read, the kinds of movies and TV shows we watch, our political leanings, our friends, our experiences, etc., etc. All of which makes us very poor readers of the biblical text. And which makes billboards like this very effective.

To this point, I have not proposed a solution to the "problem" of this billboard's interpretation of the scriptural text. I raise this as a hermeneutical problem, one which will help us address "theological hermeneutics". Why are there multiple readings of the same text? What shapes us to produce those readings? And how do we hear the Scriptures faithfully? My goal in this essay is modest. It is not to provide "the" hermeneutic for coming up with the right "answers", but to lay out a model of how the creation of meaning happens so that we can begin to assess our own, and others' readings.[7]

2   Multiple Readings of the Biblical Text

Rather than discussing interpretation in the abstract, let's turn to one specific passage as an example of the challenge of multiple interpretations and readers' goals. A classic problem passage is the account in Gal 2:11-14 of the "confrontation" between Cephas and Paul in Antioch. There, Cephas had been eating with the Gentiles, but after pressure came from Jerusalem he withdraws and separates himself. Paul will have none of this, so he publicly rebukes Cephas. Thereby, at least to many in the early church, a problem arises: Is it possible that an apostle—indeed even the first apostle, who would one day be considered the first Pope—be wrong, and in need of public correction?

Clement of Alexandria solved the problem by positing that "Cephas" and "Peter" were two different individuals (as reported in Eusebius' *Church History* 1,12,2): "This is the account of Clement in the fifth book of his *Hypotyposes*, in which he also says that Cephas was one of the seventy disciples, a man who bore the same name as the apostle Peter, and the one concerning whom Paul says, "When Cephas came to Antioch I withstood him to his face." This resolution to the problem may be reflected in the various readings in the manuscript tradition.[8]

Jerome's concern was likewise to protect apostolic authority: "Thus they give Porphyry an opportunity to blaspheme, if one believes either that Peter had gone

---

[7] I should state at the outset that I teach the "Biblical Hermeneutics" course at Concordia Seminary several times a year, including two sections that concluded ten days ago. I have taught this course some two dozen times, always using as the core text *What Does This Mean?* by James Voelz. It is impossible to summarize and defend all the issues raised in that book which influence my approach here; we might discuss these, if desired, in the question period. But I want you to be aware of my starting point, and why I head off in the directions that I do.

[8] Clement read Κηφᾶς in his text; Latin, Syriac, and bilingual Græco-Latin manuscripts as well as the "Majority Text" witnesses read a form of Πέτρος at 2:11 and 14.

astray or that Paul had impudently rebuked the chief of the apostles." He knows,
but rejects, Clement's line of rescue, for another "Cephas" is not known from Luke's
writings. But he cannot brook disharmony among the apostles. So he posits a gap
in both Paul' and Luke's narrations and argues that Peter and Paul had cooked up, in
advance and unknown to the others, a "feigned dispute". This, according to Jerome,
is common practice among lawyers (which I do not dispute) without occasioning
outcry, so why should not the apostles make use of this rhetorical device. When Paul
publicly rebukes Peter, who is in on the charade, the other Jews are actually rebuked
and thereby both the teaching of the text is preserved—that is, the Gentiles are fully
church—and, apparently at least as importantly, apostolic authority is preserved.[9]

Augustine's *Letter 28* to Jerome explicitly questions the great exegete's explanation. For if it would be admitted that the apostles carried out falsehood, that Cephas'
(Peter's) actions were hidden, and that he was acting deceitfully, then Paul would not
be "speaking the truth" when rebukes Peter. This would call into question, according to Augustine, whether any passage of Scripture was to be considered reliable.
He states his concern quite clearly: "For it seems to me that most disastrous consequences must follow upon our believing that anything false is found in the sacred
books: that is to say, that the men by whom the Scripture has been given to us, and
committed to writing, did put down in these books anything false." Rather than call
the text into question, Augustine is quite willing to sacrifice Peter. Somewhat surprising, perhaps, given that Augustine himself is a bishop. Were he the Bishop of
Rome, would he find that same argument so appealing?

Luther is not concerned about the authority of bishops. Rather, his concern is
with the teaching of Justification by Faith: "Paul had no small matter in hand, but
the chief article of the Christian religion. When this article is endangered, we must
not hesitate to resist Peter, or an angel from heaven." A different concern leads to a
different reading: The passage is about the gospel, and any thing or any person who
stands in the way of the gospel must be silenced.

Yet a fifth line of interpretation, using a "socio-scientific" approach, asks how the
actions of those involved are affected by their social setting. An influential article
by Philip Esler[10] argues that in the social context of Paul's letter an "honour-shame"
culture is operative. The agreement won by the "anti-circumcision party" at the Jerusalem council (Acts 15) would require, by nature of the unspoken social contracts of

[9] Text of Jerome's commentary available in T. P. Scheck, trans., *St. Jerome's commentaries on Galatians, Titus, and Philemon* (Notre Dame, Indiana: University of Notre Dame Press, 2010), 100–102.
[10] P. F. Esler, 'Making and Breaking a Agreement Mediterranean Style: A New Reading of Galatians
2:1-14', *Biblical Interpretation* 3 (1995): 285–314.

the day, that the "shamed" group restore their honour. So Peter is convinced by the Jerusalem church to be inconsistent in the application of the agreement by now withdrawing socially, but not theologically, from the Gentiles in Antioch. Esler argues that Peter had gone so far as compelling the gentiles in Antioch to be circumcised. Note that this reconstruction requires, just as in Jerome', some kind of machination behind the scenes which is unspoken in the text, as indeed is any mention of circumcision in Gal 2:11-14.[11] Peter is not exonerated in this reconstruction, but that is not Esler's goal. His purpose is scientific: devising an explanation of the setting that is "rooted in ancient Mediterranean rather than modern North Atlantic values".[12] One might wonder, though, despite Esler's zeal in "deliberately trying to clear [his] mind of modern presuppositions" (p. 311),[13] if he has quite succeeded. For is it not convenient to modern, non-ecclesial biblical scholarship that the founders of the church operate by brute force and backroom machinations? The very thing that Clement and Augustine were most eager to avoid?

The point of this brief review of eighteen centuries of discussion on a few sentences in Galatians highlights several of the hermeneutical problems that we raised earlier. All of these ask questions about why different readers create different "meanings". It is evident that the goals of the reader affect the reading of the text. This happens in several ways. First, a reader's goals determine which methods that the reader chooses to apply, such as textual criticism (Clement) or socio-rhetorical criticism (Esler). Second, one's situational concern produces the "meaning" that the

---

[11] As Esler, 304, acknowledges: "Since Paul himself supplies no information whatever on this question (except as to the fact that certain people were sent to Antioch by James, leading to Peter's suspension of table-fellowship with the Gentile members of the community, Gal. 2:12), it is necessary to generate scenarios and then to test them against the evidence in the text."

[12] Esler, 305.

[13] Esler claims Ambrosiaster as an ally for his view that Peter was demanding circumcision, quoting his comments (in Latin) at the conclusion of the article. I am not certain that Ambrosiaster can adduced as support, however: *"tale est [hoc], quale et illud dictum ad apostolum Petrum: si tu cum sis Iudaeus, gentiliter vivis, quomodo compellis gentes iudaizare? ita et hi cum ipsi legem non custodirent conversantes et conviventes cum gentilibus Galatas, circumcidere semetipsos cogebant, ut placèrent Iudaeis. per hoc enim molliebant sibi ánimos Iudaeorum, ut etiam de ipsis non crederent, quod gentiliter viverent."* The comment is found not at Gal 2:14, but at 6:13. My translation is: "This [referring to Gal 6:13] is the substance of what had been said to the Apostle Peter: If you, since you are a Jew, live like the gentiles, how do you compel the gentiles to Judaize? [Gal 2:14] So also these themselves ["those who are circumcised"; Gal 6:13], who did not to keep the law while living and eating with the gentiles at Galatia, compelled them to circumcise themselves in order to please the Jews. For through this they softened the attitude of the Jews to themselves, so that they [that is, the gentiles] lived on the basis of the very thing that they did not believe." It seems clear that Ambrosiaster is describing the situation in Galatia, not in Antioch.

reader draws from the text. Jerome, concerned about the authority of the bishop, created one meaning. Augustine, concerned to uphold the veracity of Scripture created a different meaning. Each "meaning" derived from the (theological) goals that they brought to the text. Third, although we have used the word "meaning" up to this point, it should be now clear that what we call "meaning" what we call "application" are inseparable. The text does not "mean" that bishops or apostles are either right or wrong, to be respected or ignored. Rather, the Scriptures become *meaningful*, that is, they take on meaning and significance as they shape our thinking and behaviour. This was both Jerome's and Augustine's concern. How does the way we read the text shape the way that we look at bishops, or the Scriptures? Fourth, there are multiple possible faithful ways to hear a text. None of the readings outlined here are necessarily "wrong", they are all different appropriations in different settings for different purposes. They operate with different theological goals, desiring to shape a specific response on the part of a specific hearer in a specific situation.

It is not "post-modern theory" which argues that different readers are likely to produce different "meanings" from a text. At the level of "words", already Augustine had tried to deal with the ambiguity inherent in signs, or words. In his *De doctrina christiana*, he uses virtually all of books II and III, nearly half of the treatise, to attempt to unravel the ambiguities inherent in "signs". He opens book II with this introduction: "Now that I am discussing signs, I must say, conversely, that attention should not be paid to the fact that they exist, but to the fact that they are signs, or, in other words, that they signify."[14] He goes on to discuss two problems in determining what words signify: that some signs/words are "obscure" (the topic of book II), and that others are ambiguous (the topic of book III). He is not able to offer a comprehensive procedure that would allow one to decipher all the signs unambiguously, however. In fact, in book III he picks up the "rules" of Tychonius—a Donatist opponent of Augustine's catholic church, mind you—and comments on them in order to find guidance. Yet even here he is not entirely successful, concluding that a single, perfect "meaning" is not attainable.[15]

In fact, Augustine has already heard the so-called "post-modern" claim that cultural diversity requires moral relativism:

Some people have been struck by the enormous diversity of social practices and in a state of drowsiness, as I would put it ... have concluded

---

[14] *De doctrina christiana* 2:1,1; translation from Augustine, *De doctrina christiana* (ed. and trans. R. P. H. Green; Oxford: Clarendon Press, 1995), 58).

[15] See David L. Jeffrey, *Houses of the Interpreter: Reading Scripture, Reading Culture* (Waco, Texas: Baylor University Press, 2003), 39–-53.

that justice has no absolute existence but that each race views its own as just. So since the practices of all races are diverse, whereas justice ought to remain unchangeable, there clearly is no such thing as justice anywhere.[16]

Yet what is Augustine's solution to this claim? Not the inerrancy of Scripture, or the revealed will of God, but an articulation of his primary hermeneutical principle:

> To say no more, they have not realized that the injunction 'to not to do to another what you would not wish to be done to yourself' can in no way be modified by racial differences (*gentili diversitate*). When this injunction is related to the love of God, all wickedness dies; and when it is related to the love of one' neighbour, all wrongdoing dies."[17]

Nearly two centuries earlier Origen had noted the multiplicity of interpretation, in particular of the Old Testament. He attributes this to the interpreter beginning with a wrong theology, that is, the "Jews" look only to a "literal meaning". So, for example, the fact that the wolf does not feed with the lamb is taken to be literal only; and since in the coming of Jesus this did not happen, then Jesus is not the Christ. (*De principiis* 4:2,8). Likewise, the "simple" believe that the Demiurge is the sole God, and identify it with the Creator God of the Old Testament (4:2,8). In 4:2,14 Origen lays out a positive approach to reading, one which argues that the first goal (*skopos*) of the Spirit is "to reveal those doctrines necessary for the perfection of the soul" the second goal (*skopos*) is to conceal "these primary teachings in the secondary story of visible creation and the Biblical account of human history".[18] Irenaeus likewise places the Scriptures into the economy of God, noting that "[i]f anyone, therefore, reads the Scriptures with attention, he will find in them an account of Christ, and a foreshadowing of the new calling (*vocationis*)" (*Adversus hæreses* 4:26,1).[19]

Even the earliest fathers knew that multiple interpretations were possible, even likely[20] and that some readings could be ruled out. When they sought to hear the

---

[16] *Ibid.*, 3:14, 22; Green, 155.

[17] *Ibid.*, 3:14,22; Green, 155.

[18] Cf. Ronald Heine, 'Reading the Bible with Origen', in *The Bible in Greek Christian Antiquity* (ed. and trans. Paul M. Blowers; Notre Dame: University of Notre Dame Press, 1997), 131--48.

[19] Cf. Maurice Jourjon, 'Irenaeus' Reading of the Bible', in *ibid.*, 105--11.

[20] In this context, it is appropriate to note that in many cases where textual variants were known, patristic commentators would comment on and interpret both variants without deciding which of the two was "original"; see Bruce M. Metzger, 'Explicit References in the Works of Origen to Variant Readings in New Testament Manuscripts', in *Biblical and Patristic Studies in Memory of Robert Pierce Casey* (ed. J. N. Birdsall and R. W. Thomson; Freiburg: Herder, 1963), 78–95.

Scriptures faithfully, they did not find refuge, primarily, in "rules", but in refocusing on the hearer, and shaping him to read with the right eyes, to hear with the right ears, and to have to right goal (viz., God's goal) in mind as he reads. Once again, we return to the problem, or more accurately, the role of the reader. For it is the reader's goals, purposes, and skills that produce "meaning". Hermeneutics must assess the ways in which a reader interacts with a text and incorporates his or her goals into the reading of the text. Theological hermeneutics seeks to hear the text with faithful goals, agendas, and methods, and expose those goals, agendas, and methods that do not produce the kind of hearer who has ears to hear.

3 Hermeneutical Models

Earlier, we defined "hermeneutics" as "critical reflection upon processes of interpretation and understanding". Here we will critique several models of the process of interpretation and understanding, in particular as these processes occur in the hearing of the Scriptures. I will acknowledge immediately that I do not find many previous discussions of "Lutheran Hermeneutics" to be sufficient for the issues that face the church in the early 21st century, especially issues involving the new life in Christ (traditionally called "sanctification") such as marriage, life and death, health care, etc. Reflections on "Lutheran hermeneutics" produced in the late 20th century do offer much of value. For example, Martin Franzmann's "Seven Theses on Reformation Hermeneutics" offers an articulate and laser-like focus on the work of Christ, which is embedded as the *cantus firmus* throughout the biblical narrative. Franzmann summarizes this "radical Gospel"[21] in this way: "God, to whom man can find no way, has in Christ creatively opened up the way which man may and must go."[22] This essay is required reading in my Biblical Hermeneutics course. Similarly, Edward Schroeder provides a helpful essay, "Is There a Lutheran Hermeneutic?" which lists many of the same Lutheran assumptions as Franzmann did, such as *sola scriptura,* "Scripture is its own interpreter", "Christ the Lord of the Scriptures", The unitary meaning of Scripture", etc. Indeed, he emphasizes a key Lutheran goal: "But any hermeneutics, however critical or simple or orthodox, if it commits the fallacy which Melanchthon saw committed by the Confutation of his day, will have to be rejected, not because Luther says so nor even because the Confessions say so, but

---

[21] "Radical" in the Latin sense of the root from which all things radiate, not in the popular modern sense of iconoclastic, extremist, or even "rad".

[22] Martin H. Franzmann, "Seven Theses on Reformation Hermeneutics", Commission on Theology and Church Relations, Lutheran Church—Missouri Synod (1969), 4.

because it buries Christ."[23] Keeping Christ and his work sole and central must be at the heart of any hermeneutic that reads the Scriptures as God's Word. Similar *foci* were articulated centuries before by Matthias Flacius.[24] But as students of Lutheran history are all to aware, articulating and coming to agreement upon Lutheran presuppositions does not result in consensus on all issues to which the scriptural text is brought to bear, in particular the social and practical issues which are so controversial today. For these essays on hermeneutics have not sufficiently recognized that in addition to *presuppositions*, one's self-selected *goals* shape and determine that meaning that the reader creates from the text.

This section will use four models, laid out as diagrams, in order to understand the process of creating meaning from a biblical text.

Diagram A
Traditional Model of
Interpretation

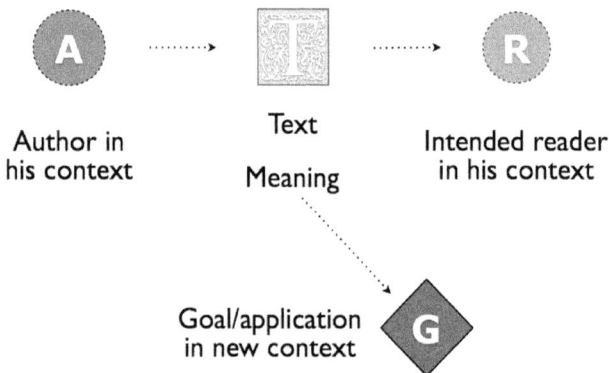

Author in
his context

Text

Meaning

Intended reader
in his context

Goal/application
in new context   G

This diagram represents what might be called a traditional view of the hermeneutical process in the production of meaningfulness via a text. First, the author in his context produces a text for an intended audience. Let's say, for the sake of an example, Paul writing to the churches of Galatia in the mid-first century.[25] This text

---

[23] E. H. Schroeder, 'Is There a Lutheran Hermeneutics?' in *The Lively Function of the Gospel* (ed. R. W. Bertram; St. Louis: Concordia Publishing House, 1966), 81–97.

[24] Now available in a recent translation, *How to Understand the Sacred Scriptures* (trans. Wade R. Johnston; Saginaw, MI: Magdeburg Press, 2011).

[25] Complications arise immediately, such as the precise location of "Galatia" and conclusions then made from the conclusions made about location such as ethnic background of the audience and date.

conveys a "meaning" which Paul desires the Galatians to apprehend and, presumably, accept. The intended audience then hears (or perhaps reads) the text and from the words then constructs a "meaning". The process of interpretation for present day readers using this model, then, is essentially the reverse of this process. One becomes as much as possible the original reader (by learning Greek, understanding the Hellenistic world, diaspora Judaism, etc.). By adopting the situation of the original audience and their perspective, one becomes able to apprehend "the correct meaning" of the text and thereby gains insight into the thinking of the original author–indeed even the mind of the divine author himself, the Holy Spirit. Often, those using this model focus upon grasping *the meaning* of the text, which is viewed primarily as *revealing* a single "truth" (usually propositional) which is unknowable apart from this act of interpretation. Once this single "meaning" or "truth" is determined, then "application" of that meaning can be made in new contexts. A clear distinction is made between "meaning" and "application". The "application" might change, the "meaning", however, does not.

I's not trying to set up a straw man in this description. Based on my interactions with pastors and teachers, this model fairly describes the way that many readers view the process of discovering the "original meaning" of a text and then "applying" it to hearers. A published example is the recent *Lutheran Study Bible* from Concordia Publishing House, which provides "interpretive notes" and "application notes" as if they were two different things. The former offer the one "interpretation", which readers then "apply" in their situations. This model does help to deal with some aspects of the problem of multiple interpretations. First, it acknowledges a distance between the original audience (in the case of the New Testament, some two thousand years distance) and our context. We are limited by our lack of familiarity with things such as the languages and settings of the New Testament. Secondly, it seeks to bridge that gap by various means. Augustine's "application" of Galatians 2 clearly differs from Esler'. Nevertheless, far more fundamental questions cannot be resolved using this model. Furthermore, readers are not able to duplicate the "moves" towards application; they remain somewhat arbitrary and unique to each interpreter. The difficulty that we raised earlier remains, the problem of multiple interpretations: not all readers will come up with the same "meaning" let alone "application". And, several of these multiple interpretations may, in fact, be "correct".

All of these are debated in the case of Galatians, though the point I am making here does not depend on one's answer to the these issues.

Diagram B
Discourse Creation

telos

Intended reader
in his context

Desired Instantiation

Instantiation

R ····▸ I ····▸ T ····▸ I

Text

A

Shared linguistic, cultural,
Author in   social, theological milieu
his context

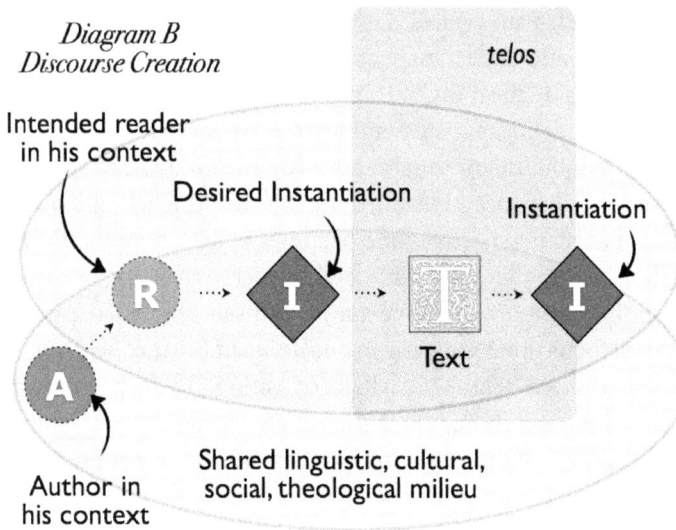

This model describes more accurately, I believe, what takes place in the production of a text, in particular of the texts of the New Testament.[26] The author begins with the reader: What needs do they have? What instruction are they lacking? What correction or encouragement do they need? For example, in the extant letters Paul discusses the Lord's Supper only in 1 Corinthians 10 and 11. Presumably, this is not because he did not think that the church in Rome or Philippi would not benefit from the Lord's Supper, but because the church in Corinth was experiencing conflict in its celebrations. The author does not write in a vacuum, into the sky. He writes for specific people, in order to accomplish specific things in and among them. This is labelled on the diagram as a "desired instantiation"—the author's desired outcome. At times this desired instantiation is more or less explicitly expressed by the author: "So then, my brothers, when you come together to eat, wait for one another" (1 Cor 11:33). At others the desired effect is less clearly signalled. In Romans, for example, Paul contrasts the "wrath of God" that is revealed to Jew and Gentile apart from Christ (Rom 1:18–3:20) with the "righteousness of God" that is revealed to all in Christ through faith (Rom 3:21–8:39). The goal of the contrast is that the church in Rome find their hope in Christ alone, not the law. But what is the desired result that follows from that? Is it limited to the sphere of salvation (vertical righteousness)? Or is an additional goal that Jew and Gentile in Rome be reconciled to one another,

---

[26] I see no reason why this model would not work for the production of any text. Since many of the contentious issues in our day involve the Pauline Letters, most of my discussion will focus on that portion of the canon.

18

as is argued in Rom 9-11? And that they end their disputes over what to eat (Rom 14)? Whether made explicit in the flow of the argument or less clearly signalled. by the rhetoric, the desired result for the hearer is in the author's mind before pen is put to paper (or, in the case of Paul's letters, dictation begins). This goal then shapes the selection of words and the argumentation of the passage in order to impact the hearers. The "meaning of the text", therefore, cannot be limited to the sum of the definitions of the words, but is, from the beginning, conceived of as producing a result in the hearer—there is more than *meaning*: the text is to be *meaningful*.

Two ovals in the diagram encompass, respectively, the author and the hearer. These two ovals represent the "shared linguistic, cultural, social, and theological milieu". So, for example, Paul writes to the church in Corinth in Greek, referring to specific situations ("A man has his father wife ..." (1 Cor 5:1); "brother goes to law against brother" (6:6); etc., in a specific social context (for example, one in which "long hair" is "glory" for the woman, but "disgrace" to the man; 1 Cor 11:14–15), in a given theological milieu. Of course, at times the "theological milieu" of the hearers is itself the problem that needs to be corrected—for example, in 1 Cor 15 where the hearers have rejected the bodily resurrection. A problem to which we must return, in due time, is that these settings are distinct and unique—Corinth in the mid-50s of the first century is a different place from Rome, with different people, issues, and circumstances. Not only is there distance between our context and that of the first century church, there were differences (geographic, cultural, etc.) among the contexts of the New Testament church. Perhaps remarkably, Paul forbids circumcision in Galatia (Gal 5:2, etc.) but himself circumcises Timothy in Lystra (Acts 16:1-3). But he refused to allow Titus to be circumcised in Jerusalem (Gal 2:3–5). Different contexts, even among the churches of the mid-first century, meant that the same action meant different things, and "contradictory" instruction is given. Later we must consider what we do with such texts—do we circumcise, or do we forbid it? But as we draw *meaningfulness* from the texts we must recognize that not even within the New Testament is the same *meaningfulness* drawn from the same passage, in this case Genesis 19 and the Abrahamic covenant's requirement of circumcision. There were multiple, faithful interpretations within the New Testament itself.

At this point we are ready to speak about the text, for it contains the "signs" (to use Augustine's term) that are written to provoke the author's desired response in the hearer. It is produced, again, within the shared milieu of the author and the hearers, so in the diagram the "text" is placed within the ovals representing both the author's and the hearers' milieu. However, the text does not inevitably produce the desired instantiation in the hearer. The church in Thessalonica, for example, took

19

the eschatology of 1 Thessalonians and over-realized it, necessitating a second letter from the apostle. We do not know if some of the baptised in the churches of Galatia underwent circumcision, in spite of Paul's words.

There is one final consideration in the process of textual creation that must be considered. On what source did Paul base his desired instantiations? Here is where theological hermeneutics comes into focus. Paul (we believe) is not inventing his "desired instantiations" capriciously, and the resultant text is not considered, from a Lutheran perspective, the mere whims of a human author, but revealing and making known of God's purposes in Christ. The Spirit is at work in the word, so that God's purposes and intentions are carried out through that word. That is to say, because the apostolic and prophetic word is at the same times God's word, these Scriptures are an effective word, bringing about the Kingdom of God and the new creation through the church in the killing and making alive of the sinner, now made saint in Christ. God is not only *saying* something in the Scriptures, he is doing something through them. What they are doing, this scriptural *telos*, or goal, will be considered below.

The strength of this model is that it incorporates pragmatics into the description.[27] The author is not merely providing information, he is attempting to persuade his hearers to a new situation, perspective, action, or belief. Theologically speaking, it allows us to incorporate the efficacy and infallibility of the Scriptures into the hermeneutical process. They functioned, for the original hearers, as the living and active Word of God. As such, they continue to function as the living and active Word of God in our day, continuing to be the means by which the Spirit kills and makes alive. Although this model does not yet account for the present-day hearer, building from this model will better situate us to understand the hermeneutical processes of the creation of meaning in our settings.

To this point we have only touched briefly on the present-day hearer's interaction with the text. The process of creating *meaning*, or better, *meaningfulness*, from the text is a separate process altogether from the creation of the text. This is illustrated in the next diagram.

---

[27] On pragmatics, see Voelz, *What Does This Mean?*, 275--88.

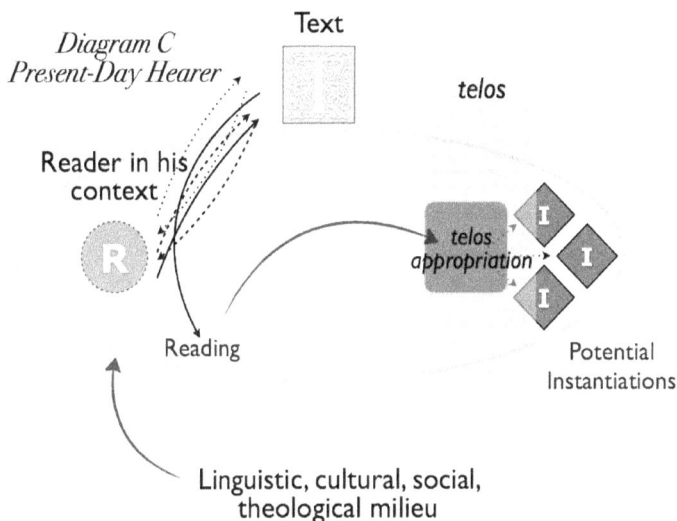

Diagram C
Present-Day Hearer

Text

telos

Reader in his context

R

telos appropriation

I
I
I

Reading

Potential Instantiations

Linguistic, cultural, social, theological milieu

The reader is situated in his or her own context, which includes again linguistic, cultural, social, and theological perspectives that shape the reader. These perspectives allow some meanings to arise and others not to be considered by the reader. The text, however, is not located in the linguistic, cultural, social, or, even theological milieu of the reader (though the latter might be debated). Most obvious is the fact that most readers of the New Testament are not native readers of Koine Greek, and so our competencies are limited, often severely. But cultural and other issuesalso come into play. An example that I used in a previous essay illustrates this well:

> Powell (14–22) relates an example ...which he encountered when teaching the parable of the Prodigal Son (Luke 15). He noticed that students, in their work, did not include all the elements of the story. So he conducted an "experiment" to figure out why. He asked 100 students, after reading the parable, to retell the story to another student. Most of the familiar elements were present in these re-tellings: The younger son asks for his share of the inheritance, the distant country, the squandering of all the money, feeding pigs, and "coming to his senses". However, of the 100 students, all Americans, only six mentioned the famine. Neither Powell, nor the students, could explain why this was so. During a sabbatical in St. Petersburg, he tried the same experiment to compare the results. Of 50 participants in Russia, 42 mentioned the famine, but only 17 mentioned the squandering of his money. Powell describes

a possible reason for this: a "collective memory" of the 1941 siege of Leningrad (as the city was then called) which resulted in the deaths of 670,000 people from starvation, one-fourth of the population. The fear of this event continued to grip those who survived and their descendants even 50 years later. Americans, by contrast, have never, in collective memory, suffered such mass starvation. What concerns Americans is money, how one spends it, and making sure one has enough. This is what is then heard in the parable; the famine, which is outside the experience of almost all educated Americans, scarcely registers.[28]

Examples from the Pauline Epistles could be multiplied; the billboard that cites the passage, "slaves, obey your masters" is only one. Hurtado notes that this is true of all readers of Scripture:

I would acknowledge gratefully the critique of naïve epistemological assumptions and the hubristic claims of some historical critics past and present. To be sure, all knowledge claims are limited and shaped by the "knower" as well as by the object of knowledge. The efforts of every interpreter are affected by his or her historicity, in time, geographical, and cultural setting, language, life-experiences, gender, values, biases, beliefs, vices and virtues. All human knowledge is "perspectival", partial, and corrigible. All inquiry is motivated and, to some degree, shaped by the acknowledged and unacknowledged interests of the inquirer. To apply words from St. Paul, "We know only in part, and prophesy only in part" (1 Cor. 13:12). Only in eschatological hope can we envision knowing "even as I have been fully known" (by God).[29]

This "partial knowing" and the inescapability of our own biases and contexts may seem to hinder "the meaning of the text". However, it must be remembered that "meaning" only happens as the text is read and heard; meaning only exists as the reader—in his context—makes sense of the marks on the page or the sounds in the air.

But the creation of "meaning" in the mind is never the sole result of interaction with any text, let alone the scriptural text. Some kind of *meaningfulness* occurs. That

---

[28]Kloha, 'Theological Hermeneutics After Meaning', 8, citing Mark Allan Powell, *What Do They Hear? Bridging the Gap Between Pulpit and Pew* (Nashville: Abingdon, 2007), 14–22.

[29]Larry W. Hurtado, 'New Testament Studies at the Turn of the Millenium: Questions for the Discipline', *Scottish Journal of Theology* 52 (1999), 173.

is to say, some kind of response is produced as a result, whether faith or unfaith, living in accordance with the text or rejecting that life. In hearing the scriptural text, an individual must find that *meaningfulness* in their own linguistic, cultural, social, and theological milieu. As we noted earlier, most present-day readers will not hear the injunctions against circumcision in Galatians to be meaningful in the same way that they were to the original hearers; a faithful hearer will desire to live out the text in such a way that "Christ benefits" us (Gal 5:2). But circumcision, in a different setting, may indeed allow Christ's work to have its way. So in the process of moving from text to possible instantiations, various possibilities will come to mind, others will not. Some will suggest themselves, others will be rejected as the hearer considers the text in his own setting. As a result, there are multiple potential instantiations (as we saw in the example of Galatians 2).

A specific example might be helpful. In 1 Cor 6 Paul rebukes the church, the "plaintiff", and the "defendant"—everyone involved—for the presence of a wrong between brothers and then having that wrong settled by unbelievers and not by the church. Particularly in our American context, such texts are very difficult to find meaningful. Are all lawsuits forbidden? What about when one is involved in an automobile accident and both parties happen to be Christian? Should the insurance company be left out of it, and all expenses paid out-of-pocket by the person at fault? But insurance is fundamental to social interactions in the Western world; for example, most states in the USA require liability insurance. Does this mean, therefore, that in an automobile accident, 1 Cor 6 is irrelevant? I would suggest that such a move is inappropriate, both because it rejects the authority of the text and because the text is shaping hearers to relate to one another at a more fundamental level than simply setting up "rules" which "apply" only in some situations, not others. So Paul's question "Why not rather be wronged? Why not rather be defrauded" (6:7) shapes the hearer, as in the Sermon on the Mount, to "turn the other cheek" (5:39), even at the risk of having that one slapped also. And Paul's rebuke, "But you wrong and defraud, and this to brothers" (6:8) shapes the hearer to not wrong or defraud in the first place, This coheres with the Seventh Commandment. Finally, the rebuke of the entire church, that there is "no one wise among you" (6:5), corresponds to instruction elsewhere regarding the role of the church in restoring the lost brother (Matt 18; Gal 6:1; James 5:19–20). So, while there are specifics in this text, in particular the problem of having the ways of thinking present in those who do not have the Spirit be allowed to shape and define relationships in the church with respect to disputes, there are multiple potential instantiations of this text in a present-day setting. In some cases (I would hope, rather rare cases), a lawsuit between brothers might be deemed appropriate. In others, some mechanism for resolving disputes *within* the church may be appropriate—and there may be many different ways that such "dispute resolution" might occur. That is to say, there is not only one, single outcome generated by a text as it is heard is new contexts.

The final element in the process of the hearer creating meaningfulness is that there is a prior goal, or *telos*, which shapes and defines the possible instantiations of the text as it is appropriated in its new context. This will have a profound impact on the hearing of the text, and decisively influence the result. For example, many present-day readers of the biblical text have a *telos* that is derived from their milieu that then determines their hearing. In the example of the billboard that I used earlier, "slaves, obey your masters" sounds like a "bronze-age ethic" to our modern, enlightened society. Within a *telos* of inclusivity and egalitarianism, notions of submission and vocation are foreign. And so it becomes impossible to hear that phrase as anything other than something to reject.

Examples in biblical scholarship and ecclesiastical life abound. A recent set of essays, *Studying Paul's Letters: Contemporary Perspectives and Methods* lays out the many different goals which readers bring to the text, thereby shaping their reading. The essays are clear about these goals. For example, in an essay on "Feminist Approaches", the goal is to

> provide a more involved demonstration of a feminist kind of ideological criticism in the section to follow. By making visible the ideology of gender and slavery in the biblical text, the biblical interpreter is able to analyse how it operates in the text and its interpretations, raise critical questions about it, and envision ways to resist or transform it.[30]

The "resisting and transforming" of the biblical text inevitably has in mind its own ideology before it approaches the text, and becomes a lens through which the text is viewed and possible instantiations are envisioned. In the case of the author cited here, it is not possible to have any instantiation result from reading Paul other than to "resist and transform" towards a *different goal*.

Other approaches outlined in the book have a different *telos*, but the results are similar. An essay on "Queer Approaches" argues that "the exercise of queer reading can become an efficacious exercise, not solely for how it produces meaning but for

---

[30] Cynthia Briggs Mittredge, 'Feminist Approaches: Rethinking Histories and Resisting Ideologies', in *Studying Paul's Letters: Contemporary Perspectives and Methods* (ed. Joseph A. Marchal; Minneapolis: Fortress, 2012), 127.

how it generates effects, how it is involved in the production of new concepts of self and society".[31] Notice that the goals is to generate "new concepts of self and society", which are generated by this approach. With a different goal, a different result ensues.

Other ideological approaches may be cautiously considered however. For example, a "postcolonial approach interprets with suspicion but also towards retrieval or restoration. Interacting with colonial history and its aftermath a postcolonial optic focuses on histories of repression and repudiation, but through exposé engages also in restoration and transformation".[32] In some respects, this approach is more helpful than a feminist approach, for it seeks a similar goal to that of the Scriptures: that the hearers "love their neighbour as themselves", and the apostolic message, in many ways, itself was a message of God tearing down the powers and principalities of this age.[33] What must be considered, however, is the extent to which a post-colonial *telos* coheres with a biblical *telos*. This is the goal of theological hermeneutics: to consider the divine goal of reading/hearing, and then testing our readings to see if they cohere with the divine goal.

Lest I give the impression, however, that having a "divine goal" is all that is necessary to faithful hearing of the Scriptures, we should consider examples where (to use Luther's phrase) an "orthodox" reading is produced, but not an accurate one. I will use, anonymously, a sermon preached recently on Mark 6:45-56 (I do not know the author, nor his ecclesiastical affiliation, but his sermons are regularly posted on a web site frequented by Lutherans). The text is a challenging one; it is the second time in Mark that Jesus calms a storm; the disciples are alone on the lake in a storm, again fearful. The oddest part of the text is in verses 48–50: "And about the fourth watch of the night he came to them, walking on the sea. He meant to pass by them, but when they saw him walking on the sea they thought it was a ghost, and cried out, for they all saw him and were terrified." Leaving aside the problem that a modernist would have with the depiction of Jesus walking on water, other questions arise, such as, Why is he about to pass by? Why would he leave them abandoned to the storm? Why did they think he was a ghost? Why were they terrified, this second time that they were in a storm? And, most importantly, what *meaningfulness* should we draw from the text? That we not fear in our (allegorical) "storms":? The sermon, unfortunately, ignores every one of these aspects of the text. Here is the "application" that the sermon makes:

---

[31] Joseph Marchal, 'Queer Approaches: Improper Relations with Pauline Letters', in *ibid.*, 224.
[32] Jeremy Punt, 'Postcolonial approaches: Negotiating Empires, Then and Now', in *ibid.*, 195.
[33] An excellent study that highlights this them in Acts is C. Kavin Rowe, *World Upside Down: Reading Acts in the Graeco-Roman Age* (Oxford: OUP, 2009).

He makes His way to the Boat that the boat may make its way to the other side. Without Jesus there is no way. With Jesus, He is the Way. He is the only way. And His Way is to be carried along by the Wood. The Wood on the Water bearing Jesus to the other side—to safe ground—to a promised Land—to paradise. There is no way to cross over unless you are carried by the Wood. There is no way to heaven, unless you cling to the cross of Christ by faith, receive His baptism in your baptism, hold His Word dear to your hearts. The cross is your bridge. The Body of Jesus is your nourishment. The blood of Jesus is your drink. The passion is your hope. His Church is your ARK.

The sermon, entitled "No Crossing Except by Water and the Wood", is "orthodox" in that it focuses on the cross and encourages participation in the sacrament in the church. This reading is "orthodox" in the sense that it has selected one aspect of the Kingdom *telos* and forced the text to urge that aspect. In this example, the preacher knows that in the Kingdom of God salvation happens only by Christ, the Lord's Supper sustains one in salvation, and the church is the place where Christ and his Supper are found. In the mind of the preacher–the locus of meaning, as we discussed earlier–"boats" evoke wood, from which the cross is made, and the "water" that Jesus walks upon evokes baptism. Body and Blood are absent from the text, but the preacher chooses to emphasize that from within his understanding of the Kingdom.

But is any of that actually found in the text? The fact that the preacher fails to mention that Jesus is about to pass by the struggling boat while offering neither a word of encouragement nor a finger of assistance, which seems to be a significant element, suggests that the scriptural text is merely a pre-text for the preacher. Is it textually defensible to label the "boat" as the cross, or the church (I am not sure which metaphor he is working with, it seems to be both)? This allegorical move, which rejects some textual features into order to fit, Procrustean-like, into his *telos*, is orthodox, but not textual. For it distorts and ignores key elements of the text. To return to my diagram, the preacher is operating on the right side of the diagram, but not on the left. Theological hermeneutics exposes this kind of reading as shaped, unhelpfully, by ideology in the same way (though not with the same result, of course) as a feminist or queer reading.

The problem with such readings is that they abandon and leave behind the text. The text has no normative function, even though an "orthodox" sermon has been preached. The pragmatics of the biblical text have been ignored; as a result, the goals of the preacher have replaced the goals of the text and its divine author. The preacher runs several risks here. First, how will his own reading be normed? How does he know, ultimately, that he is preaching with a Kingdom *telos*? For if all his readings of the text are this influenced in this way by his own agenda, can any reading of the text actually penetrate his thinking? Second, he runs the risk of neglecting sections of the Scripture which do not suit his self-selected goals. The result will, over time, be congregations who have not heard much of the biblical account of the good news of the Kingdom. A more self-critical approach is needed.

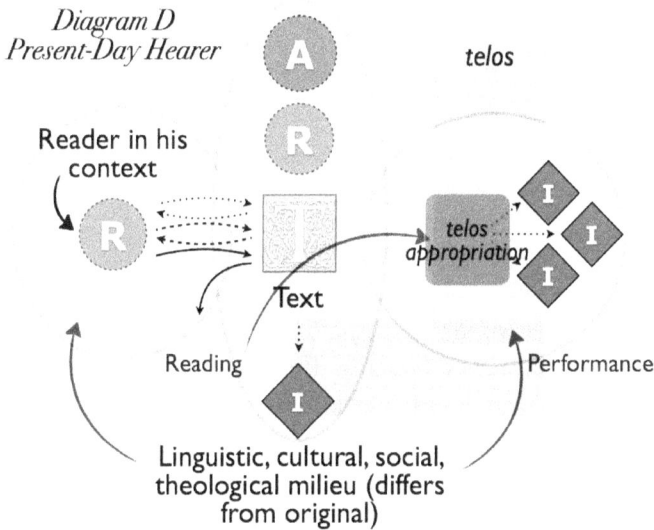

Diagram D
Present-Day Hearer **A**   *telos*

Reader in his   **R**
context

R   *telos*   **I**
                                             appropriation   **I**
                                                               I
      Text

      Reading   Performance
              I

Linguistic, cultural, social,
theological milieu (differs
from original)

A fourth model incorporates the theological nature of Scripture in accordance with the Spirit's purposes for the Word, and is able to account for new hearings of the word. In this diagram, it is made evident that our setting is different from the setting of the original hearers of the Scriptures. This is obvious, and is the basic hermeneutical problem. But we continue to hear the word, because in it the Spirit continues to shape and form us in our setting. Nevertheless, faithful hearing occurs in every generation of the church, even if, as the multiplicity of interpretation and the history of the church demonstrate, faithful hearing may look different in different times and places.

In this diagram, the previous diagram (C) is rotated to the vertical axis. This is done in order to make clear that while we, the present-day readers, have the text in common with the original hearers, nevertheless we have different contexts and therefore different instantiations of the goal (*telos*) of the text.

Unfaithful hearing may occur for any number of reasons. On the left side of the diagram, it might occur because of my context, my social setting, my lack of ability with the Greek and Hebrew, etc. On the right side of the diagram, unfaithful hearing might occur because I cannot conceive of a way that the text might shape my thinking and life, either because it is too foreign and "antiquated" or because I do not agree with the results that the text will produce in me. My ideology, my prejudgement, my theology, my ideology might prevent the Word from having its way with me. At the same time, this model is helpful in explaining why I regularly use profitably commentaries and studies on the biblical text by authors that do not share my theological foundations. They might illuminate issues that focus on the left side of my diagram; they help reshape my thinking in order to understand the language, structure and setting of the text. For example, it is fair to say that feminist approaches have made clear that women were more involved in the early churches than had been considered before. When these studies move towards what that they believe the instantiations should be as a result, this is where theological hermeneutics becomes critical: Do they produce a faithful hearing, consistent with the *telos* of the divine author and his Word?

In the diagram, notice that while the setting of the original hearers is different from our setting, the Kingdom *telos* is the same. That is to say, the Spirit' work is to keep the hearers of the Word faithful until the day of our Lord Jesus Christ, whether that hearer lives in the first century or the twenty-first. The Scriptures are a means by which faithful hearers of every generation are taught, reproved, corrected, and trained in righteousness through that God-breathed word, "so that the man of God may be complete, equipped for every good work" (2 Tim 3:16–17). The instantiation of life in the Kingdom formed by the word in every new context will, inevitably, be both different from and, in some respects, identical to the instantiation that the word forms in the original (and subsequent) hearers.

4   Towards a Theological Hermeneutic

In conclusion, I will focus on what I believe is most critical for the present-day situation of the church: What theological hermeneutic provides the correct *telos*, or goal, that generates faithful hearing? This is not to say that presuppositions such as infallibility, the Christocentric nature of Scripture, the unity of Scripture, etc. are not important; indeed, they are essential. However, even agreeing upon these foundational matters has not always resulted in faithful hearing.

What is the proper *telos* of the Scriptures? "Christ" is the answer, but simply stating that is not sufficient. For which Christ do you have? Christ as lawgiver? Christ as one who frees, completely, from any law? Christ as model? The Small Catechism in the explanation to the Third Article of the Creed provides a simple summary of both "which Christ" and "which *telos*". Christ's work is for a purpose: "that I may be his own, and live under him in his Kingdom, and serve him in everlasting righteousness, innocence, and blessedness." In order that we might be his own, the Spirit was sent, "who spoke by the prophets", who "calls, gathers, enlightens, sanctifies", and "keeps". The Catechism, like the creeds, embeds Christ in a narrative, a credal narrative, in which God creates and preserves, Christ redeems, and the Spirit calls and sanctifies, until the last day, when the dead are raised and the resurrection bodies are bestowed on those who believe in Christ. The apostolic and prophetic word is a part of this credal narrative; its *telos* is the Triune God's *telos*: to bring us, righteous, to the last day. Therefore, a Christocentric hermeneutic which eliminates the new life in Christ cannot produce a reading which will "keep me in the one true faith", for with such a hermeneutic I will be free to design my own *telos*, my own goal. This is the shortcoming of feminist approaches, queer approaches, etc.

The Scriptures must be understood within the economy of salvation. God can only be partially, hiddenly, known through his creation. He dwells in "unapproachable light" (1 Tim 6:16). Apart from God's initiative, we cannot know God, know how we stand before him, fear him, or love him. But God is a speaking God. "The gods are mute, but the Lord speaks" are the opening lines of Sasse's unfinished work *Sacra Scriptura*.[34] In the economy of God, this speaking occurs by the Spirit, who makes known Jesus Christ, the Son of God. Jesus himself does not begin his public ministry until the pouring out of the Spirit in his baptism (Mark 1:10–11 pars.). His authority, to forgive and to heal, is the same authority that belongs to the one God (Mark 2:1–12). In the wisdom of God, the world could not know him, but he makes himself known through the foolishness of what was preached, the foolishness of the cross (1 Cor 1:20–25). This Jesus, and his authority, was rejected and crucified by the world, but through the Spirit of holiness he was declared to be Son of God by his resurrection (Rom 1:2–4). God makes himself known, he speaks in power, only in Jesus Christ in order to make for himself a holy and righteous people.

The Spirit, then, continues to call to Christ. The Spirit is the active agent throughout the life and ministry of Jesus (Luke 1:35; 3:22; 4:14, 18–21; etc.), and the Spirit speaks the Word about Christ through his Apostles (Acts 1:8) and, as the narrative

---

[34]Hermann Sasse, *Sacra Scriptura: Studien zur Lehre von der Heiligen Schrift von Hermann Sasse*, hrsg. H Hopf (Hermannsburg: Verlag, "Lutherische Blätte", 1981), 11.

of Acts unfolds, through the church. "Deacons" such as Stephen (7:55) and Philip (Acts 8:29), "prophets" like Agabus (11:28), indeed the church gathered, as at Antioch (13:2–4), even individuals without title such as Priscilla and Aquila "explain the way of God more accurately" (18:26). This speaking of the Spirit always occurs through people to people, who all have their own backgrounds, beliefs, and questions. So Peter's speaking to those in Jerusalem will sound different from Paul's speaking to those in Athens which will sound different from Paul's letters, which are addressed to the baptised.

A Trinitarian, credal framework also allows us to recognize that God works among us as Father, Son, and Holy Spirit. The work of the Father, the creator, in the words of the first article of the Small Catechism, is to "still preserve" us and his creation. As his creatures we live within, and indeed are blessed through, the created realm even in its groaning condition (Rom 8). His reign in his left-hand kingdom is through rulers, who mete out justice as agents of God (Rom 13). Therefore, as his people we will find that, in Christ, the world as we experience it may be in accord with his revealed will. The biblical texts frequently appeal to "the way things are" as genuine expressions of God's will. For example, in 1 Cor 11 Paul notes that "In the Lord woman is not independent of man nor man of woman; for as woman was made from man, so man is now born of woman." God's creation shapes and defines relationships between woman and man (or, perhaps in this passage more narrowly, "husband" and "wife". Furthermore, in the same passage, "nature itself", that is, the "way things are" still "teaches" within the church. Of course, teaching drawn from creation alone is insufficient to know God, who is revealed only in the "word of the cross" (1 Cor 1) or "in Christ" (Rom 3). Nevertheless, God's work as Father reminds us that God's will for his people is not always in conflict with, and in fact is at times worked out through, his creation and his left-hand rule.

The work of the Son, the redeemer, is usually in a more antagonistic relationship to the fallen creation. Jesus himself describes his activity using imagery of someone robbing a strong man's house—in his casting out of demons he is stealthily stealing people away from the dominion of Satan (Mark 4). Christ's work is described in like manner in the epistles: By Jesus Christ giving himself up for our sins he has rescued us from the "present evil age" (Gal 1). Christ's work as redeemer presupposes a "Christ against culture" orientation between the Kingdom of God and the kingdoms of the world. We are called to battle radically against "the rulers, against the authorities, against the cosmic powers over this present darkness, against the spiritual forces of evil in the heavenly places" (Eph 5). This is the language of the second article of the Small Catechism: "Who has *redeemed* me … *purchased* and *won* me

…" Notice that God's First Article work might seem to contradict his Second Article work—is the ruler one who is to be "obeyed", as in Rom 13? Or is the ruler to be regarded as an agent opposed to Christ's Lordship, as in Acts 4? Because scriptural passages which use different credal discourses may seem to contradict each other, we must account for the ways that we choose which direction to follow, and why we choose not to follow the other.

The work of the Holy Spirit, the Paraclete, is to make all things "new" and to "transform". He "calls, gathers, enlightens, and sanctifies", that is, takes me from where I am now to a new place, thought, and life. This transformative work of the Spirit, however, remains incomplete both in the individual and in the church until the Last Day, so that some part of the old remains. When the Scriptures focus on the work of the Spirit, the discourse will focus on what God is doing in the individual and in the church in order to achieve his purposes. We are "straining forward to what lies ahead" (Phil 3), living in the present in the light of the future. As the great chapter on the resurrection concludes, because Christ has risen and we will be raised, "our labour in the Lord is not in vain" (1 Cor 15). When the Scriptures urge sanctification and the Christian life, the teaching and preaching will necessarily adopt third-article rhetoric, since it is only by the working of the Spirit that such living in the present happens, whether in the individual or in the church.

These three perspectives are not, of course, contradictory or mutually exclusive, any more than are the persons of the Trinity. All three describe ways that God works in the world still today; in our teaching and preaching, however, we often find ourselves gravitating towards one or the other of the articles; Lutheran preachers tend towards a second-article framework. If one were to err, better to err on preaching Christ. But such a focus runs the risk of failing to, for example, preach "sanctification". Or to neglect creation, within which we have been placed as stewards. Others, including Lutheran, will tend towards a Third Article framework. The reign of Christ over creation is highlighted, with its emphasis on renewal and eschatological hope. This, of course, is entirely consistent with the New Testament, but even in the apostolic age the danger of "over-realized eschatology" plagued the church (1 Cor 4; 2 Thess).

Above all, the Scriptures, because they are Word of God, are performative. That is, they accomplish God's purposes. Although the Scriptures convey information, the information provided is never solely for the purpose of filing away in a dogmatics text that is placed on a shelf. For this reason, remarkably, we keep hearing the Scriptures, day upon day, week upon week. The revelation of the Word of God is like no other. How many of us go back and read Plato and Aristotle weekly or daily, even though virtually all the epistemological and ontological questions still discussed in Western thought were raised and addressed by them? We do not go back to those texts to find new insight, new modes of being. If we read them at all, it is for historical purposes; moreover I could more easily read someone else's expert summary of them to get what I need. Again, it is very unlikely that any of us have read Foucault in the original, yet to a person our thought patterns are shaped by his work and even assume, without realizing it, that all language and relationships are, as he described it, negotiations of power. Unlike these seminal texts, we keep going back to the Word of God. We do not read other people's summary of the Scriptures. We keep hearing the Scriptures because something happens: God works—again and again—when we hear his word.

When I hear the gospel reading appointed for the Second Sunday in Advent, for probably the thirteenth or fourteenth time during a gathering of God's people in worship, I will hear it differently from how I did the twelfth or eleventh time that I heard that same reading. Because I am different. Because my circumstances have changed. My struggles have been resolved, and new ones press to the fore. Yet in my changing circumstances, God's Word speaks again. And we run to hear it again and again and again because we know that the hearing will be different this time—I will hear it differently this time. Like no other writing, God speaks in this Word. I am addressed. And even against my will I am made into his faithful child, that I may live under him in his kingdom, and serve him in everlasting righteousness, innocence, and blessedness. As Wingren describes it:

> To speak of the last day, of the final victory and the full redemption, is to speak of something that is being accomplished by the Word and mediated by the preaching that is now going on throughout the world, which is the link between Christ's resurrection and our own. Redemption is not just something of which we hear in the Word. It is something which is even now happening to us, when we encounter the Word; the Word is the creative Word which brings its work to birth in us.[35]

Our struggle, then, is to determine when our hearing of the Word of God is indeed proper hearing. When is the life that we live and urge upon others indeed formed by the Word? And when, in fact, is it merely the sinful imposition of my will upon others?

---

[35] G Wingren, *The Living Word: A Theological Study of Preaching and the Church* (Philadelphia: Fortress Press, 1960), 94.

Turning again to our predecessors in the study of the Scriptures, I would like to draw upon Augustine, Flacius, and Luther to help define an appropriate *telos* towards which the Spirit through the Scriptures is working. Augustine summarizes the *telos* in this way:

> Whoever, therefore, thinks that he understands the divine Scriptures or any part of them, but cannot build up this double love of God and neighbour, has not yet succeeded in understanding them.[36]

And again,

> So when someone has learnt that the aim of the commandment is "love from a pure heart, and a good conscience and genuine faith" [1 Tim 1:5], he will be ready to relate every interpretation of the holy Scriptures to these three things and may approach the task of handling these books with confidence. For when the apostle said "love" he added "from a pure heart", so that nothing is loved except that which should be loved.[37]

This "double-love" is the *sine qua non* of faithful hearing of the Scriptures. Several authors have pointed this out in Augustine. Francis Watson, in his summary of Augustine's hermeneutics, places at the top of the list: "A firm grasp of the *telos* of Holy Scripture and its interpretation, which is to engender the love of the Triune God and of the neighbour and nothing else."[38]

Seeing "double-love" as the *telos* of God's work in scripture is not unique to Augustine. Flacius' essay *How to Understand the Sacred Scriptures* likewise recognizes that unless one understands the overall purpose or goal of the Scriptures, one cannot hear properly:

> It is useful right in the beginning to understand what one ought to get out of the proposed work, not only so that he might be more clear with respect to the work, but also so that he might recognize what to pluck from it and deposit securely in his heart. All that is written, therefore, is written for us, so that Scripture first binds us under sin and condemns us; then, testifies to us about Christ; third, consoles us so that we might

---

[36] *De doctrina christiana* 1:36,49; Green, 49.
[37] *Ibid.*, 1:40,44; Green, 53; cf. 3:14,22; Green, 155, cited above.
[38] Francis W. Watson, 'Authors, Readers, Hermeneutics', in *Reading Scripture with the Church: Toward a Hermeneutic for Theological Interpretation* (Grand Rapids: Baker Academic, 2006), 122.

have patience and hope; and finally teaches, rebukes, corrects, and instructs, so that the man of God may be perfected, equipped for all things (2 Timothy 3:16,17).[39]

The purpose of scripture is, for Flacius, summarized in a four-fold goal: Law, Gospel, comfort, and, based on 1 Tim 3:16–17, teaching, rebuking correcting and instructing "so that the man of God may be perfected, equipped for all things". These would correspond to Augustine's "double-love" in that "Law, Gospel, comfort" accomplish the love of God, while "teaching, rebuking correcting and instructing" accomplish love of neighbour. The necessity of recognizing that a goal of Scripture is to produce a "perfect life—love both God and neighbour—is reflected in the summary "Guidelines" which he provides at the conclusion of his treatise:

> [I]t is therefore especially necessary in this regard for one to consider and keep in view the attainment of the true and genuine meaning of the Sacred Scriptures, with the desire to use it with the best faith for the glory of God, for your benefit, and for the benefit of others, especially the spiritual and eternal benefit.[40]

This comes tantalizingly close to Augustine's *telos* of double-love of God and neighbour. However, in his treatise Flacius does not develop or emphasize in any significant way that hearing of the Word results in love of neighbour. The nearest he comes is in section 51, where he teaches that our speaking "should always be salted by the Word of God, so that we and others are edified" and that we are "to be prepared always to give a reason for our faith" which is "above all the end product to be sought and derived from this study [of the Scriptures]".[41]

Though not laid out as a treatise on hermeneutics, Luther's catechism works with the same double-love *telos* in his "meanings" of the commandments in the second table of the law: "We should fear and love God so that we do not hurt nor harm our neighbour ..." "We should fear and love God so that we do not take our neighbour's money or property ..." This double-love, of God and neighbour, serves as the key to hearing the word faithfully.

Finally, Jesus himself operates with this double-love in his teaching of the Scriptures. When asked of the "greatest law", his response was love of God and love of

[39] Matthius Flacius Illyricus, *How to Understand the Sacred Scriptures* (trans. Wade R. Johnston; Saginaw, MI: Magdeburg Press, 2011), 70.
[40] *Ibid.*, 105.
[41] *Ibid.*, 98–99.

neighbour; "On these two commandments depend all the Law and the Prophets" (Matt 22:34–40; cf. Mark 12:28–34). When asked by the "lawyer" in Luke 10 what he must do, Jesus asks him, "What is written in the law? How do you read it?" The man cited the correct passage from Leviticus, and Jesus replies, "Do this and you will live." But the man did not know how to read the law, even though he could read the law, because he had only love for himself; he could not show mercy. So Jesus tells a parable, ending with the instruction: "You go, and do likewise." Perhaps even more striking is the rich young man of Matthew 19, to whom Jesus gives a list of commandments, all from the second table. The man, foolishly, declares that he has kept all of them, but in Jesus command to sell all and give to the poor, he walks away from Jesus. This demonstrates that in fact the man loved neither God nor his neighbour. Likewise, the apostle hold up this double-love as "summary" (Rom 13:9) and "fulfilling" (Gal 5:14) of the entire law (Torah?), and James calls it the "royal law" (2:8).

How does this double-law function hermeneutically? How does the text shape our life of love of God and love of neighbour, even in situations which are so vastly different from those of the Apostles? Here we refer again to Diagram D. Notice again that our context or milieu does not correspond to the milieu of the text; but what does overlap, what does correspond, is the same *telos*. That is to say, the same God is working to bring about the same kingdom in and among us through the same text. And, what is produced in us by the Spirit through the Scriptures is the same life in the kingdom. What is shared between us and the original hearers is the text, and the *telos*, the Spirit's text which produces the Spirit' goal. Therefore, any hearing of the Scriptures which does not produce love of God (faith, worship, obedience) and love of neighbour does not reflect the purpose of the Scriptures, nor produce the faithful response that the Spirit is working through that Word. In a sense, this double-law is eschatological. Through the Scriptures the Spirit produces for God a people of faith, who live faithfully in this age and will be proved faithful on the last day. It is a hermeneutic which allows the Scriptures to function according to the Spirit's purposes, even if in this age only in a tentative, provisional way, even with multiple faithful interpretations of the same text. Just as the Kingdom of God is manifest in the world only hiddenly, tentatively. This may not lead to exactly the same instantiations of the text in every time and place, but this has always been the case. Augustine has a faithful reading of Galatians 2, as did Jerome, as did Luther. They produced a different instantiation of the text, but they were all faithful instantiations, because they resulted in love of God and of neighbour. We might demand circumcision, in accordance with the covenant, or forbid it. Either one may obscure Christ; either one may result in not loving neighbour, as it did in Galatia ("It is those who want to make a good showing in the flesh who would force you to be circumcised, and only in order that they may not be persecuted for the cross of Christ" Gal 6:12). But the goal, the kingdom goal of the text, is to love God and love neighbour.

We may crave singularity, the one perfect reading so that, once captured, we might put the Scriptures aside. But we are called to hear ever again, daily, weekly, the Word, so that the Spirit might shape us in our ever-changing situations and circumstances. This is the nature of faith. It is always struggling, always seeking, always trusting. God's Kingdom comes indeed without our prayer; but we pray in the Lord's Prayer that it comes to us also. It comes by the power of God, by his Word, towards his goal. As Kolb and Arand describe God's *telos*:

> Luther's reminder that God calls Christians in the midst of a sinful world to turn from their mistakes, failures, and disobedience each day of their lives reminds theologians of their need to return to Scripture continually to check out whether they are faithfully reproducing God's message. This is true not only because students of God's Word can make false formulations but also because Satan's deceptions take so many forms and God's gift of humanity has so many facets. In different situations and in confrontation with various forms of evil, God's message for a fallen world takes on new and different expressions. The unchangeable truths of Scripture must be proclaimed to specific human beings in their specific environments as the gospel addresses their realities and brings its power to change those realities through forgiveness and the promise of new life in Christ. God's Word not only describes reality but also creates it.[42]

The Scriptures are generative, they are creative. They open new possibilities. They create a new, righteous person in the place of a sinner. They create faithful people who "walk in newness of life" (Rom 6:4), who have "crucified the flesh with its passions and desires (Gal 5:24). The Spirit by this word is at work, bring about new life. Life which loves God and does his will, and life which loves the neighbour; imperfectly yet in this age, but perfectly in Christ in the coming age.

---

[42] Robert Kolb and Charles P. Arand, *The Genius of Luther's Theology: A Wittenberg Way of Thinking for the Contemporary Church* (Grand Rapids: Baker Academic, 2008), 13.

Chapter 2

End of Solo: Hearing as a Limb. A response to Jeffrey Kloha

Rev. Dr. Boris Gunjević

It is my privilege to be with you today here at Westfield House. I would like to express gratitude to the ELCE pastors and leadership and particularly I would like to thank all of you who organized this theological symposium and to Dr. Kloha for his thoughtful and stimulating paper. Thank you very much for this opportunity to respond to the material you have just presented.

> How many of us go back and read Plato and Aristotle weekly or daily, even though virtually all the epistemological and ontological questions still discussed in Western thought were raised and addressed by them? We do not go back to those texts to find new insight, new modes of being. If we read them at all, it is for historical purposes; moreover I could more easily read someone else's expert summary of them to get what I need'.[1]

How does the Word of God enter into us? What shapes us to hear what we hear in the Word and how to apply the text to ourselves and to our ecclesial bodies? These are the simple questions, but it is not easy to give simple answers. We live in a time defined by absence of meaning. Meaning is constantly in flux and shifting

---

[1] Kloha, p. 31.

and this can be applied to every text, including human lives. Every text is reduced to endless interpretations characterized by the postponing of truth. We live in a time of competitive and violent interpretations in which regimes of power are producing models of meaning and truth, to put it in Foucaultian terms.

In order to respond to such ultramodern interpretations, we need to make one step back into pre-modernity and then we will be able to make two theological steps forward, beyond modernity. In that case we shall take into consideration some of Dr. Kloha's insights and conclusions. Dr. Kloha thinks that Gadamer can be a big help on the way. Later we will show how.

But before we come to Gadamer it is important to take a methodological distance from historical criticism and Kant's modern epistemology. For historical criticism ultimately reduces every interpretation of text to philology and linguistics. Everything ends in the counting of improper verbs and repetitive nouns. The opposite is true with Kant's critical project. It is not critical enough, as Hamann put it in his *Metacritique* of Kant. In Kant's epistemology, the emphasis is always on the subject, on me and how I perceive an object, detached from the object as such. In the end, whatever I do, I want to be able to "see things in themselves". If there is only "how I perceive things", I am left with my assumptions and uncertainties and I want to be able to recognize truth only interpretations.

Hamann described that as Kantian self-referentiality of reason that does not need the subjective grace of faith or the objective grace of revelation. Instead of Kant, Hamann's metacritical project is based on "knowledge by faith alone". It means that we need to distance ourselves from historical criticism and modern epistemology for a while in order to hear and to recognize the truth in the Word among many words. This process of hearing of the Word starts with assumptions, with knowledge by faith alone.

If we want to hear the voice of the Shepherd, we need somehow participate in his community. We need to allow ourselves to be not only informed by the Shepherd but transformed by him and his Word. Transformation begins when we assume that there is authorial intention in the text and that that intention is possible to understand. It means that the process of interpretation and transformation starts as a process of searching for authorial intention. This is a crucial assumption. All other questions come afterwards, especially if we talks about pre-modern authors. They did not write their texts to expose an original and new system of thought but to produce an effect and to transform readers and hearers. In that context Jules Michele said that "antiquity contains ideas in a state of concentration, in the state of elixir". In order to drink this elixir in spite of our situatedness, prejudices and or socio-political determinations, Dr. Kloha suggests that we need to adopt certain modalities of discourse and some conceptual tools. These discourse and tools can help us to hear and interpret the voice of the Shepherd in spite of our own assumptions and prejudices.

First of all, Dr. Kloha suggests that we should take seriously post-liberal theologians from the so-called Yale school and their emphasis on the importance of story and history in the process of interpretation.[2] Secondly, he suggests that we should consider a certain aspect of John Seral's philosophical project called 'Speech-Act Theory'. And thirdly, he suggests that we should adopt hermeneutical practices of translation and performance which I do not want to explain here. With these modalities of discourse and conceptual tools we can take one step back into pre-modernity, is what Dr. Kloha with his reading of Gadamer is partially suggesting. Gadamer is very important in this case. In his (ground-breaking) book, *Truth and Method*, he pleads for a serious rehabilitation of three pre-modern modes, or we should call them categories of interpretations. The first are prejudices, the second is allegory and the third is tradition. For us Lutherans, this is tragically important, not to say very problematic.

Now we are entering into the irresolvable Lutheran aporia of the relationship between Scripture and tradition. (This still unresolved in Roman Catholic Theology after the Second Vatican Council as well.) The first generations of Reformers had their own strategy to resolve this question, but unfortunately their questions are not our questions, simply because we live in a different time and a totally different context. Nevertheless, we try to continue to live with that aporia as nothing had happened. We are still pretending that we are at war with Tridentine theology and we try to answer questions in a pietistic style and mood. We have adopted the semi-pietistic attitude that if we accept tradition and allegory we will degrade the authority of Scripture and that we will lose the chance to hear truly what the Shepherd speaks to us. The truth is exactly the opposite.

Every time we open our Bible and when we start our reading, we are locating ourselves (immediately) in some interpretative tradition. Well, we are not lone readers (like Lone Rangers), and we are not the first ones to read the Scriptures. The reading of Scripture does not start with us. If we by any chance deny the importance of the authority of tradition in our reading, it means that we create our own tradition and our reading becomes the authoritative reading. As Pelikan put it, "Tradition is the living faith of death. Traditionalism is the dead faith of the Living."

---

[2] "[A] heresy is often the sign that orthodoxy has sacrificed the elements of mystery, and along with it tentativeness or open-endedness, to an oversimplified consistency." Hans w. Frei, *Theology and Narrative: Selected Essays* (George Hunsinger and William C. Placher, eds.; Oxford: OUP, 1993), 49.

Honestly speaking, our own tradition cannot be compared with the tradition of the Church Fathers. We cannot pretend that we understand the text better than Origen, Gregory of Nyssa or Augustine. Reading with them is reading with traditional tools. It means help. Because they give us appropriate tools for making our interpretation better and maybe more practical, as Augustine put it: "So anyone who thinks that he has understood the divine scripture or any part of them, but cannot by his understanding build double love of God and neighbour, has not yet succeeded in understanding them" (*On Christian Teaching*, I, XXXV, 86; Kloha p. 33).

In the same text Augustine is far more modern then any post-structuralist authors.[3] He said that in reading we make mistakes because we do not understand the nature of signs. This is a very post-modern statement. The meaning of signs may be veiled either because the signs are unknown or because they are ambiguous. For every sign is literal or metaphorical, and if we do not understand this simple instruction we will by enslaved by the sign. In that case we can easily agree with Augustine today because we live in a world of signs, metaphors, symbols, and we are daily called critically to interrogate, interpret and redefine signs. This is the reason why in our hermeneutical strategies and procedures we need to two two steps forward, beyond late modernity. This is our task today in order to redefine once again the doctrine of allegory (what Origen called 'spiritual sense' of Scripture) and Tradition. We can also add some other things, such as *Lectio Divina* and the importance of the memorization of Scripture. But everything is connected with a new understating of Tradition.

This is reason why I found Dr. Kloha's insights very valuable, especially the insights into the importance of narrative theology, Speech-Act Theory, translation and performance—and his conclusions that we should be humble hearers of the Word, credal people of the Church who are able to recognize how God is doing something new in spite of us. All of these conclusions are important categories for an interpretative tradition.

We are hearing the Word in community with others who belong to the Body of Christ. We are hearing the Word as limbs in the Body of Christ. It means that we are ready to hear the Word with our fellow brothers and sisters who, too, have died in

---

[3] "Life in the world is like a manuscript of writings that is still in rough draft. When a man wishes or desires to do so, he can add something or subtract from it, and make changes in the writings. But the life in the world to come is like documents written on clean scrolls and sealed with the royal seal, where no addition or deletion is possible. Therefore, so long as we are found in the midst of change, let us pay heed to ourselves; and while we have power over the manuscript of our life, which we have written by our own hand, let us strive earnestly to add to it by leading a good manner of life, and let us erase from it the failings of our former life." St Isaac the Syrian, from Homily Sixty-Two.

Christ. We are ready to hear how they lived, how they struggle with Scripture and in that sense we are in dialogue with them. In this dialogue it helps us that through the liturgy and the sacraments we are enacting the Word of God. Consequently, we are enacting whole history of salvation which is what ecclesiology is all about. It means that before anything else we are seeing the external marks of the Church, symbols, and metaphors, and then gradually we become led and initiated into the specificity of the Christian doctrine of God, man, salvation and resurrection.

Maybe this aporia of authority is not a totally irresolvable in Lutheran theology and practice.[4] The question of authority in the Western Church prior to 1300 was not about the Bible on the one side and Tradition and reason on the other. Quite the opposite. Scripture, tradition and reason were one authority. Under the influence of nominalistic philosophy and voluntaristic theology at the beginning of the fifteenth century, this threefold authority began to deteriorate into Scripture *versus* tradition and reason. The disintegration was continued via Spinoza, Hobbes and Jansenism up to the Enlightenment, where we come to the position of modern-day Manichæism of faith against reason, Scripture against tradition, nature against grace.

It is important to conclude that the nominalism and voluntarism of the late mediæval era did not just inaugurate Church Reform and the Reformation but, more importantly, they inaugurated Protestantism and Tridentism. Following Michel De Certeau, John Milbank concluded that Protestantism and Tridentism are primordially two unfinished modern models of authority in the Western Church. In front of us is the task, which is not easy, of findind our way out of the labyrinth beyond protestant Biblicism and post-Tridentine catholic authoritarian positivism.

Hearing the Word as a limb means to live life in harmony with the incarnate Logos. This allegorical perspective of a life lived from the Christian tradition is different for every generation of Christians. Every generation must re-invent this allegorical perspective, and this invention must be founded in the Word and constantly redefined by the Word in the community of the faithful. Not because this community owns the whole truth but because it lives truthfully in communion with the Logos who described himself as the Way, the Truth and the Life.

This communion does not have some particular ethics, because church is ethics; it is a radical mode of living for the neighbour. Hearing the Word of God in the community of the faithful does not mean having answers to all questions, to be always right and have one hundred percent certainties that we own the final truth. In a quite paradoxical way, the Word of God teaches us that it is possible to live in

---

[4] Someone once defined Lutheranism as "the history of the rejection of theology of Martin Luther", and he wasn't really wrong.

truth even if we do not know all answers. It teaches us how to live in the absence of answers, asking right questions.

Part II

The Word Was God: Inerrancy or Christology?

Chapter 3

The Word Was God: Inerrancy or Christology?

Rev. Dr. David P. Scaer

As the story goes, when Karl Barth on a visit to the University of Chicago was asked what was the greatest theological truth, he responded, "Jesus loves me this I know, for the Bible tells me so." His response implied that he had been asked how he knew of God's love in Jesus and he answered that it was found in the Bible. Theologically this would be expressed by holding that the conviction that the Bible is revelatory word of God comes before and provides the basis for faith in Jesus. In terms of this essay, what we think about the Bible as the inerrant or more accurately the infallible word of God is the presupposition for faith in Christ. Neo-orthodoxy of which Barth was a leading exponent subsumed history into revelation. Biblical history (*Historie*) was insulated within revelation and thus immune to historical critique. Faith in Christ came from confronting him in the Bible as a supernaturally revealed book and not in the historical person of Jesus. Within these boundaries biblical inerrancy cannot be tested. Since Evangelicals are prominently involved in the historical research of the gospels, they do not fit the neo-orthodox mould, but like Barth their commitment to the Bible precedes their faith that Jesus loves them. For Evangelicals the Bible testifies to its being God's word but does not create justifying faith. Recognition of the Bible as the word of God gives the Spirit occasion in a parallel, but separate, action to create faith directly.[1] Biblical inerrancy confirms that it is the word of God and provides faith with the knowledge of what it believes but it does not create it. Acknowledgement of the Bible as the inspired, inerrant word of God precedes Christology. Lutheran Orthodoxy held to a similar but not identical view that the Scriptures were *autopistia* in creating the faith that believes they are God's word.[2] This is an argument in a circle. Since it did not allow for historical critique, it provided a haven for some from the negative results of historical criticism that appeared in The Lutheran Church—Missouri Synod (LCMS) in the 1950s.[3] Demonstrating the Bible is inerrant has a role in apologetics, a discipline to convince unbelievers that it is factually reliable and thus its call to faith is worthy of their attention. Evangelicalism sees apologetics in the same way, but it also demonstrates biblical inerrancy to confirm the Spirit's inner testimony. Inerrancy for Lutherans is defensive in refuting claims that the Bible has errors. Beginning theology with Jesus, as Lutherans do, shares common ground with beginning with an inerrant Bible, as the Reformed and Evangelicalism do, in that both begin with the historical and so can be historically validated. Evangelicals do not hold that the biblical revelation is in every instance christological. Lutherans do. Barth like Lutherans held that theology is christological but without coming to terms with Jesus of Nazareth as an historical figure. His is in every sense a 'word of God' theology.

Cordoning theology off theology into four distinct areas and further subdividing dogmatics into loci allows a topic by topic discussion, but in terms of the biblical revelation these divisions are artificial and less than fully productive. Though speaking of first, second or third article Christianity is *chic* and so common that it is now cliché, God's self-revelation is not given in loci. No doctrine is presented in isolation. God's redemption of Israel from captivity assumes that she already recognizes him as creator (Ex 20:2,11). Atonement is presented in Jesus' discourse on humility (Matt 20:20–28) and his sacrifice for sin is fundamental in recognizing that bread

---

[1] The Reformed scholastic Heidigger writes, "The word is the same which man preaches and which the Spirit writes on the heart. There is strictly one calling, but its cause and medium is twofold: instrumental, man preaching the word outwardly; principal, the Holy Spirit writing it inwardly in the heart." Quoted by Heinrich Heppe, *Reformed Dogmatics*, trans. G.T. Thompson (3rd reprint ed.: London: Allen & Unwin, 1978), 518.

[2] Robert D. Preus, *The Theology of Post-Reformation Lutheranism: A Study of Theological Prolegomena* (Saint Louis: Concordia Publishing House, 1970), 296–300. Unlike the Evangelical or Reformed view, the Spirit works through and not along side of the Scriptures.

[3] See Valen Sendstad, *The Word That Can Never Die* (Saint Louis: Concordia Publishing House). In Lutheran theology this conviction is worked by the preaching of the law and the gospel. Guilt over sin worked by the law is a sign to the hearer that God is working in him/her. This is confirmed by a sense of relief worked by the gospel.

and wine are Jesus' body and blood (26:28). Luther commended Melanchthon for his *Loci Communes*, but how he thought emerged in his Lectures on Genesis (1535–45), which were a cocktail of what is now divided in systematics, exegesis, history and pastoral theology, including homiletics.[4] Preaching has to do with biblical inerrancy and Christology. Unless a preacher assumes the former, he expounds on the texts that for him may not even be true to fact and so he beings to graze in other pastures to look for other things on which to preach. Within a Christian context, he is obligated say something about Christ or at least mention his name. He may find that the assigned text does not yield the high Christology to which he is committed to preach. To compensate for a text's deficient Christology, he borrows from other sections of the Bible which he inserts to his sermon. Doctrines that make a particular church distinctive, e.g., Lutheran, Roman, Anglican, Reformed, will determine these biblical references, whose interpretations will be determined by a church's official theology. By repetition these passages, the *sedes doctrinae*, soon constitute a mini-canon. So it is also in debate with each side advancing its position its favoured passages.[5] So by itself biblical authority, of which inerrancy is a component, is not adequate. Conclusions drawn from abstract principles can give birth to false doctrine.[6]

---

[4] Jaroslav Pelikan describes Luther's Genesis Lectures as an indispensable source into the Reformer's thought. Martin Luther, *Lectures in Genesis* in *Luther's Works*, ed. Jaroslav Pelikan (Saint Louis: Concordia Publishing House, 1960–70), 1:12. Ulrich Asendorf refers to the Genesis lectures as Luther's *Summa Theologiae*. "Die ökumenische Bedeutung von Luthers Genesis-Vorlesung (1535–1545) *Caritas Dei: Betrage zum Verstandis Luthers under der gegenwartige Ökumene: Festschrift fuer Tuomo Mannermaa zum 60. Geburtstag*, eds. Oswald Bayer, Robert W. Jenson, Simo Knuuttila (Helsinki:Luther-Agricol-Gesellschafter, 1997), 19. Also see S. J. Munson, 'The Divine Game: Faith and Reconciliation of Opposites in Luther's *Lectures on Genesis*', *Concordia Theological Quarterly* 76/1–2 (April 2012).

[5] For Luther the critical passages were found in Galatians and Romans and for his opponents in James. In defining the ministry 1 Pet 2:9 is the trump card for the LCMS. Proponents of women's ordination favour Galatians 3:28 and disallow 2 Timothy 2:12, which is dismissed as less than authentically Pauline.

[6] Evangelical Calvinists and Arminians agreeing to biblical authority are irreconcilably divided over whether God's or man's will is the cause of salvation and damnation. Twin volumes, *For Calvinism* by Michael Horton and *Against Calvinism* by Roger E. Olson (Grand Rapids, MI: Zondervan, 2011) with each author providing a preface for the other's book, go *tête à tête* on this issue. In each case consistency of principle contravenes biblical passages and classical Christian doctrine as noted in side-by-side reviews in *First Things* 119 (January 2012:63–64). Disruptions in the LCMS in the early 1970s were partially caused by differences on how consistently the Lutheran law-gospel principle was to be applied in theology and biblical studies.

Infallibility is a divine attribute and by extension applies to what God says. In so far as the Bible is recognized as God's word, it is not subject to historical critique. On the other hand the Bible is also a human book and can be historically critiqued to determine its authenticity. To err is human but not necessarily so. Human beings may be expected to carry out most tasks and convey information without error. An administrative assistant prone to error will soon be replaced. We might be living in an age of electronic inerrancy, e.g, financial and credit card statements. Apologetics assumes and demonstrates the trustworthy character of the biblical documents. Historical-criticism begins at the opposite end of the pole and assumes that the like other documents the biblical ones are subject to error. Their authenticity is subject to critique. To advance their causes both apologetics and historical criticism work with historical evidences rather than abstract doctrines. Historical critical methods are of two types. Some recognize only those biblical events with parallels as historically probable. Others take the opposite tack in holding probable those biblical events without parallel. Lack of an agreed-upon definition of historical criticism is the fuel keeping the engine searching for the historical Jesus running. Such opposing principles in determining probability suggests that historical principles are better understood as philosophical ones. Apart from how particular methods define themselves, they do not venture beyond what can be observed and so do not identify supernatural causes. They can examine the biblically reported event, but recognizing God as a cause is off-limits.[7] It can be noted that the biblical writers present historical arguments for their positions and engage in historical critique.[8] Matthew

---

[7] Jenson argues that, since without the faith of the church there would be no Bible, so what the church believes cannot be separated from a historical-critical study of the Bible: "The final reason that one cannot interpret the Bible independently of the church and its dogma is that without these there is no such book." Jenson goes on to say, "The modern attempt to interpret Scripture 'historically' has been intrinsically self-defeating and has now defeated itself, since it has curiously supposed that to interpret the Bible historically we must abstract from the history for whose attestation the church assembled this collection in the first place, the Incarnation and Resurrection of Christ." Robert W. Jenson, *The Triune God, Systematic Theology 1* (New York and Oxford: OUP, 1997), 1:59. Historical critique belongs to the human experience in that on basis of past experiences we find some things to be more probable than others.

[8] Matthew in refuting deniers of the virgin birth and the resurrection (27:2–8; 28:12–15) with the intent that his Jewish hearers would abandon their leaders resembles a modern apologist. Luke describes how he critically how he dealt with his sources (1:1–4). Similarly Paul's names witnesses of Jesus' resurrection (1 Cor 15:5–7) would have been useless, unless they were known to the Corinthians. For Luke ἀπολογία is arguably synonymous with his gospel (12:11; 21:13). Paul uses ἀπολογία in a judicial sense in defence of the conduct of his life (Acts 1:33; 22; 2 Tim 4:16). 1 Peter 3: 15 is used to show that what is called apologetics was in vogue in apostolic times, but it would be difficult to show ἀπολογία from which apologetics is taken had this meaning.

presents Jesus' resurrection as the reason for the empty tomb as the right one. Report of a nightly escapade to steal his body is wrong (28:11–15).

In preparing his sermon the preacher assumes the integrity of the biblical text, *i.e.*, its inerrancy, and its christological content necessary for creating and confirming faith which is the sermon's purpose. Robert D. Preus (1924–1995) typically introduced his sermons, which were unexcelled in their magnificent Christology, with an ode to the inspiration and inerrancy of the text, but without relating one to the other. An inerrant text can be christological but not necessarily so, as in the case of the Evangelicals. Along with its commitment to biblical inspiration, Lutheran Orthodoxy also held that the Logos, the hypostatic Word "is the heart and content and meaning of the prophetic Word; He is the heart and purpose of all the Scriptures,"[9] but its theologians "refused to debate about how Christ is present in the Word of Scripture and how Scripture brings Christ to us".[10] Abraham Calov went so far as to equate Christ with the Bible: "the Word of Scripture and the Word of Christ, Old Testament as well as New Testament, are identical,"[11] a position that can also be credited to Luther but unlikely to be found among Evangelicals. Just as Christ is the sole content of the sacraments and the Scriptures, he is the subject of all theology. Without inspiration, *i.e.*, the Spirit's work, Scriptures would not be word of God and without Christ they would not be worth reading.[12] Preus says nothing about how for Lutheran Orthodoxy the Bible's christological content was connected to or a necessary result of its inspiration.[13] In dogmatics courses inspiration is presented separately from and prior to Christology. A deceased colleague required students to place one Bible passage on every page of a sermon to give it the ring of "thus saith the Lord". For him Bible as Bible had authority. Similarly without an acceptable context, inclusion of the word 'Christ' does not make a sermon christological and can even be a covering for false belief.[14] An egregious example is Harry Emerson Fosdick's hymn "God of Grace and God of Glory". Its second stanza, "Lo, the hosts of evil round us Scorn the Christ and assail his ways!" seems to fit the *Christus Victor* theme that God conquers Satan, until one learns that Fosdick was the lead-

---

[9] Preus, *op.cit*, 270.

[10] *Ibid.*, 374.

[11] *Ibid.*, 373–75.

[12] *Ibid.*, 373–75.

[13] One cannot dismiss the haunting suspicion that the organizers of his conference chose the title of this essay in light of a controversy that arose a quarter century ago over whether all theology is Christology. Otherwise, it is an amazing coincidence that can only be explained by an act of direct inspiration.

[14] The 'Christ' party in Corinth may have been an early Gnostic group (1 Cor 1:12).

ing modernist preacher of his day and believed in neither devils nor Christ's deity. Its title "God of Grace" had no Reformation meaning for him. Hearers' properly informed dispositions can cover a multitude of poetical (homiletical, theological) transgressions. Apart from an orthodox context, inclusion of the word 'Christ' does not satisfy the christological component required for preaching.

A pastor's weekly challenge is forging a sermon that is biblically dependent and christological in content. When the search for an adequate Christology in what for the preacher might be the barren places of the Old Testament and Synoptic Gospels fails, he can fall back on John and Paul and if all else fails, Luther's Small Catechism which by frequent citation serves as a functional authority. Maybe this is not a *homoousion* with the confessions matching the Bible in authority, but it is surely *homoiousion*. So a sermon can become acceptably christological by a dogmatic transfusion with the narrative of the assigned pericope is relegated to background material for pre-packaged doctrinal conclusions. Such sermons typical of seminary students resemble poorly constructed dogmatics lectures. With skill, a great christological sermon can result without the preacher seriously coming to terms with the text. For Lutherans the law and gospel cures all. Commitment to church theology compensates for not coming to terms with a biblical text. This calls attention to the staggering task faced by pastors who every week first have to come to terms with the biblical texts and then put the results into intelligible and convincing sermons. Inspiration and inerrancy of a text are givens. Locating its christological content is challenging. Faced with a variety and contrary interpretations from the commentaries, a preacher can find relief in Paul's proposal that "the gospel" is Christ's death for sins and being raised for our justification (Rm 4:25), but on second glance Paul said this was only the beginning of the gospel (1 Cor 15:3–4) and not its totality. Should the preacher be content with Paul's initial minimal definition, he may conclude that he has met the christological obligation for a sermon. Challenging is that some preachers might find that some biblical sections, especially in the Old Testament and the Synoptic Gospels, e.g., the Sermon on the Mount, are devoid of even a minimal Christology necessary to create justifying faith.

The 1975 report of the Fact Finding Committee appointed by J.A.O. Preus to examine the theology of the faculty of Concordia Seminary, Saint Louis, may show that a minimal christological definition is not adequate. Essential to the faculty position was the gospel as the principle of biblical interpretation. If this was extricated from the text, other matters including its historical hull were up for grabs. This the committee did not accept, but commended them for adherence to justification or the gospel, the christological principle, a belief the committee said they happily shared with them. Overlooked was that the faculty defined gospel as the proclamation of Christ for the forgiveness of sin, but it was not necessarily derived from to the historical character of the events the gospels reported, *i.e.*, that Jesus was born of a virgin and performed this or that miracle. Agreement on the gospel may have only been superficial, since forgiveness created by the gospel was seen as coming to terms with oneself, a concept in vogue at the time.

Disruptions pinnacling in 1974 were rooted in a christological dispute in the 1950s over whether Psalms 2, 45 and 110 were originally intended as direct linear messianic prophecies. Their christological content was later read into them by the New Testament writers, so it was held. In response the traditional view was affirmed, but this raised the question of how the remainder of the Old Testament was christological, if at all. An age old solution consigns Israel's history, rituals, institutions, and leading persons to typology, an amorphous category that allowed for more latitude than explicit predictions. New Testament citation (e.g., Matt 1:23) of an Old Testament passage (e.g., Is 7:14) suggested that a passage was a linear prophecy, but not always. Crossing of the Red Sea was more like a type of a baptism (e.g., 1 Cor 10:2) than direct prophecy. Designating something or someone as a type had the advantage of not requiring that the prophet wrote with christological intent. Like beauty in the eye of the beholder, christological meaning was in the minds of the New Testament writers and later in the even more active imagination of the early fathers. Typology was not really a solution in recognizing the christological character of these passages, since they were afterthoughts of those who lived centuries later. Old Testament Christology became *ex eventu*. This created a two tiered Christology between direct messianic prophecies and types. Prophecies served as christological oases in an Old Testament desert. They were like boulders left behind by retreating glaciers, made of a different substance from the ground on which they rested.[15]

---

[15]Direct linear prophecies are the christological gold standard, just like the homolegoumena are the gold standard in the canon. Types are more like the antilegomena or the apocrypha, useful but lacking certainty in regard to their christological grounding. In the New Testament messianically interpreting Old Testament passages, the Spirit is only explaining what he said, so the argument goes. Inspiration becomes a hermeneutical principle and it is assumed that the Old Testament writers wrote with messianic intent apart from any arguments. Israel's history plays a lesser role in messianic interpretation. Apart from passages designated as direct prophecies or consigned to the universal limbo of types, the majority of the Old Testament, *i.e.*, laws, histories, stories, genealogies, institutions, heroes and rituals, are acknowledged as inspired word of God but without necessary christological intent on the part of the writers. These may be evidences of God's beneficial favour on Israel as his particular people, but these were not messianically intended.

Perceived and real threats in the LCMS that the Scriptures were only of human origin led to an increased reliance on Evangelicals in assuming agreement on biblical inspiration and inerrancy.[16] Perhaps unrecognized was that for Evangelicals biblical authority precedes Christology,[17] a doctrine of such major disagreement that were it not for the Reformed doctrine of the Trinity the Lutherans would have considered them a non-Christian religion.[18] Evangelicals require prior allegiance to the canon as a constitution preserved by providence evident in God's 2000-year faithfulness. Preservation of the canon is reason to trust God.[19] Testimony of the Spirit and not the Bible's christological character, as it is for Lutherans, causes it to be recognized as authoritative.[20]

---

[16] An example was my participation with Robert D. Preus in The Chicago Statement on Biblical Inerrancy (1978), a document still cited by Evangelicals. Coming out of the LCMS controversies that peaked in 1974 and lingered for the next few years, confessional minded Lutherans recognized common positions with Evangelicals. The Statement acknowledges "the limitations of a document prepared in a brief, intensive conference" and that it would not have confessional status. In retrospect the Statement belongs to the Reformed tradition of Evangelicalism. Consider its Article XVII that "the Holy Spirit bears witness to the Scriptures, assuring believers of the truthfulness of God's written Word". This is followed by what seems at first glance an acceptable statement: "We deny that the witness of the Holy Spirit operates in isolation from or against Scriptures." As quoted in Wayne Grudem, *Systematic Theology: An Introduction to Biblical Doctrine* (Leicester, England: Inter-Varsity Press and Grand Rapids, MI: Zondervan Publishing House, 1994), 1200. This satisfies the Reformed belief that the Spirit work along side of the word, but not the Lutheran belief that he works through the word.

[17] The first articles of the Westminister Confession of Faith (1643–46) and the New Hampshire Baptist Confession (1833) and Baptist Faith and Message (Southern Baptist Convention (1925, 1963) deal with biblical authority. Scriptural authority in The Thirty-Nine Articles of the Church of England appear first in the sixth article with a listing of the Old but not the New Testament books. The Westminster Confessions lists books of both testaments.

[18] Michael Horton argues that just as a constitution undergirds a community, so the Scriptures undergirds the church as a covenant community. *The Christian Faith: A Systematic Theology for Pilgrims on the Way* (Grand Rapids, MI: Zondervan, 2011). Also Wayne Grudem, *op.cit*, 77. "Our ultimate conviction that words of the Bible are God's words comes only when the Holy Spirit speaks *in* and *through* the words of the Bible to our hearts and gives us an inner assurance that these are the words of our Creator speaking to us." (Italics in original.) Also, Johann Gerhard: "We therefore believe the canonical Scriptures because they are the canonical Scriptures, that is, they have been brought about by God and written by the direct inspiration of the Holy Spirit." As quoted in Robert D. Preus, *op.cit.*, 305.

[19] Grudem, *Systematic Theology*, 50, 54–64. By making providence as evidence that Scriptures are God's word, they are placed under the natural knowledge of God in the sense that such recognition does not come from the documents themselves.

[20] Compare the Reformed (Evangelical) view to Luther's commitment to the christological principle, as it was defined for him by Paul, which led him to reject, Hebrews, James and Revelation. If the Sermon on the Mount had been a separate book, it probably also would have fallen under his canonical ax.

A heightened interest among Evangelicals (and Lutherans) in liturgy, the historical creeds and the early church fathers may spring from an awareness of a christological deficit in a theology chiefly defined by inspiration and the Spirit's testimony.[21] Commitment of the fathers to the thoroughly christological character of the Bible led them into what was labelled an extravagant allegorising, against which seminary students were warned. The historical-grammatical method was the method of choice. Analysis of a text's grammatical structure along with acknowledging its historical character is the key to the meaning necessary for preaching, but the results were so christologically meagre that frustrated preachers ran for refuge to Paul and Luther. Further hobbling the quest for Christology was the *tertium unum comparationis est* hermeneutic for the parables. When an acceptable christological meaning could not be extricated from a text, law and the gospel became the hermeneutic for nearly every pericope.[22] Affirming the historical character of the Bible is essential for a religion that defines itself according to the *incarnatus est*. Without this its narratives were hardly different from ancient mythologies. Gospels could be seen as formed by the imaginations of those committed to the cause of Jesus. In the light of the LCMS controversies (1955–74), historical affirmation of the gospels was absolutely necessary, but this does not necessarily translate into a theology that can be preached.[23] This approach surrenders the critical role in formulating Christo-

---

[21] Recent conversions to Catholicism and Orthodoxy may also be belong to a search for a more christological defined basis for faith. Mickey L. Mattox and A.G. Roeber, *Changing Churches: An Orthodox, Catholic, and Lutheran Theological Conversation* with an Afterword by Paul R. Hinlicky (Grand Rapids, MI & Cambridge, U.K.: William B. Eerdmans Publishing Company, 2011). Bravos Theological Commentary on the Bible published by Baker Book House under the Bravos Press logo and the Ancient Christian Commentary series published by Inter-Varsity Press are doing just this. Editors R.R. Reno, Robert W. Jenson, Robert Louis Wilken, Ephraim Radner and Michael Root and George Sumner of the Bravos Theological Commentary are recognized for their historical and theological expertise. This may reflect frustration with the results of historical criticism.

[22] Each parable is unique and no one key interprets all. They are extended metaphors or, as someone has called them, figures. If a parable has only one point of comparison, why are they so long?

[23] Coming to terms with the christological content of a gospel is accomplished by locating the method of each evangelist.. Not only may the writer of the first gospel been unaware of his own method, but the second and third evangelists may not have recognized the techniques used in the gospels which they may have known and from which they borrowed. Failure to recognize uniqueness of each gospel resulted in blending the gospels as if they were one gospel, which after all they were, in the hearing and minds of the earliest Christians. Signs of this can be detected in the *Didache*. Just as there was one word of God so there was one gospel. In the second century Tatian produced the first known gospel harmony, as did John Calvin and Andrea Osiander in the 16þcentury. See David Laird Dungan, *A History of the Synoptic Problem* 40–41; 181–84; 306–16. If Mark was the third synoptic gospel, it may have been created as a harmony. Its contents were seen as so similar to what could

logy to the epistles and the confessions. Hermeneutical insecurity is compensated by confessional commitment.

For Lutherans Scripture effects faith by its inspired character,[24] but also "derives its power from its contents, Christ,"[25] who speaks not only in the New but also in the Old Testament.[26] Later Lutherans dogmaticians understood the Bible's inspiration and christological content as an extension of the Trinity, a view shared with the Reformed,[27] but the logic of this argument is defective. A trinitarian origin for the Scriptures would account for its perfection in being inerrant, but does not imply their christological origin which must have incarnation and humiliation at its core.[28] If inspiration is ascribed to Christ because he is the Son of God, it would be ascribed only to his divine but not his human nature. That's the crux of the problem. A christological and not a trinitarian view of inspiration necessarily includes incarnation and humiliation. Such a view has an advantage in not having to face how an infinite God becomes incarnate or speaks in ordinary words. So in reading the Scriptures, one confronts not a bare word of a sovereign God, the Reformed view, but the word of Christ apart from which there is no other word of God. This

---

be found in Matthew and Luke, it was largely ignored until the 19th century. Differences that were the clues to recognizing their methods and their unique Christology of each became less important than recognizing that they constituted one gospel, one word of God. Available in English translation is Martin Chemnitz's *The Harmony of the Four Gospels*, trans. Richard J. Dinda, 3 vols. (Malone, TX: The Center for the Study of Lutheran Orthodoxy, 2012.

[24] Preus, *op.cit.*, 371: "The power of the Word is due to its divine origin (it is inspired by God) and to its divine nature (it is the word of very God)." "Inspiration is so vital to the character of the Scriptures that without it, "it would no longer be the Word of God but a mere human word" (375).

[25] Preus, *ibid.*, 373.

[26] Preus, *ibid.*, 373.

[27] Preus, *ibid.*, 1:275. For the dogmaticians inspiration is "an act of the triune God whereby He communicates to men that which He wishes written for men's sake",

[28] Inspiration understood apart from Christology is characteristic of Reformed theology already with Ulrich Zwingli for whom God's unity precedes his trinitarian existence in *Fidei Ratio*. As translated by Gottfried W. Locher, *Zwingli's Thought: New Perspectives*(Foreword by Duncan Shaw; Studies in the History of Christian Thought; Leiden: Brill, 1981), 172. "'I believe and know there is one only God. He is by nature good, true, mighty, just and wise. He is the creator and sustainer of all things visible and invisible. There are the Father, Son and Holy Spirit, three persons, but they have one simple being.'" Locher, *Zwingli's Thought*, 172–73, n. 98. Locher notes that beginning theology with the divine unity, as Zwingli, Calvin and Karl Barth do, tends toward modalism. Preus notes that Melanchthon, Chemnitz and the earlier dogmaticians began with the doctrine of the Trinity under which the attributes are subsumed. Johann Gerhard, followed by Quenstedt, begins with God's attributes and then the Trinity. Preus says that since all of the divine attributes belong to the Triune God, the earlier method is preferable, but the latter was more logical. *The Theology of Post-Reformation Lutheranism*, 2:54–55. No mention is made of whether Gerhard and Quenstedt were influence by the Reformed model.

can ben seen in how our gospels begin with Christ and not God. This might be the key to choosing Christology over inerrancy.

John begins with the Word who is with God and then identified as God (1:13). Luke begins with those who were eyewitnesses and ministers of the Word (upper case; 1:2). Mark describes his narrative as "the gospel of Jesus Christ" (1:1). A scribe uncomfortable in finding ultimate authority in Jesus may have added "the Son of God". Matthew presents Jesus as the God who is already incarnated by explaining that Emmanuel means "God with us" (1:23). Only in the voice's identifying Jesus as his Son in his baptism is God presented as Father by inference (3:17). Matthew's introduction is not bare genealogy but a summary of God's redemptive activity in Israel's history and as such is christological. So each gospel begins not with God but Jesus. Inspiration is not simply the work of Spirit (Zwingli) or the Spirit of the Son of God, but the Spirit of Christ.[29] Biblical perfection, of which inerrancy is part, is to be understood only in reference to the *incarnatus est, homo factus est* and *crucifixus,* which offend the world's understanding of perfection (1 Cor 1:18; 2:2).

Coming to terms with Scriptures as totally christological and yet inspired (inerrant) distinguishes Lutheran theology from Reformed theology which is pneumatological, a religion of the Spirit.[30] Since the Reformed deny the *genus apotelesmaticum,* for them the Holy Spirit is the Spirit of the Son of God according to the divine nature, the *extra Calvinisticum,* but not the Spirit of Jesus according to his human nature.[31] Lutheran differences with the Reformed over the person of Jesus should be recognized in each's respective doctrines on inspiration, but they are not. The Spirit who speaks through the prophets, *qui locutus est per prophetas,* is the Spirit who proceeds not only from the Father but also from the Son through whom alone he is accessible. Christ's resurrection according to the Scriptures, *et resurrexit tertia die secundum scripturas,* attests to their christological character.

Hunnius and Gerhard spoke of Christ as the author of the Scriptures, but did not connect his authorship with their inspiration by the Spirit,[32] leaving two theological conclusions laying side by side unconnected. Christ's words by which the world will be judged (Matt 7:24–28) and which the disciples are to preserve (28:16–20) are God's words (5:2). Words spoken by the apostles will be those spoken by the

---

[29] John 16:13–15. Rom 8:9; Phil 1:19; 1 Pet 1:11.

[30] Lochner characterizes Zwingli's theology as pneumatological, having to do with the Spirit, and his thought as spiritualistic. *Zwingli's Thought*

[31] Also Zwingli: "It does not divide his person to say that the human nature is in one place and the divine nature is ubiquitous." As translated by Locher, *Zwingli's Thought,* 176.

[32] Preus, *The Inspiration of the Scriptures,* (Mankato, Minnesota: Lutheran Synod Book Company, 1955), 29; *The Theology of Post-Reformation-Lutheranism,* 1:34 .

Spirit of the Father (10:20), a passage the Lutheran dogmaticians knew but did not apply to biblical inspiration. By not coming to terms with how the words spoken through the apostles by the Spirit of the Father were those first spoken by Jesus, they saw inspiration as an internal, virtually mystical process, as Calvin did, rather than a historical act.[33] Thus the historical witness of the apostles was an accompanying, subsidiary factor to biblical inspiration and did not create faith. A christological view of inspiration requires that the words inspired by the Spirit are those of Jesus to whom the Father entrusted them.[34] Jesus speaks the words of God by which man lives (4:4) as his own as God (5:20) and in this speaking he gives the Spirit.[35] This inspiration is sealed in his giving of the Spirit in his crucifixion (Matt 27:50 and John 19:30) followed by a liturgical bestowal in the resurrection (John 20:22). Pentecost

---

[33] So Quenstedt. "[The writers] were inwardly enlightened by the Spirit with a supernatural light; and they were inwardly supplied by the Holy Spirit with all that was necessary for their writing, both with respect to the content and with respect to the very words." Preus, *The Theology of Post-Reformation Lutheranism*, 1:273. See also his *The Inspiration of the Scriptures*, 19, "Inspiration is generally defined by the dogmaticians as the act whereby God conveyed to men both the context of that which He wished to be written for man's sake and the very words expressing that content." For Calvin the Spirit's inward inspiring of the Bible was parallel to his inward testimony to convince the reader that it was true, a belief that persists among the Reformed. See Richard A. Muller, *Post-Reformation Reformed Dogmatics*, 2 vols., 2nd ed (Grand Rapids, Michigan: Baker Book House, 2003), 2:235. "The two issues—testimony of the spirit [sic!] and inspiration—are, therefore, intimately related in Calvin's theology despite their formal separation." This view also appears in Francis Pieper's *Christian Dogmatics*.

[34] On the basis of Matthew 10:20, the Lutheran dogmaticians held that the oral words of the apostles were inspired but did not connect this passage to the written word, though this passage would have an opportunity to do so. Here Jesus speaks of "the Spirit your Father," when "my Father" might be expected and preferred, since the apostles are told that their words will be God's. "Your Father" suggests the disciples knew that Jesus was the Son of God (Matt 16:16), and that they had been authorized and invited by him to address his Father as their own Father, *i.e.*, "Our Father" (Matt 6:9). They are already a gathered community with the Lord's Prayer and a creed that Jesus was God's Son in place as a liturgy. All this has happened not through an inward, mystical activity of the Spirit, as the Lutheran dogmaticians held, but through and because of the preaching of Jesus (Matt 11:27). Here the insight of the Augsburg Confession is right on target: "*Nam per verbum et sacramenta donatur spiritus sanctus*" (5:2). See Levity Alexander, 'Ancient Book Production and the Circulation of the Gospels,' *The Gospel for All Christians*, ed. Richard Bauckham (Grand Rapids, Michigan: Eerdmans, 1998),71–105. There can be no quibble here; however, if the Scriptures were dictated by the authors to scribes, as is most likely the case, the written word was first the oral word and so this may be a distinction with no difference.

[35] "He opened up his mouth" (Matt 5:3) is reminiscent of Isaiah's "for the mouth of the LORD has spoken" (40:5). What the Lord's mouth has spoken the Spirit accomplishes: "For the mouth of the LORD has commanded, and his Spirit has gathered them" (Isa 34:16).

culminates Jesus' giving the Spirit with the terms laid down by the resurrected Jesus (Luke 24:49; Acts 1:8; 2:33).[36]

Jesus' authority is derived from the Father (Matt 28:16) but is also inherently his (7:28). The Spirit gives to the disciples what he takes from the Son and originally and always belongs to the Father.[37] In inspiring the disciples the Spirit does not give them new data but he causes them to remember what Jesus said during his ministry and thus provides a fuller perspective (John 14:26). The Spirit inspiring the Scriptures is not autonomously sovereign act but ratifies what Jesus has spoken (John 20:22). In Luke the Spirit confirms the witness of the disciples to what they have seen Jesus do (24:49). For Matthew inspiration covers Jesus' words (28:20) and for Luke his deeds. John covers both (21:25). In the gospels inspiration finds its source in Jesus' humiliation (*homo factus est*) and not in a mystical process.[38]

Some Anglican and Lutheran churches now allow for the elimination of the *filioque* from the creed, but it is crucial in any doctrine on biblical inspiration. In his giving the Spirit to the disciples, Jesus gave what was eternally and essentially

---

[36] Preus notes that inspiration for the Lutheran dogmaticians applied also to the preached word of the apostles and prophets, but they "would not have broadened inspiration to include the whole historical process that antedate the writing of the various Scriptures or the research the writes may have done or the traditions and sources and other writers may have used". *The Theology of Post-Reformation-Lutheranism*, 1:276. Perhaps this assessment is too broadly stated. Putting aside how Moses came across his materials, the prophets who followed him drew from the Pentateuch and later prophets took from the earlier ones. Some were chosen by others, e.g., Moses and Joshua and Elijah and Elisha. There was a prophetic succession, if we dare speak in these terms. Writers of the New Testament were not blank slates which needed to be supernaturally informed of the commonly held beliefs of the early communities, but they were immersed in the traditions which came from Jesus and which were in every sense the Spirit's words.

[37] "For [the Spirit] will take what is mine and declare it to you. All that the Father has is mine; therefore I said that he will take what is mine and declare it to you" (16:14–15).

[38] A comparison of Matthew 28:20 to Acts 1:1–2 allows for seeing how the Spirit's words are first Christ's. The disciples have been told that their words are really those of the Father' Spirit (Matt 10:20), but in 28:20 they told to preserve all the words Jesus commanded. Matthew's readers already know that the Father's Spirit will be speak through the apostles (10:20). The words of the Spirit of the Father and Jesus are the same words that with the crucifixion threaten eschatological judgement (Matt 27:50–53; comp. Acts 2:17–21) . Inspiration is trinitarian, though it would be hard to show that the Lutheran dogmaticians argued precisely in this way. In Acts Jesus gave command to the apostles through the Holy Spirit (1:2). Dissimilarities complement each other. In Acts the teachings commanded by Jesus are given through the Spirit: "after he had given commandment through the Holy Spirit to the apostles" (1:2). Within the context this commandment refers to Luke's gospel in which the words of Jesus are recorded (Acts 1:1). For both Matthew and Luke Jesus' words given to the eleven are characterized as command (not law as in 'law and gospel'). Matthew's disciples (20:16) become Luke's apostles (Acts 1:2), whom Matthew has already identified as apostles (10:2).

his and not something given to him either before or in time, the view of Arius.[39] Words spoken by Jesus are the Father's because he is the Father's Son. Unless this were so, the Son would not be the Son and the Father would not be the Father. Words entrusted by the Father to the Son are already his, because he is the Son and words spoken by the Spirit are those of the Father given to the Spirit by the Son. The Spirit's inspiration of the Scriptures is an extension of the trinitarian life in which the Son is begotten by Father and because the Son is in the Father the Spirit proceeds from both.[40] The Son is the source of the Spirit's procession because he is the Son of the Father and in the Father. If the procession came only from the Father without the Son, the Father would not be the Father.[41] Words inspired by the Spirit are God's word, not only because they are first the Father's but also the Son's. With the crucifixion the Son's words are given to the church by the Spirit's inspiration as the words of Jesus.[42] Remove the *homo factus est* and the *filioque* from the Spirit's inspiration of the Scriptures and they are no longer inherently christological and are only a bare word of God, but with the crucifixion and resurrection God's word is

---

[39] What each divine person does in the world reflects and must reflect and cannot contradict what he is in relation to the other two persons. Matthew L. Becker notes that Augustine held any person of the Trinity could be sent as the Redeemer. Rahner holds the proper view. "Rahner develops the issue that mission of the Son is proper only to the Son. Only the second person of the Trinity became a human being and thus his 'mission' is unique to the Logos, to his particular history." Matthew L. Becker, 'The Self-Giving God: The Trinity in Johannes von Hofmann's Theology', *Pro Ecclesia* 12:4 (Fall 2003), 420. See the paragraph heading "The Renewal of Trinitarian Theology" (419–24). By extension biblical inspiration had to be accomplished by the Spirit, but as we have argued, this must be seen in relation to the other two Persons." What God does in the world (*opera externa*) reflects what he is in himself (*opera interna*).

[40] Jesus' giving of the Spirit cannot be identified with the *filioque*, but as Robert W. Jenson says, "For it is the very function of the trinitarian propositions to say the relations that appear in the biblical narrative between Father, Son, and Spirit are the truth about God himself." *Systematic Theology* 1:150.

[41] See Jenson, *Systematic Theology*, I, 149–51. Since the Spirit proceeds from the Son, and not only from the Father, he is distinguished from the Son whose origin is only in the Father and answers the question of how the begetting of the Son is different from the procession of the Spirit, a question that mystified the dogmaticians. *Quid sit nasci, quid processus, me nascire sum professus.*

[42] Paul's determination to define his theology by the crucifixion also applies to how he understands God's word. "The word of the cross" is the word of God (1 Cor 1:18; 2:2). Biblical inspiration is defined by crucifixion and resurrection events which supply its content. These events define what the Spirit does and says. Matthew locates the giving of the Spirit in the death of Jesus (Matt 27:50), as does John (19:30), who focuses a specific giving of the Spirit by Jesus to the apostles after the resurrection (20:22). A double giving of the Spirit is not a problem, if crucifixion and resurrection are seen as two sides of one event. The Spirit who is active in establishing the apostolic ministry (Matt 10:1–2; 20; John 20:22) is the Spirit who accompanies Baptism and Eucharist (19:31) and forms the community of believers (Acts 2).

now the gospel to be preached all (Matt 24:14 [οἰκουμένη]; 26:13 [κόσμος]; [πάντα τὰ ἔθνη]28:20).[43] By its being given from the cross as apocalyptic event, inspiration threatens judgement on all who ignore the gospel (27:50–53; cf. 7:24–27).[44] What the Spirit inspires is completely and inherently and not partially or incidentally christological. The one who has the Spirit, is conceived by the Spirit, is endorsed by the Spirit and accomplishes his work by the Spirit (Matt 12:28; Luke 11:20) is the Father's Son and gives the Father's Spirit to the church as His own Spirit. Jesus possesses the Spirit fully and gives it to his church: "'When he ascended on high he led a host of captives, and he gave gifts to men'" (Eph 4:8). The Spirit is the gift and the gifts.[45]

Understanding inspiration as an historic process rather than an internal one allows for that history in which inspiration is given to be critically examined with the understanding that the method employed does not have prior bias against the supernatural being encased in history. (For the Reformed, what is divine is never encapsulated in history.) Will Durant's definition that the study of history is more of an art than a science is reason enough to hold that no historical method is ultimate. Like Solomon's rivers flowing into and returning from never-full seas (Eccl 1:8), one method replaces another in a perpetual cycle.[46] Conceding that the supernatural,

---

[43] ὁ δὲ Ἰησοῦς πάλιν κράξας φωνῇ μεγάλῃ **ἀφῆκεν τὸ πνεῦμα**. Καὶ ἰδοὺ τὸ καταπέτασμα τοῦ ναοῦ ἐσχίσθη ἀπ᾽ ἄνωθεν ἕως κάτω εἰς δύο καὶ ἡ γῆ ἐσείσθη καὶ αἱ τέτραι ἐσχίσθησαν καὶ πολλὰ σώματα τῶν κεκοιμημένων ἁγίων ἠγέρθησαν, καὶ ἐξελθόντες ἐκ τῶν μνημείων μετὰ τὴν ἔγερσιν αὐτοῦ εἰσῆλθον εἰς τὴν ἁγίαν πόλιν καὶ ἐνεφανίσθησαν πολλοῖς.

[44] The loud voice of Jesus, the tearing of the temple curtain, the earthquake, the splitting of the rocks, the opening of the tombs, the resurrection of the saints and their entry into the Holy City and appearing to many are events of the end times. See Kenneth L. Waters, Sr., 'Matthew 27:52–53 as Apocalyptic Strophe: Temporal-Spatial Collapse in the Gospel of Matthew', *Journal of Biblical Literature* 122/3 (Fall 2003), 489–515.

[45] In commenting on the Holy Spirit as the gift of God, Jenson says that this is both a subjective and objective genitive: "the Holy Spirit is God given by God." *Systematic Theology* 1:147.

[46] There is no certain agreement on who the historical Jesus was. For Ernest Renan he was a revolutionary (*The Life of Jesus* [New York: Random House, 1972], 194–96; first published 1863); for Albert Schweizer, he was a disillusioned mystic (*The Quest for the Historical Jesus: A Critical Study of Its Progress from Reimarus to Wrede* [Introduction by James M. Robinson; New York: Macmillan, 1968]; first published 1906); and for John Dominic Crossan he was a peasant cynic (*The Historical Jesus: The Life of a Mediterranean Peasant* [San Francisco: HarperSan Francisco, 1991]). See 421–22. "The historical Jesus was, then, a peasant Jewish Cynic. His peasant village was close enough to a Greco-Roman city like Sepphoris that sight and knowledge of Cynicism are neither inexplicable nor unlikely. We add, "Nor proven." Quests for the historical Jesus seem to be directed by the Zeitgeist and so their conclusions are not startling.. Some hold that Jesus had a self-awareness of his special relationship to God, but might have been more apparent to the early communities of his followers than to him.

including inspiration, is not historically demonstrable,[47] the Word's becoming flesh (John 1:14) invites and even requires historical inquiry. Inerrancy and apologetics have a place alongside of historical criticism, since each examines the data from a different perspective and goal. A method attempting to locate Jesus within a shared world history cannot be totally unattractive to Lutherans for whom theology begins with the God who is found in the history of Israel, Jesus and the church.[48] A theology beginning and solely based on inspiration without a thoroughly penetrating Christology assumes that the Spirit's inspiration comes from a God in a transcendental realm that is philosophically inaccessible. To this God are attributed attributes that make a full incarnation impossible and to which the biblical narrative must be conformed. Evidence for the biblical truth becomes the biblical truth itself and the Spirit's inner testimony. Examination of the historical data in the documents and the methods proposed to do it are relegated to an auxiliary position. The Spirit's inspiration comes from Jesus and so inspiration should be understood christologically. A theology beginning with a non-christologically defined doctrine of inspiration allows for coming to ideas about God, e.g., his sovereignty, that compromise the incarnation and make his redemptive purposes an afterthought. Without knowledge of these, some biblical events may be seen as at odds with what God is in himself and one event at odds with the other. Theology's purpose has less to do with locating its Christology and more to do in demonstrating biblical perfection. Gospel harmonies now become a necessity to compensate for the unevenness of the four gospels.[49] A caveat about critical methods: Redaction, literary, social, narrative, feminine and ethnic criticisms are not strictly speaking historical methods. Rather than addressing historical question to the biblical documents, they subject them to cultural and literary standards, which at times seem arbitrary. By sidestepping the Scriptures as historical documents with historical data, they are strangely caught between what Jenson calls a kind of fundamentalism[50] and, I would add, historical agnosticism.

---

[47] Critical methods may allow for the Spirit's inspiration, but for some of these the Spirit is understood as the Spirit of the community (Schleiermacher) and not as he is confessed in the creed as the one "who with the Father and the Son is worshipped and glorified" or "who spoke by the prophets." Bart Ehrman's *The New Testament: A Historical Introduction to the Early Christian Writings*, whose popularity is attested by its being published in a third edition, may be more typical of critical approaches in making no mention of the Holy Spirit at all as a factor in the production of the New Testament.

[48] This contrasts with to the Reformed who begin with God and moves immediately to the Holy Spirit For the role of the Holy Spirit in Zwingli's theology, see Lochner, *Zwingli's Thought*, especially 178–80.

[49] Preus, *The Theology of Post-Reformation Lutheranism*, 1:352–53.

[50] Jenson, *Systematic Theology*, 1:172. "A remarkable feature of many proposals of narrative or structural or reader-critical exegesis is their fundamentalism. The proposers, no longer believing in the

Methods now in vogue cannot be here analysed, but it is hard not to mention N. T. Wright's argument that the resurrection may be the best possible explanation for the absence of the body of Jesus of Nazareth from the tomb.[51] In coming to terms in choosing between inerrancy and Christology, this essay has proposed that inspiration belongs to Christology, because God's word come from Jesus' mouth and the Spirit who inspires proceeds from the Son and not only from the Father. Though Lutherans are aware of our christological and sacramental differences with the Reformed and Evangelicals, our real differences are rooted in different understandings of God, Christ and inspiration. On biblical christology Jenson says,

> Christ is the not the content of the proclamation merely as a passive object, that *about* which the proclamation speaks. That he is risen, and so can himself speak now in the church, is part of what is narrated. It is the Father whose words are the gospel, but the Son, who is the content of the gospel, is not mere object but himself speaks in his church, and that he speaks is part of what the Father says.[52]

Inspiration, which is what the Scriptures as the word of God is all about, should be understood historically in the sense that this word was spoken by the prophets in anticipation of Christ's coming and by the apostles in their witness to him. Hence they are thoroughly christological. Since this speaking takes place within the historical life of Israel and the church, historical-critical methods and demonstrating biblical inerrancy belongs to what Christology is all about.[53] Remove the christological character from inspiration and the God who inspires becomes a *deus ex machina*, appearing and reappearing over a 2000 year period, intruding into history to disrupt the psyches of the chosen writers. (In Lutheran terms, eliminate Christology from inspiration and the Old Testament contents become a collection of historical data and poetry and with the remainder the scales are tipped against the gospel in favour of the law.) Inspiration has its origin in not only a dogmatic but an historically defined Christology, grounded in the history of Jesus as confessed in the *incarnatus est* and *homo factus est*.

Resurrection to which the Bible bears witness, nevertheless persist in supposing that the book itself must somehow be a blessing, if only we can find an unthreatening way to read it."

[51] N. T. Wright, *The Resurrection of the Son of God*, Christian Origins vol. 3 (Minneapolis: Fortress Press, 2003).

[52] Jenson, *Systematic Theology* 1:175.

[53] Some time back I proposed that inspiration should be seen as subcategory under apostolicity. David P. Scaer, *The Apostolic Scriptures* (Saint Louis: Concordia Publishing House, 1971).

While the christological character of the New Testament is a given, that of the Old Testament it is often limited to messianic predictions and types imposed on the texts centuries later. This christological limitation typifies Evangelicalism in holding that the Bible is christocentric but not thoroughly christological. A case in point is an article examining Samson as a messianic figure that finds he comes up short.[54] Should christological standards be strictly applied to Adam, Noah, Job, Abraham, Isaac, Jacob, the twelve patriarchs, David and Solomon, none would make the grade. As with saints old and new, good intentions lie side by side with bad ones, what Lutherans call *simul iustus et peccator*. Tamar plays the harlot to preserve the line of Judah, Rahab in saving herelf and family provides refuge to the spies from Joshua's invading army and in following Naomi back to Bethlehem, Ruth perpetuates the messianic lines by offering herself to Boaz. Good intentions can have bad results. On the hand, Abraham takes Hagar to provide an heir, but God intends to work through Sarah. They all believed God's redemptive purposes were found in Israel. Their messianic beliefs were as tinged with sin and imperfection as were the christological beliefs of Peter and the other disciples, as well as ours still are. Christ who is the Old Testament's content appears in the New Testament as Jesus and so all the Scriptures are christological.

Even if some have difficulty in recognizing the christological character in Old Testament persons, Luther did not. Neither did some hymn writers. In the fourth stanza of "See, the Conqueror Mounts in Triumph", Christopher Wordsworth sees Jesus as Enoch, Aaron, Joshua and Elijah. In "Lo, Judah's Lion Wins the Strife", Jesus is portrayed as David slaying Goliath. Luther in "Christ Jesus Lay in Death's Strong Bands" sees Jesus as the true paschal lamb. In "Lo, Judah's Lion Wins the Strife", the writer sees Christ in Samson.[55] Along with Samson, Solomon is often not seen a Christ figure. Of course the Greater Solomon saw things otherwise (Matt 12:42).

---

[54] Benjamin J. M. Johnson, 'What Type of Son is Samson', *The Journal of the Evangelical Theological Society* 53/2 (June 2010), 269–86. His lifestyle suggests to Johnson that he is not what Christ is supposed to be (285). This could also be said about all of them, especially David, who along with Samson, " through faith conquered kingdoms, enforced justice, received promises, stopped the mouths of lions" (Hebrews 11:32–33).

[55] "Like Samson, Christ great strength employed And conquered hell, its gates destroyed."

Chapter 4

A Response to David P. Scaer

Dr. Daniel Johansson

This response is divided into three brief sections. First, I ask some questions in regard to the main thesis of this paper. Second, I highlight some questions which are suggested by the title of this paper but which were not discussed, questions that are highly relevant at least in the Scandinavian context. Finally, I make some brief comments on some details in the paper.

The thesis of this paper is that inspiration and Christology cannot be separated, that inspiration belongs to Christology. Two main arguments are put forward to defend this thesis: First, God's word comes from Jesus' mouth and second, the Spirit who inspires proceeds both from the Father *and* the Son. Essential in this argumentation is a critique of a "Trinitarian" view of inspiration since this would ascribe inspiration of the Scriptures only to Christ's divine nature and not his human nature (12). Thus, if I have understood Dr. Scaer correctly, the crucial point of this paper is that Christ's human nature, not merely his divine nature, is involved in the inspiration of Scripture. This, in turn, guarantees both the central message of Scripture, that is, incarnation and humiliation, but also its historical character (contra Barth's view) so that it can be both critically examined with historical-critical methods and its inerrancy demonstrated.

I have four questions in regard to this.

1. Why is it necessary for a historical-critical study and examination of the Scriptures that Christ according to his human nature participates in inspiration? Why is not the participation of human authors sufficient enough to guarantee its historical

and incarnational character and therefore also a historical study and verification of its truthfulness?

2. Dr Scaer seems to suggest that our view of inspiration has consequences for what we encounter in Scripture. It was claimed that a Christological view of inspiration necessarily includes incarnation and humiliation, but that this is not the case with a merely Trinitarian doctrine of inspiration. But is that so? Does it really matter whether one encounters the "bare word of God" or the word of Christ if the very word we encounter nevertheless assures us that God took on flesh and died and rose for our sins? If Christ is the content and core of the entire Scripture, the one we encounter in the New as well as the Old Testament, does it then really matter whether its inspiration is Spirit-given or Christ-given?

3. It seems to me that this paper assumes a rather strong distinction between the two natures of Christ. Is not Christ involved in a Trinitarian inspiration according to both his divine *and* his human nature, once the two natures have been united in the incarnation? Given our understanding of the relationship of the two natures do we then have to reject a Trinitarian origin of inspiration in favour of a Christological one?

4. If Christ's human nature is essential in a biblical understanding of inspiration, then what about the inspiration of the Old Testament which took place before the incarnation took place? Is that essentially different from the inspiration of the New Testament?

Now to my second issue. The title of this paper suggests that one may choose Christology over inerrancy or vice versa. Scaer affirms both, but choosing Christology over inerrancy has been a common approach in liberal as well conservative circles in the Scandinavian Lutheran churches. Some pastors may hold the Word of God with capital W, that is, Christ in high regard, but has less regard for the word of God as in the Old and New Testament. Thus the Word of God rather than the words of God is Spirit and life. A conservative version of this view can be encountered where most of you probably do not expect it. Let me read a couple of sentences from a book which most of you probably have read:

> Personally I simply believe that the Bible is just such as God wished it to be. Perhaps, it does not mean that every detail is arranged for scientific research in such a way that it would in a doctoral dissertation, but it means that every detail is shaped in such a way that it helps a person, who is seeking salvation, to the truth. [Translation mine]

This is senior pastor Bengtsson speaking to pastor Torvik in Bo Giertz's *The Hammer of God*. The two friends are discussing the doctrine of Scripture and the young fervent Torvik is defending "a historical view of the Bible". The older and more experienced Bengtsson for his part states that he has "a religious doctrine of Scripture". For Bengtsson, who here serves as the voice of Giertz, this means that the Bible is infallible in theological matters, but not necessarily so in historical and other matters. Now those of you who have read the *Hammer of God* in English have not encountered this discussion, because this was one of the parts the English translator chose to not include in his translation. Why, I do not know. But I mention this for it illustrates an ongoing discussion among conservative theologians and pastors in the Scandinavian churches where some have defended what has been labelled an ortho-dox doctrine of Scripture: the Bible is seen as inerrant in all matters, theological and historical. This would if we use a terminology common in Evangelical circles, be those who defend "inerrancy". The view of the other group, where Giertz was one of the most well-known figures, has been labelled a conservative doctrine of Scripture: the Bible is regarded as inerrant in all matters theological but not necessarily so in historical, scientific and geographical matters. This would be the equivalent to those in the English speaking world who hold to infallibility. This discussion is not a past reality, but these two views exist side by side in Scandinavian Lutheran circles.

Here are some questions in regard to this:

First, I was left without a definition of what Dr. Scaer means by inerrancy. What does it include or not include?

Second, in whatever form, you seem to take inerrancy for granted. But is it ne-cessary for Christian theology, confessional Lutheranism, for a true Christology, for being faithful to the historical witness of the early Church or the inspired Scripture? And why? Is not sufficient to hold inerrancy in theological matters? Giertz could put it like this: "There are no errors in the Bible if it is properly used, when it is read with the intention to become saved, that is to hear God himself speak about salvation through Jesus Christ, but one should not expect that God speaks through it when one uses it as textbook for natural sciences or as a history of the world." Giertz, it would seem, had answered "Christology" to the question of this paper.

Third and finally, I would like to make some brief comments on some of the biblical passages Dr. Scaer cites and some he does not cite.

In the argumentation for a Christological view of inspiration I expected a dis-cussion of couple of other passages than those that are actually discussed. First, Rom 10:14. Here Paul does not say "And how are they to believe in him *of whom* they have never heard?" as some translations take it, but actually, "How are they to believe in him *whom* they have never heard?" What Paul here seems to say is that people hear Jesus himself in the proclamation of the apostles, just like Jesus himself says in Luke 10:16: "The one who hears you hears me." This would, if anything, guarantee that Jesus is the author of the New Testament writings.

In my view, however, John 1:18 takes this a step further by ascribing not only the New Testament revelation to Jesus but also the revelation of the Old Testament. "No one has ever seen God; the only God, who is at the Father's side, he has made him known." This passage seem to suggest that the figure the prophets, for example Moses, encountered in various theophanies was not the Father but the pre-incarnate son and that he made God known not only after the incarnation but also prior to it, that is, he is the source of revelation also in the OT. The OT word is not only spoken by the prophets in anticipation of Christ' coming but are in fact words revealed by the pre-incarnate Son himself. Furthermore, the Son is not present in the OT just through messianic prophecies or typological figures, but also really present in the OT. This is a claim made not only by the early fathers, but by John in several passages, for example, his claims that Abraham saw Jesus (John 8:56-58) or that Isaiah saw the pre-incarnate Son in the temple (John 12:41), and Paul when he speaks of the wilderness wandering (1 Cor 10:4, 9).

For my own part, I doubt that Matt 10:20 (p. 56) is relevant to biblical inspiration as these words seem only to speak about Christians defending themselves at trials. But I note that the Lukan parallel passage (21:15) is a stronger support for Scaer's thesis. Jesus does not say, as in Matthew, "Your Father's spirit will speak through you", but, "I myself will give you a mouth and wisdom, which none of your adversaries will be able to withstand or contradict."

Finally, a brief comment on the discussion of the beginnings of the four Gospels (p.55). If the Gospels are Græco-Roman biographies as most scholars seem to agree today, then it is perhaps not so significant for our view of inspiration that they begin with their main character Jesus (Luke is in this regard an exception who has readers to wait a chapter or so before he introduces Jesus). This is what we should expect and God's presence and existence is probably presupposed and taken for granted. Nevertheless, I also note that Mark, to take one example, relates in a strategically placed passage how God authorizes Jesus as a source of revelation: Listen to him (the Transfiguration scene; Mark 9:7). Thus, I think God's authorisation of Jesus' speaking is more important for the doctrine of inspiration than the significance of that the Gospels begin with Jesus, which is simply natural for a Graeco-Roman biography. Given the format of books (the scroll), it is necessary that the author immediately states what the book is about.

Part III

Quia—Quatenus: Scripture and Confession

Chapter 5

Quia—Quatenus: Scripture and Confession

Rev. Dr. Armin Wenz

> Non est autem firma fides, quae non ostendit se in confessione.[1]
> There is no certain faith which does not show itself in confession.

1 Scripture and Confession—a referential framework

If one confesses to be confessional, one faces many challenges, especially in our time. Very often, even in churches that claim to be bound to certain historic confessions in their church orders, the confessions are considered a problem or even a burden rather than a benefit for the church and her members.[2] According to Jörg Baur, retired Professor of Systematic Theology in Göttingen, the "average protestant resentments" against a pledge to the confessions are voiced as follows: "the confessions are instrumental in turning the dogmatic results of the Reformation and of the Early Church into a taboo zone beyond criticism, in making Scripture immune over against renewed critical approaches, and thus in conserving an understanding of the Scriptures of the past. The confessions are experienced as an obstacle for connecting the faith of our time with the Scripture of the past, which is a most difficult

---

[1] Apol. IV.385 (264); BSLK 232.20f.
[2] Especially the Lutheran Church "has always been reproached for valuing confessions too highly and indeed for putting them above the Bible". Hermann Sasse, *We Confess Jesus Christ* (St. Louis: Concordia Publishing House, 1984), 83.

task anyway."[3] Jörg Baur rightly makes the point, that such "pious scruples concerning the appearance of a third player between Scripture and the church, between the Word and faith, between Christ and the believer" grow from an "act of the free will, by which the judging person leaves the factual connection between Scripture, as it is interpreted and proclaimed, and faith which lives from the word, within the historically contingent fellowship of church."[4] "Everything must and can look totally differently, if the confession finds its place in a referential framework, *i.e.*, in the dynamic connection of Scripture, proclamation, faith, and ecclesial fellowship."[5]

The difference between these two opposing viewpoints, described by Baur, can also be observed concerning the question of the understanding of Holy Writ which is closely connected to our topic. If the Scriptures are considered to be mere texts of antiquity whose relevance for today has to be critically ascertained by an allegedly neutral recipient, then the historic confessions turn into merely time-bound attempts of interpretation by past generations, which can be of paradigmatic relevance for our present-day perception of processes of understanding at best. If, on the other hand, the biblical Scriptures are considered the effective word of the living God, who personally reveals himself as the triune God[6] by drawing the justified sinner into a communicational community with himself through these very Scriptures, then the confession is no additive, but the only fitting form of expression of that faith in

---

[3] "Können die gängigen protestantischen Einwände – durch die Bekenntnisse wird ein bestimmter dogmatischer Ertrag der Reformation und der alten Kirche tabuisiert, die Schrift gegen erneuten kritischen Umgang immunisiert und ein vergangenes Schriftverständnis konserviert – wirklich in dem Anspruch unabweisbarer Notwendigkeit ... auftreten?" Das Bekenntnis "wird nur noch als Hindernis für die sowieso schon prekär gewordene Verbindung von heutigem Glauben und vergangener Schrift erfahren." Jörg Baur, *Einsicht und Glaube: Aufsätze* (Göttingen: Vandenhoeck & Ruprecht, 1978), 285.

[4] *Ibid.*: "die Sorgen über das Auftreten eines Dritten zwischen Schrift und Kirche, Wort und Glaube, Christus und dem Glaubenden, erwachsen aus einem Akt des liberum arbitrium, durch den sich der Urteilende aus dem faktischen Zusammenhang von ausgelegter, verkündigter Schrift und aus dem Worte lebendem Glauben innerhalb einer geschichtlich kontingenten Gemeinschaft von Kirche gelöst hat."

[5] *Ibid.*, 286: "Alles aber muß und kann sich sehr anders ansehen, wenn ... das Bekenntnis ... seinen Platz im Verweisungsgefüge, im dynamischen Zusammenhang von Schrift, Verkündigung, Glaube und kirchlicher Gemeinschaft hat. ... Es ist in seinen Aussagen selbst Aufforderung, Anweisung, Ermutigung, eben in seinen Sätzen die Aussage der Schrift an uns neu zu entdecken; es warnt mit seinem Anspruch vor der gewiß nicht a limine unmöglichen Möglichkeit, daß wir die Schrift anders hören und also selbst anderes sagen und hören wollen; es fügt konsentierend Hörende zu bekennender Kirche zusammen und hält den Stachel der Differenz angesichts dissentierenden Hörens im Fleisch der konkreten Kirchen lebendig; es erlaubt den voneinander geschiedenen Konfessionskirchen also nicht die Entspannung ihres Verhältnisses zum neutralen Phänomenvergleich."

[6] Cf. Reinhard Slenczka, *Kirchliche Entscheidung in theologischer Verantwortung. Grundlagen, Kriterien, Grenzen* (Göttingen: Vandenhoeck & Ruprecht, 1991), 262.

God which is effected by the Scriptures. Holy Scripture—intrinsically perceived as
the word of the living God—is the very authority, which empowers and obliges its
readers and hearers to join in the confession of its very contents. Thus the essence
of a faithful confession is nothing but the rendering of an account concerning the
truth perceived through the Scriptures by its recipients. A faithful confession of the
church never goes beyond Scripture, but as a summary of the gospel of Christ as it is
proclaimed in Holy Writ it points and guides into the Scriptures. Thus confessional
obligation also is a result of the insight, that a special form of Biblicism does not do
justice to the nature of Scripture as the word of the triune God. It was Hermann
Sasse who emphasized that a Biblicism denying the necessity of binding confessions
regularly leads to enthusiasm.[7]

Both the external effects of the biblical message as well as its internal structure
make confessions an intrinsic necessity. Externally, the message of the Bible is a
message creating conflicts in this time and world, including conflicts concerning a
faithful interpretation of the Scriptures, thus forcing the recipients to differentiate
and to take sides in the struggle between God's truth and that mixture of truths and
lies as we find it in our world and which can spoil the very interpretation of the Bible.
Internally, the Bible in itself is not an indifferent enumeration of rational truths,
but it is characterized by complex, in some respects even conflicting, relations of
divine institutions, works and effects such as the Old and the New Testaments, Law
and Gospel, God's wrath and God's grace, God's works in creation and its orders
and God's works in salvation and the orders of the church. A faithful confession
mirrors the very theological thrusts and movements, revealed in these relations and
tensions in the context of the whole biblical Trinitarian framework and confronts it
with alternative understandings of Scripture which do not do justice to the described
framework and thus at least endanger the church's communion as it is effected by
Scripture.

---

[7]Cf. Hermann Sasse, *In statu confessionis II: Gesammelte Aufsätze und Kleine Schriften* (ed. F. W.
Hopf; Berlin und Schleswig Holstein: Die Spur, 1976), 258: "Der Ruf zum Bekenntnis ist … nichts anderes als der Ruf zum Worte Gottes, das es auslegt und von dem allein es seine Autorität erhält. Kein Bi-
blizismus kann Ersatz dafür sein, wie die tragische Geschichte aller biblizistischen Bewegungen zeigt,
deren Ende immer das Schwärmertum ist, weil es ohne Bekenntnisbildung keine Unterscheidung von
wahrer und falscher Schriftauslegung gibt."; Slenczka (*Entscheidung*, 278) refers to Werner Elert, who
shows that the opposing theological wings of Liberalism and Biblicism have a strong anti-dogmatic
resentment in common.

2   The marks of the Christian confession according to the Scriptures

Throughout Holy Scripture time and again the reader is confronted with encouragements and obligations to make a confession, because the divine words and deeds proclaimed and brought about in Scripture and through it do not take place on neutral ground, but constitute the difference between faith and unbelief, between the community of salvation and a lost world. This is highlighted when we look at two central key-texts from both the Old and the New Testaments, one concerning the first commandment and one concerning the question posed by Jesus to his disciples: "But who do you say that I am?" (Matt 16:15)

If we look at the first commandment we first hear God's self-presentation to man which is at the same time a word of promise: "I am the LORD your God" (Ex 20:2). The other side of the coin is the commandment: "You shall have no other gods before me" (Ex 20:3). This revelation constitutes God's relation to his people and therefore results in Israel's confession: "Hear, O Israel: The LORD our God, the LORD is one!" (Deut 6:4) And the disciples' response to their Lord's question (Matt 16:16) is no multi-perspective formula of consensus between formerly opposing viewpoints, but an exclusive formula. According to Jesus himself, this confession is only possible through the Father's revelation to his disciples (Matt 16:17). The manifold opinions and interpretations of men are excluded as sources of truth. At the same time ambiguity is excluded by the one revealed truth. Thus in both passages we find the fundamental twofold act of assent (*assertio*) and exclusion or contention (*contentio*), which runs throughout Holy Writ, and which is repeated in all articles of faith and is therefore also essential for a scriptural understanding of confession. The connection between the Old and the New Testaments is specifically manifest in the fact that the New Testament repeats and consents with the confession to the God of Israel as it corresponds to the First Commandment,[8] while at the same time unfolding this very confession by presenting an exclusive framework of relations between the persons of the Trinity. The Father exclusively reveals himself through the Son.[9] The Son is perceived and confessed as God and Lord (*Kyrios*).[10] The internal Jewish conflict concerning the legitimacy of this confession and of the closely connected understanding of the Old Testament runs throughout the New Testament. The criteria, decisive for salvation in the last judgement as declared by Christ, is not a formal belief in Scripture, which was also shared by the Scribes and the Pharisees, but the

---

[8] Mark 12:29; 1 Cor 8:4–6.

[9] Matt 3:17; 17:5; John 10:30; 14:6–9 and many more passages.

[10] John 20:28; 1:1ff. and many more passages.

confession to the person of Christ as true Son of God.[11] At the same time, however, Christ himself points to the Scriptures of the Old Testament as the unique and exclusive key for the true understanding of his person and his work of salvation.[12]

It therefore cannot be emphasized often enough that it is Christ crucified and risen who made the Canon of the Old Testament and the New Testament writings mandatory for his church, by opening the Scriptures of the Old Testament to the disciples[13] and by sending them out as apostles in order to proclaim the gospel the church is founded upon, thus constituting the New Testament.[14] The one saving faith, which articulates itself in the confession of Christ, is effected and protected through the Holy Scriptures and the proclamation based upon them.[15] The binding of his church to the Scriptures by Christ himself goes hand in hand with the sending of the Holy Spirit who builds and assembles the church by guiding her into Christ's truth and by thus empowering and authorizing her to do both, to confess Christ and to pray to the Father in Jesus' name.[16] It is this confession of Christ, effected by the Holy Spirit, that distinguishes and separates the true church from the false church and all those who share different beliefs. In the New Testament it can be clearly seen that even single aspects of Christ's person and work like his incarnation (John 1; 1 John) or his bodily resurrection (1 Cor 15) do belong to the doctrines which are decisive for our salvation and thus separate Christians from those who deny these aspects.

The existential and ecclesiological necessity and relevance of such confessions can clearly be seen where the question of legitimate access to the divine worship and the sacraments is discussed in the Bible. The one who communes at the table of the Lord and thus partakes in the body of Christ cannot at the same time have communion with the table or worship of the demons.[17] Even from the New Testament beginnings of the church we see the close connection between the celebration of Holy Communion with formulas of curse and excommunication against those who deny

---

[11] Matt 10:32–33; cf. Rom 10:9–10.

[12] John 5:39; Luke 24:27, 44; 2 Tim 3:15–17.

[13] Luke 24:27.45-47.

[14] Matt 28:18–20; cf. Luke 10:16.

[15] Cf. John 20:31; Luke 1:4; Matt 28:20 etc.

[16] 1 Cor 12:3b: "No one can say that Jesus is Lord except by the Holy Spirit." 1 John 4:2: "By this you know the Spirit of God: Every spirit that confesses that Jesus Christ has come in the flesh is of God." Concerning prayer to the Father cf. Rom 8:14–17; Gal 4:6–7.

[17] 1 Cor 10:14–22.

the truths proclaimed in the act of Christ's Supper.[18] Johannes Wirsching, the late Berlin systematician, writes: "From the very beginning the sacrament of the altar was connected with doctrine, that is, with the claim to state the salutary truth of Jesus Christ in a binding way. Thus the refutation of error has not become a historical fact only through later confessing churches fighting each other, as is often presupposed, but is something given together with the sacrament already."[19] The same is true for baptism according to Mark 16:15–16 and other New Testament passages. The Christian, who by the power of his baptism lives in a union with Christ and in His Spirit, cannot at the same time confess himself to be a loyal follower of sin, the flesh, or the world.[20] In the baptismal liturgy this is manifest in the combination of confession of Christ and renunciation of the devil which are inseparably connected according to Christ's own paradigm in Matt 4. Based on these observations the following fundamental aspects of a scriptural understanding of confession can be expounded:

1. The *christological-trinitarian* aspect: Christ himself challenges his disciples to confess and sends them his Spirit without whom no such confession would be possible. Therefore the confession is the oral or written expression of that saving faith in Christ which is brought about through the revelation of Christ in the gospel. Faith and confession are inseparably connected (cf. Matt 10:32–33; Rom 10:9–10). The foundation of such unanimous confession therefore is the clarity of the Scriptures as testimonies of Christ, through which God's Spirit effects that one faith whose contents is identical with the contents of the gospel proclamation in its biblical fulness. The alternative or opposite of such confessing faith is not neutral nonunderstanding, but the denial of the truth in unbelief, which can only be overcome through a miracle of the Holy Spirit. The decisive mark for the presence and efficacy of the Spirit, therefore, is the confession of Jesus as the Christ and Son of God and the prayer to the heavenly Father in Jesus' name (1 Cor 12:3; 1 John 4:2–3; Rom 8:15; Gal 4:5–6).

2. The *existential* aspect: Unbelief and belief, however, dare not be attributed to certain groups of people only. Rather, they mark the radical breach and discon-

---

[18] 1 Cor 16:22; Rev 22:20; cf. Did 10:6; Rom 16:17–20; Gal 1:8–9; Johannes Wirsching, *Kirche und Pseudokirche: Konturen der Häresie*, (Göttingen: Vandenhoeck & Ruprecht, 1990), 158.

[19] *Ibid*, 159–160: "Zum Sakrament des Altars hat darum von Anfang an die Lehre gehört, d.h. der Anspruch, die Heilswahrheit Jesu Christi verbindlich auszusagen; so ist die Abgrenzung gegen den Irrtum auch nicht erst durch spätere, einander bekämpfende Konfessionskirchen entstanden, wie immer wieder behauptet wird, sondern bereits mit dem Sakrament selbst gegeben."

[20] This is the *ceterum censeo* of the paraenetic New Testament passages, which are all based on baptism.

tinuity in every man's existence, which is experienced by every believer in Christ through baptism and through the word of Scripture, proclaimed as law and gospel. This discontinuity is called *mortificatio* and *vivificatio* in the Apology of the Augsburg Confession, the killing of the sinner through the law, and the resurrection of the believer through the gospel. This event or experience is identical with the justification of the godless sinner by faith for Christ's sake. This is the reason why a true confession of Christ always goes hand in hand with the confession of sins. Theology as doxology and anthropology as repentance (Edmund Schlink) are two sides of the same coin. This existential breach is experienced in baptism and in every divine service. And this is the reason why baptism and the divine service including communion is the normal and original setting or context not only of justification but also of that confession which results from justification as an expression of that faith which receives justification.

3. The *ecclesial* aspect: Grammatically, the subject of the biblical confessions is always ultimately collective. Each individual confessor joins in the choir of those who confessed before him, who confess at the same time with him, and whose confession is yet to come. A true confession, therefore, is not a proclamation of a Christian's or a theologian's private opinion. It is the church who speaks in the confession, thus accounting for her belief before God and the world. To confess is a primal function of the church of all times and places.[21] The confession names and expounds the church's belief in Christ which in its substantial identity is shared beyond times and places. At the same time the confession is the demarcation line, beyond which the authentic faith in Christ is lost. Since the message of Scripture brings about the distinction and separation of belief and unbelief, already in the New Testament confession of truth and exclusion of falsehood are inseparably joined together as can be seen in the texts concerning baptism and communion. Johannes Wirsching says, "The confession of Christ proves to be a living one by putting up norms or demarcation lines. This also belongs to its very essence. Thus it separates at least virtually truth from error, the church from the pseudo-church. This is true not only for the later doctrinal conflicts in history, but even for the early New Testament age of the

---

[21] Cf. Wirsching, 'Bekenntnisschriften', *TRE* 5, 487: "eine Urfunktion der Kirche aller Zeiten und Zonen".

church."[22] Therefore, as Dietrich Bonhoeffer coined it, the concept of confession necessarily implies the concept of heresy.[23]

4. The *eschatological* aspect: Each genuine confession responding to Christ's revelation is presented in view of the risen Christ who is present in his church through word and sacraments and who is expected to return for the last judgement day.[24] Only then the essential conflict between faith and unbelief will be settled and the final separation will be executed. Since it is in this context that true faith and true doctrine intrinsically are necessary for salvation, the confession of the church also has an often forgotten eminent relevance for the care of the souls,[25] since in the final analysis the confession is nothing other than an exercise in dying faithfully and a preparation for the last judgement. In this horizon the confessor, according to the testimony of the New Testament, can and must be assured of his salvation **because** by faith he is inseparably attached to Christ.[26] It is this eschatological aspect that is most relevant for the care of souls which once more lays open the close connection between Scripture and a salutary confession. Understood as the word of the triune God who speaks and works through law and gospel, Scripture is clear and effective enough in and of itself in order to bring about a faith which has certainty of salvation and thus a confession which has certainty of those truths it relies upon. This **qualitative** relation between the clarity of Scripture and the certainty of salvation is the very foundation and the central reason for the conviction concerning the normativity of the confessions which is in effect not only insofar (*quatenus*) they are in accordance with Scripture, but because (*quia*) they are in accordance with Scripture.[27] Since Scripture is clear and perfect, our confession is not unclear or conditionally clear, but unconditionally certain. Jörg Baur writes, "In the confession, testimony is given and proclamation made concerning how the word of God

---

[22]Cf. Wirsching, 'Bekenntnisschriften', 490: "Das Christusbekenntnis erweist sich lebendig nur, indem es Normen, d. h. Grenzbestimmungen aufstellt; es hat immer *auch* Abgrenzungs-Charakter und scheidet (zumindest virtuell) Wahrheit von Irrtum, Kirche von Gegenkirche. Das gilt nicht erst für die späteren großen Lehrkämpfe, sondern bereits für die neutestamentliche Frühzeit der Kirche."

[23]*Ibid.*

[24]Cf. Armin Wenz, *Das Wort Gottes Gericht und Rettung: Untersuchungen zur Autorität der Heiligen Schrift in Bekenntnis und Lehre der Kirche* (FSÖTh 75; Göttingen: Vandenhoeck & Ruprecht, 1996), 17, including note 25.

[25]Cf. Jochen Eber, 'Seelsorgerliche Verantwortung für die Gemeinde: Das Trostamt des Pfarrers in den lutherischen Bekenntnisschriften', *Lutherische Beiträge* 4 (1999), 41–58.

[26]Rom 10:9–10: "… if you confess with your mouth that Jesus is Lord and believe in your heart that God raised him from the dead, you will be saved. For with the heart one believes and is justified, and with the mouth one confesses and is saved."

[27]Cf. Sasse, *In statu II*, 250.

establishes the glory of Christ and gives consolation to confused consciences. Thus it is obvious that wherever this happens final decisions have commenced. Thus the confession is part of the struggle of Christ's kingdom against the devil's kingdom. Since it is committed to doctrinal instruction, the confession realizes the unity of the church in its historical continuity."[28]

3 Confession in the history of the church

Following the earlier example of Werner Elert,[29] Karlmann Beyschlag and Johannes Wirsching, who both passed away not long ago, teach us to perceive the history of dogma primarily as a history of decision-making ("Entscheidungsgeschichte"[30]). In this view the thrust and result of the dogma of the Early church should not be labelled as a Hellenization of the original gospel, but as a critique of mythologizing and rationalizing depravations of Christ and a return to the biblical truth concerning Christ in its fulness.[31] Instructed by the New Testament, the dogma of the two natures of Christ ascertains that Jesus is not like one of us, but that he is the one

---

[28] Baur, *Einsicht*, 288: "Im Bekenntnis wird bezeugt und ‚proklamiert' …, daß und wie das Wort Gottes die Ehre Christi aufrichtet und verwirrte Gewissen tröstet (vgl. Apologie zu CA IV). Dabei wird deutlich, daß, wo immer dies geschieht, letzte Entscheidungen anbrechen. So gehört das Bekenntnis selbst in den Kampf des regnum Christi adversus regnum Diaboli … Insofern es dies als Anleitung zu Lehre tut, nimmt es die Einheit der Kirche in ihrer geschichtlichen Ständigkeit wahr."

[29] Werner Elert, *Der Ausgang der altkirchlichen Christologie: Eine Untersuchung über Theodor von Pharan und seine Zeit als Einführung in die alte Dogmengeschichte* (Berlin: Lutherisches Verlagshaus, 1957). Concerning the close connection between church unity, communion fellowship, and christological dogma or confession, cf. Werner Elert, *Abendmahl und Kirchengemeinschaft in der alten Kirche hauptsächlich des Ostens*, 2nd edition (Fürth: Flacius Verlag, 1985); English: *Eucharist & Church Fellowship in the First Four Centuries* (St. Louis: CPH, 1966).

[30] Cf. Johannes Wirsching: 'Menschwerdung: Von der wahren Gestalt des Göttlichen', in *Die Weltlichkeit des Glaubens in der Alten Kirche. Festschrift für Ulrich Wickert zum siebzigsten Geburtstag* (Berlin/New York: Walter de Gruyter, 1997), 412, *passim*; Karlmann Beyschlag: *Grundriß der Dogmengeschichte. Band II: Gott und Mensch. Teil 1: Das christologische Dogma* (Darmstadt: Wissenschaftliche Buchgesellschaft, 1991), 2–3: "Normgeschichtlich dagegen läßt sich die D(ogmen)g(eschichte) keineswegs einfach als fortlaufender Evolutionszusammenhang vorstellen, vielmehr wird ihr eigentlicher Atem erst dort spürbar, wo die vorwärtsdrängende Masse theologischer 'Entwicklungen' (und Verwicklungen) im Augenblick der Glaubenskrise vom *Ursprung der christlichen Wahrheit* her eingeholt und zur normativen dogmatischen Gestalt gebracht wird."

[31] Cf. Wirsching, *Kirche*, 52: "Kirchentrennung wird dann unvermeidlich, wenn Christen anfangen, einander den ganzen Christus zu verweigern. Das kann ‚reduktiv' geschehen, durch Loslösung einzelner Wesenszüge, aber genausogut 'produktiv', durch Eintragung fremder Wesenszüge in das Bild Jesu Christi."

coming to us from outside in a way none wanted him to be.[32] Both in the Early Church conflict concerning the divine nature of Christ and the relation of his two natures, as well as in the conflict over the deity of the Holy Spirit, the question of salvation is at stake. Had Christ and his Spirit been perceived as repeatable manifestations of human possibilities or abilities, salvation would have taken the form of human ascent towards God through the power of man. Only if the true divinity of Christ incarnate and the divine efficacy of the Holy Spirit through the word and the sacraments are perceived, our salvation radically remains something to be received.

At the same time the Early Church, when formulating its christological dogma, held on to the authority of Scripture. Because when the Early Church confesses Christ and the Spirit to be external persons whose very substance and authority is and remains prior and superior over against the church, in the simultaneous act of acknowledging the canon of the Scriptures, she perceives the very presence and efficacy of Christ and the Spirit mediated through these Scriptures. It is not a church free from dogma, but the dogmatic church which acknowledges the biblical canon. She thus humbly points away from herself towards the biblical canon as a distinct, objective rule for her doctrine and practice.[33] Only in this twofold acceptance of the dogma concerning Christ and of the authority of Scripture does the church subordinate herself under the rule of the risen and exalted Christ.

Whereas the Early Church expounds the theological implications of the confession of Christ in the form of the Trinitarian doxology, the Reformation, as it were, had to get to the bottom of its anthropological implications in the form of the confession of sins. This can be seen in the Augsburg Confession and in Luther's Catechisms as the fundamental confessions of the Reformation. Since in both cases, we perceive an unfolding of the Early Church dogma on the Trinity and on Christ which is undertaken by expounding the soteriological and ecclesiological consequences of that dogma. At the same time the Lutheran confessors were able to resume a history of conflict concerning these consequences that already takes place in and through the biblical texts. For in the understanding of the confessors, the Old Testament prophets as well as the New Testament apostles had already fought in the same struggles

---

[32] Cf. Wirsching, *Menschwerdung*, 406: "Jesus ist nicht einer von uns, er *kommt* zu uns. So wie er ist, hat ihn keiner gewollt."

[33] Cf. Wirsching, *Kirche*, 89: "Nicht die dogmenlose, sondern die dogmatische Kirche legt einen Kanon biblischer Bücher fest; *sie* ist es, die von sich selber auf einen anderen Maßstab, auf den Schriftenkanon verweist."

against the works' righteousness of the Pharisees and against the antinomianism of the Enthusiasts.[34]

Thus the 'sola fide' and the 'sola gratia' Reformation principles do not add anything substantially new to the Christological dogma of the Early Church and to her reception of the authority of the biblical canon ('solus Christus' and 'sola Scriptura'). More so, the confessors perceived their confession as a repetition and approval of the confessions of the Early Church against the errors that had crept into the church in their own days. The Lutheran confessional writings are eager to prove that they take the confession of Christ and of the Holy Spirit more seriously and draw the respective consequences for the proclamation and for the pastoral care of the church more diligently than their Roman and Enthusiast opponents. This is expressed nicely in the many passages in the confessional writings explicitly naming the honour of Christ and the consolation of tempted consciences as the fundamental motivation for the confessions made and as the material criterion for the true doctrine. Again we meet the inseparable biblical union of the confession of sins and of the praise of God.

4 Confessional hermeneutics and the hermeneutics of the confessions

It has been pointed out by many observers that in later historic stages, both of the Early Church as well as of the Reformation, there is a slight adjustment in the formal structure of the confessions which might imply a different understanding of confession itself. Whereas the Apostles' and the Nicene creeds take on the form of an existential first person confession, in the Athanasian creed, an objective intellectualization in form and contents can be perceived.[35] To a certain extent this is repeated in the 16th Century when we look at the Formula of Concord. The early confessions of the Lutheran Reformation, by using the form of plain reports, in the case of the Catechisms the form of instruction, give an account concerning the very contents of the proclamation and catechesis which already takes place in the churches even before and independently of the explicit composition of confessions.[36] In the Formula of Concord the written expression of what is actually taught and therefore confessed now also turns into a norm of convictions and a doctrinal obligation. What at first glance appears to be an adjustment in the understanding of confession, is caused by

---

[34] Cf. Wenz, Wort Gottes, 46–53.

[35] Cf. Wirsching, 'Bekenntnisschriften', 492

[36] Cf. Heinrich Bornkamm: Das Jahrhundertder Reformation: Gestalten und Kräfte, 2nd edition (Göttingen: Vandenhoeck & Ruprecht, 1966), 220: "Die Confessio Augustana konstituiert nicht eine schriftgemäß lehrende Kirche, sondern bezeugt ihr Vorhandensein."

the needs of a new historic situation[37] and is even reflected upon by the Formula of Concord itself. Thus the confessors emphasize over and over again that they do not want to confess anything substantially new that would go beyond what has been confessed before,[38] but that they want to repeat especially the Augsburg Confession as the most prominent Symbol of their time[39] over against new misconceptions and changes in doctrine, that is, they want to clarify its true understanding over against errors that have been spread more in the time since the formulation of the Augsburg Confession. By pointing back and approving of the earlier confessions of the Early Church and of the Reformation **and** by explicitly repeating the '*Sola Scriptura*' -principle, the Lutherans of the Formula once more consciously join in the '*magnus consensus*' from Augsburg Confession Article 1.[40] This way their confession remains a true existential and catholic expression of the biblically sound certainty of salvation which is especially obvious in their earnest eschatological focus on the last judgement[41]

Thus the Lutheran church also in this respect holds the middle line, taking seriously both the existential and the catholic dimensions of the true biblical confession. In the Reformed church the total focus is on the existential and actual aspect of confessing, an approach which, in the last resort, turns the confessions into time-bound pieces of history. And on the other side in the Roman Church the dogma of the church is not considered substantially identical with the contents of Scripture, but it is perceived as a collection of mandatory credenda to which the church can add

---

[37] Cf. Wirsching, 'Bekenntnisschriften', 497: "Weder das schriftbezogene Zeugnis zu 'Gottes Lob und Ehren' (*BSLK* 759, 52; Preface to the Book of Concord 22; A.W.) noch die ökumenische Ausrichtung des Bekennens sind aufgehoben, sie werden aber neu (und nun partikularkirchlich) motiviert."

[38] Cf. *BSLK*, 761 (Preface to the Book of Concord 23); 833–834 (FC, Comprehensive Summary, 1). Especially relevant for the perception of the confessors' awareness of the problem is the following passage from the preface to the Book of Concord, 16: "We hope, therefore, that our adversaries will hereafter spare both us and the ministers of our churches, and not employ these customary and most grievous accusations, that we cannot decide among ourselves upon anything as certain concerning our faith, and that, on this account, we are forging new confessions almost every year, yea, even every month." (*BSLK* 751, 21–28)

[39] FC SD, Comprehensive Summary, § 5: "our symbol for this time" (BSLK 835,18: "als dieser Zeit unserm Symbolo"; cf. 768,30).

[40] This is also obvious in the Formula of Concord' refutation of the Anti-Trinitarians and other sects (an extensive repetition of AC I) and in the *Catalogus Testimoniorum* attached to the confessions.

[41] Cf. Wirsching, 'Bekenntnisschriften', 494: "Daß die Männer der Konkordienformel sich zur Heiligen Schrift, zu den altkirchlichen Symbolen, zur Augustana und deren Apologie, zu den Schmalkaldischen Artikeln und den Katechismen ,bekennen', bedeutet demnach ein innerliches Ergreifen und Aneignen der dort niedergelegten Inhalte und bleibt damit in der Spur der lebendigen *confessio* der reformatorischen Frühzeit."

more and more. The Reformed understanding of confession is not compatible with the catholicity of the church. In the Roman understanding, however, certainty of salvation is lost because faith and confession are in danger of being turned into human works even if these are considered to be accomplished with the help of the Spirit; a Spirit, however, who is bound not to Scripture alone, but also to the tradition of the church.

5   The relevance of the confessions in ecclesial life and practice

In the course of history, the Reformed concept of confession has been victorious in the realm of 'Protestantism'. Under the growing rule of a mindset shaped by Pietism and Enlightenment notions, the concept of an objectively true and legally safeguarded confession has succumbed to the concept of personally subjective convictions[42] This development was instrumental in the many Protestant attempts to reach church unions between the Lutheran and the Reformed Churches, including the Leuenberg Concord. But once the balance between the existential and the catholic aspects in the understanding of confession is lost, it comes as no surprise when the pendulum sooner or later swings back to the other end of the spectrum. This can be seen in the attempt to reach a common understanding on the doctrine of justification between the Roman Church and the Lutheran Church by ignoring the mutual condemnations in the confessions of the 16th Century, while at the same time combining the doctrinal concerns of both sides in a merely additive way.[43] That branch of the Lutheran Church which considers this method and its results as ecclesial progress thus has succumbed to the Roman understanding of dogma.

But in our modern age, the Lutheran understanding of confession is not only challenged by other denominations but also by the opposing forces of theological Liberalism on one side and of a formal Biblicism on the other side. Both tend to take a more or less negative approach over against confessions, dogma, and doctrinal obligation.[44] In this situation of being tempted and torn apart from many sides between Protestant unions and a doctrinal convergence with Rome on the one hand and anti-dogmatic and anti-sacramental Liberalism and Fundamentalism on the other hand, a rediscovery and re-acknowledgement of the Lutheran confessions

---

[42] Cf. Wirsching, Bekenntnisschriften, 499.

[43] Cf. Gottfried Martens, 'Ein ökumenischer Fortschritt? Anmerkungen zur "Gemeinsamen Erklärung zur Rechtfertigungslehre"', Lutherische Beiträge 3 (1998), 164–187.

[44] Both groups, represented by the enthusiasts and the anti-Trinitarians, so to speak already play a role in the Reformation century and are refuted in the Lutheran Confessions.

could open up for us and for our churches salutary experiences of liberation and processes of healing and reformation.

1. This concerns first of all the factual proclamation, catechesis, and pastoral care in the parish. Hermann Sasse writes in his 1941 essay on Church and Confession: "It is the task of the church's confession to express the right understanding of Scripture which the church has reached (...) Thus pastors are helped to proclaim only the pure doctrine, and congregations are protected against the whims of the preacher and the misinterpretation of Scripture. In this sense the church's confession is servant of the Word."[45] As a clarification of the understanding of Scripture in all questions concerning our salvation the confession protects parishes and preachers against all authoritarian and monopolistic claims concerning the interpretation of Scripture. This protective function, however, is not only important over against the magisterial office of a juridical Papacy, but also over against the spiritualistic magisterial office of an introverted church of the Enthusiasts as well as over against the scientific magisterial office of a hyper-hermeneutical church of the theologians.[46] It is therefore mandatory to make the history and contents of the confessions including their biblical foundation the central object of theological studies and parochial instruction.[47] Only in such a setting, the obligation to the confessions in the ordination vows as well as the joining in in the "yes" and the "no" of the Christian confessions in the baptismal vow find their fitting context. Only the serious binding to the confessions guarantees the continuity of doctrine when new pastors are called into parishes. To maintain such continuity is a central right and obligation of a Christian congregation for the sake of the certainty of salvation and of the reliability and steadfastness of their faith. According to the Augsburg Confession, it is the Bishops' or church councils' obligation to watch over the actual proclamation in their churches which includes the public refutation of open violations against the doctrinal consensus as it is put forth in the confessions.[48] Doctrinal discipline is ut-

---

[45] We Confess Christ, 84. Cf. the German original in In statu confessionis I: Gesammelte Aufsätze (ed. F.W. Hopf; Berlin und Schleswig Holstein: Die Spur, 1975), 22–23.

[46] Cf. Johannes Wirsching, Glaube im Widerstreit: Ausgewählte Aufsätze und Vorträge, Band 3 (Kontexte 29; Frankfurt am Main: Peter Lang, 1999), 47–48. Wirsching here coins fitting terms in German: "das Amtsmagisterium der juridifizierten Papstkirche", "das Geistmagisterium der introvertierten Schwärmerkirche", "das Wissenschaftsmagisterium ('Gelehrtenapparat') einer hermeneutisierten Theologenkirche".

[47] Cf. Werner Klän, 'Lutherische Pfarrerausbildung heute: Das Bekenntnis; Wesentliche Bestandteile der Ausbildung lutherischer Pastoren', Lutherische Theologie und Kirche 28 (2004), 81–100.

[48] Cf. AC XXVIII,21–22: "Again, according to the Gospel or, as they say, by divine right, there belongs to the bishops as bishops, that is, to those to whom has been committed the ministry of the Word and the Sacraments, no jurisdiction except to forgive sins, to judge doctrine, to reject doctrines contrary

terly impossible without being bound to confessions on a quia-basis. Confessional commitment without doctrinal discipline, including public refutation of public false teachers, results in hypocrisy and in the long run undermines the discipline and the unity of the church. Sasse writes, "Whether a church is still a confessional church is decided not by the number of old confessional writings it still possesses but by its living proclamation in preaching, instruction, and pastoral care. If it is a genuinely confessional church in this sense, then it is also a Biblical church."[49]

2. *Being bound to the confessions helps the church to remain different and distinguishable from the world.* If the doctrinal consensus according to AC I constitutes ecclesial unity, all earthly or human qualities or entities are excluded from being fundamental for such unity (cf. AC VII).[50] Thus the confessions serve as a protection against the temptation to draw false borderlines around the church and against the temptation to blur the necessary limits of the church. Johannes Wirsching coined the thesis: "It is the confessional church, not the national church, which represents the fundamental pattern of the new [= eschatological; A.W.] mankind."[51] This exclusion of criteria for the unity of the church drawn from creational conditions or from sociology also concerns the temptations to see the church as a cosmopolitan extension of a likeminded avant-garde community on the one hand,[52] or as a small, convenient family-like church on the other hand, in which even blatantly unbiblical and unconfessional positions or practices are tolerated or even promoted, as soon and as long as these positions or practices are held by "someone coming from our own circles." Thus confessional obligation reminds the church that the criteria for the integrity of doctrine and the unity of the church must not be the question of what is harmful or beneficial for the social atmosphere or for the emotional well-being, be it in the large context of territorial or even globalized churches, or in the small, family-like context of so-called free or independent churches. But the cri-

---

to the Gospel, and to exclude from the communion of the Church wicked men, whose wickedness is known, and this without human force, simply by the Word" (BSLK 123f.).

[49] *We Confess Christ*, 84 (*In statu I*, 23).

[50] Concerning the often abused "*satis est*" from AC VII, see Hermann Sasse, *We Confess the Church* (St. Louis: Concordia Publishing House, 1986), 67: "*Satis est* does not then postulate a minimum of agreement, a consensus, which we achieve in the course of our discussions, but a maximum ... Not the agreement in doctrine ... but only the consensus in the pure doctrine and in the right administration of the sacraments is the consensus demanded in the Augsburg Confession." (*In statu I*, 68)

[51] Cf. for the full quote: Wirsching, *Kirche*, 64: "Die Konfessionskirche ist die eigentlich theologische Kategorie der Ökumene." Sie, "nicht die Nationalkirche ist die Grundgestalt der neuen Menschheit."; cf. *ibid.* the quote from Fritzsche: "Die Konfessionskirche hat die Nationalkirche verhindert." Cf. Sasse, *In statu I*, 268.

[52] Wirsching, *Kirche*, 64, *passim*.

teria should only be those things which are harmful or beneficial for the certainty of salvation.[53]

3. *Confessional obligation helps the church avoid false concepts of ecclesial unity*, insofar it excludes what Johannes Wirsching calls the three historical patterns of ecclesial enthusiasm which were perceived most clearly by Martin Luther: "the introverted spirit-church of Enthusiasts as a paradigm of self-righteousness; the juridical church of the Papacy as a paradigm of a works-righteous formalism; the rationalized church of the Qur'an as paradigm of a literalistic law righteousness".[54] All these patterns ignore the gospel and turn the church into a human construct. All these patterns which also represent perennial temptations for each church body must, however, be fought not through external means of power, but through the word alone, according to AC XXVIII: *sine vi humana, sed verbo*.[55] At the same time, though, the word has to be allowed to accomplish and exercise its very discriminating and separating power in the fulness of the biblical testimony to Christ and must not be blurred or silenced by some overzealous and uncritical obedience over against external authorities other than the Scriptures. The confessions serve as a reminder that the Christian truth is a truth in an 'either-or' pattern, an eschatological truth, which is decisive for eternal life and eternal death.[56] Neither church unions which operate on the basis of the smallest common confessional denominator construed by men, nor doctrinal reductions which result in short unifying formulas shared by those present at a certain point in time, can be instrumental in reaching a true concord of hearts and consciences. This true concord or consensus can only be reached by a common, patient and diligent examination of Holy Writ and can thus be received as a fruit and a gift of the gospel truth.[57]

---

[53] Wirsching, *Kirche*, 9, *passim*, coined the terms 'Sozialschädlichkeit' versus 'Heilsschädlichkeit'.

[54] Wirsching, *Kirche*, 128, 126: "drei empirisch-ekklesiologischen Grundgestalten des Enthusiasmus": "die introvertierte Geistkirche als Urbild der selbstgerechten Innerlichkeit; die juridifizierte Papstkirche als Urbild der werkgerechten Äußerlichkeit; die rationalisierte Korankirche als Urbild der buchstabengerechten Gesetzlichkeit".

[55] AC XXVIII,21. Cf. Wirsching, *Kirche*, 128; Baur, *Einsicht*, 288: "Das Bekenntnis nimmt überdies teil an der Leidensgestalt des bekennenden Glaubens. Es erduldet wie dieser die Gewalt des Irrtums. Darum kann es seine Wahrheit zwar wohl unter Scheidung, doch nie mit Gewalt durchsetzen."

[56] Cf. Johannes Wirsching, *Glaube im Widerstreit: Ausgewählte Aufsätze und Vorträge* (Kontexte 4; Frankfurt am Main: Peter Lang, 1988), 127: "Daß aber gerade die christliche Wahrheit eine Wahrheit im Entweder-Oder, eine eschatologische Wahrheit" ist,"durch die über Leben und Tod entschieden wird".

[57] Cf. Wirsching, *Bekenntnisschriften*, 505: "Weder Unionen, die mit dem Konstruktivismus des kleinsten gemeinsamen Bekenntnisnenners operieren, noch Reduktionen auf bloß aktualistisch einigende Kurzformeln können eine echte Konkordie der Herzen und Gewissen herbeiführen; sie kann

4. *Confessional obligation protects the church's integrity and the rights of the justi-fied sinners over against any allegedly necessary improvements or depravations of the merely biblical faith in Christ.* If the confessions help the church to remain conscious concerning its difference from the world and from worldly powers, this does not take place for its own sake, but enables the church to keep up faithfulness concerning her specific mission which is entrusted only to her. The church of the confessions is neither a social agency nor another supplier of leisure events. She is but the only place in the world where forgiveness of sins, true life, and salvation effectively are given and received through the word and the sacraments. This unique place is mainly endangered by inner-churchly attempts of enhancing the biblical faith which are meant to be improvements but always turn out to be depravations. It is Johannes Wirsching's merit to have pointed this out very clearly that a heretic is a person who wants to be "a better Christian in a better church":

> The heretic is not able to believe without coming to help the supposed poverty of his faith with additional proofs. ... He therefore does not perceive his confession of Christ as a testimony to the truth of Christ Jesus in the communion with the fathers and the brothers (horizontal catholicity), but as the program of an avant-garde communion enjoying a special calling to surpass the fathers and the brothers (vertical or futuristic individualization). Thus the heretic is not satisfied with giving a testimony of something beyond himself, but he wants to achieve something (new). .... In all this, heresy proves itself to be revolutionary instead of reformatory. The Christian revolutionary in the end always establishes a party, ... despite the fact that he wants to remain part of the church and to preserve or to restore it as a pure community of faith. ... The heretic is not satisfied with justification of the sinner, that is, he takes offence when he hears that his salvation and the fulfilment of his human nature is not a matter of his decision at all. ... He does not like the thought of needing certain external means in order to receive his salvation, but demands and maintains that it is possible to have immediate access to salvation. Basically his position is outside the community of faith, he, however, perceives himself—as the true believer—in its very midst, thus being able to show how this community has to be improved, enhanced, and made perfect. ... Man's salvation always

---

nur in gemeinsamer Befragung der Heiligen Schrift von der Wahrheit des Evangeliums erwartet werden."

already *is* at hand (without means). The only thing which is left is that it is lived out and executed ethically, socially, politically. Yet he is unable to perceive the perforating cruelty which is the result of such an understanding and the connected transformation of grace into a demand of the law."[58]

Over against such pious activism and success-minded pragmatism the confession is the advocate of the justified and tempted sinners, whose right it is to receive what they need for a salutary life and death in the communion with Christ.

5. *Confessional obligation helps the church to be prepared and ready for the Last Day of Judgment.* The confessions admonish the church not to confuse our salvation in Christ with earthly experiences of happiness, but to remain steadfast in the midst of the unresolvable tension between a faith which depends on external means of grace and the immediate seeing of God in our heavenly future, a tension which is experienced in the manifold temptations of the believers and of the church as a whole. This serves also as reminder that all practice of the church should not be judged according to democratic consent concerning progress towards an earthly manifestation of God's kingdom, but must be accountable in the light of Christ's return at the end. He alone is "Lord and Judge of us all",[59] as Luther points out most clearly in the preface of the Smalcald Articles which are both his personal and the church's confession rendered before the "judgement-seat of Christ".[60] The "seri-

---

[58] Wirsching, *Kirche*, 176–179: "der bessere Christ in einer besseren Kirche": "Er kann nicht glauben, ohne der vermeintlichen Armut seines Glaubens durch Zusatzevidenzen aufzuhelfen. … Darum versteht der Häretiker sein Christusbekenntnis auch nicht als Zeugnis für die Wahrheit Jesu Christi in der Gemeinschaft der Väter und Brüder (horizontale Ökumene), sondern als das Programm einer Auswahl- oder Vortruppgemeinde in Überbietung der Väter und Brüder (vertikale oder futurische Vereinzelung). So gesehen, will der Häretiker auch nicht etwas bezeugen, sondern vor allem etwas erreichen … In alledem erweist sich Häresie als revolutionär, nicht als reformatorisch. Der christliche Revolutionär gründet am Ende immer eine (Kirche sein sollende) Partei, obwohl er doch in der Kirche bleiben und sie als die reine Gemeinschaft des Glaubens erhalten, wenn nicht wiederherstellen will … Er nimmt Anstoß an der Rechtfertigung des Sünders, das heißt, er stößt sich daran, daß dem Menschen die Entscheidung über sein Heil und damit über die Vollendung seines Menschseins aus der Hand genommen sein soll. … Ein Heil aber, das der Häretiker sich selber nicht mehr vermitteln zu lassen braucht, kann er auch nicht anders als unvermittelt zur Geltung bringen. Im Grunde steht er damit außerhalb der Gemeinschaft des Glaubens, sieht sich jedoch—als der wahre Gläubige—erst recht in ihr, um ihr nunmehr vorzuhalten, wie sie verbessert, überboten und vollendet werden muß. … Das Heil des Menschen ist immer schon vermittelt, es muß nur noch als solches gelebt und—ethisch, sozial, politisch—durchgesetzt werden. Die hierin durchbrechende Gewaltsamkeit wird ebensowenig empfunden wie die vollendete Umkehrung der Gnade in eine Forderung".

[59] SA, Preface, 8; BSLK 411,11: "unser aller Herr und Richter".

[60] SA, Preface 8; BSLK 411,8: "fur dem Richtstuel Christi".

ous and salutary office",[61] perceived by the Lutheran confessors demands clarity and faithfulness in proclamation and faith[62] and excludes all fear and complaisance of men. It is not vague promises concerning the church's or theology's processes of self-purification in a distant future that deserve to be trusted, but Christ alone who obliges his disciples to confess faithfully.

Let me conclude with words saturated with experience and wisdom by Hermann Sasse who on the occasion of the 1500th anniversary of the dogma of Chalcedon wrote the following, which to this day is as relevant as when it was first printed:

> Now let no one come with the excuse that confessional formulations and church regulations cannot guarantee pure doctrine, that to use these to bolster the church is evidence of little faith …. We must respond that no theologian expects the church to be saved by confessional writings …. However, we declare it superstition to suppose that He [God] will produce a miracle to do what He has entrusted us, the servants of the church, and what we in our laziness and cowardice, in our love of ease, and in our fear of men again and again fail to do. He has commanded the servants of the Word, the shepherds of his flock, for the sake of the eternal truth and for the sake of the souls entrusted to their care, to testify against false doctrine and to exclude it from the church. We must call it blasphemy to expect the Holy Spirit to set aside the obstacles with which we willfully hinder His work. We know that no confession can guarantee purity of doctrine. … But we also know that where confession of the truth is forgotten the church's doctrine must suffer complete corruption, the Gospel must die. … The world, also the Christian, also the Lutheran world, does not want to hear it. Today there are only a few groups, mostly small, who say all this and are not ashamed to be called confessional and orthodox. Yet on their faithfulness depends far more than most of us can imagine."[63]

---

[61] Small Catechism, Preface 25: "Our office is now become a different thing from what it was under the Pope; it is now become serious and salutary." (BSLK 507,12–15). Cf. the Preface of the Apology.

[62] "Moreover it is required in stewards that one be found faithful." (1Cor 4:2)

[63] *We Confess Christ*, 69–70 (*In statu I*, 36–37). Cf. Wirsching, *Glaube* (1988), 71: "Vielleicht sind es, wie Martin Luther gemeint hat, gelegentlich nur arme Demütige, geringe einzelne, die in den Gemeinden und stellvertretend für sie erfassen und vorleben, was an Erbe uns überkommen, was an Hoffnung uns geschenkt, was in der Fülle Jesu Christi verwirklicht ist. Wahrscheinlich ist es so, und wahrscheinlich muß es so sein. Denn nur wenige Menschen kennen die Geschichte, die meisten irren mit ihrer Zeit."

Chapter 6

A Response to Armin Wenz

Rev. Dr. Joseph Randrianasolo

1   Introductory Appreciation

It is a great honour for me be invited at such an important and timely debate. A pastor or theologian must take a stand concerning the relationship between Scripture and the Confession. Our time is marked by the fluidity of relativism and indifferentism stemming out of the progress of history and of discoveries of modern exegesis. Pfarrer Höppl in his interchange on the nature of confessional subscription with Hermann Sasse, says,

> I take the side of *quatenus* because I cannot see how I can honourably remain a theologian and pastor in any other way…If there is to be a decision between the *quia* and the *quatenus*, an ordination understood simply leaves no other choice but the *quatenus*. This remains my approach to the Confessions, and even to the Bible itself.
>
> For if the approach leads to Christ as the final goal, then a *quatenus* is valid also over against the Bible. My basic position allows me freedom not only to acknowledge a declaration of the Confessions as being capable of being corrected and in need of correction in the basis of Biblical exegesis. Also in biblical exegesis the *quatenus* which aims for Christ gives to me that free possibility of seeking Christ through the Bible.[1]

---

[1] Pfarrer Höppl & Hermann Sasse, '*quatenus* or *quia*, An interchange on the Nature of Confessional subscription', *Logia, A Journal of Lutheran Theology*, Vol.VIII Number 2 (Eastertide 1999), 5–6.

Hermann Sasse responds to it as follows,

An actual and serious doctrinal pledge can never consist in pastor's pledging himself to a confession "insofar as" this confession agrees with the Word of God. For it is self-evident that a confession, in any church that stands upon the "Scripture alone" (sola scriptura), has authority only so far it agrees with the Bible as the norma normans and correctly explicates the same... Of course, I am prepared to surrender any assertion of Confessions, or the Confessions in its entirety if it is shown to us that the doctrine contained therein is contrary to the Scripture. If the *quatenus* is meant to say nothing more than this, then we find no difficulty with it. But the distinction must be made between the question of what we would have to do if our confession did not teach Scriptural truth, and the entirely different, and for us essential question, namely, whether they in fact do teach truth or falsity. We reject the *quatenus* because it is used to avoid or minimalize the seriousness of this question. I can only preach with conviction when I, with Luther, am convinced that what I preach is the pure doctrine of the Word.[2]

The conjunction "or" between *quia* and *quatenus* is short and small in letters, but long and important in spirit. Why do we need to choose between them and what are the doctrinal reasons for our choice? Dr Armin Wenz leads us to respond to that question by first describing the contextual framework of the issue and next by explaining the marks of a Christian confession according to the Scriptures, the place of confession in the history of the church, the content of a confessional hermeneutics, followed by the relevance of the confession in ecclesial life and practices. At one point in his paper, he clearly confesses that he is on the *quia* side[3] by holding the middle line between those who reject the understanding of confession as of paradigmatic relevance for the present day and those who take it as being still subject to change because of historical contingencies.

In our response to Dr. Wenz' paper, we shall confine ourselves to approach it from three fronts: Confession and Scripture, Scripture—Hermeneutics and Confessions, and Scripture—Confession and Contextualization. Obviously, we shall approach Dr. Wenz' paper with our own presuppositions and theological baggage. The way we have ordered the approach is a transparent interpretation of it.

---

[2] 6.
[3] Wenz, 76.

2   Confession and Scripture

Right from the first sentence of its paper, Dr. Wenz takes the way of treating the whole topic through the scope of confession. It is indeed true that a "clear and binding summary and form in which a general summary of teaching is drawn together from God's Word"[4] but the confessors confess that they adhere to "the prophetic and apostolic writings of the Old and New Testaments, as to the pure, clear fountain of Israel, which alone is the one true guiding principle, according to which all teachers and teaching are to be judged and evaluated".[5] First, his starting point begs the question of the primacy of Scripture, that is, its author, its authority and its unity. The use the term "conflicts" itself, while talking about "conflicting relations of divine institutions, works, and effects such the Old and the New Testaments, Law and Gospel…"[6] piques our curiosity in such a way that it invites us to know more about the Scriptures in the paper. Second, it is no surprise that related descriptions and reactions to Scripture are expressed as perception, consideration, understanding, belief, unbelief, effect, experience, Biblical canon and so on. This comes from the angle through which the topic is dealt with.

Does this mean that Scripture is not the word of the living God? Yes, it is indeed, but defined from the recipient's side. Let me just quote some sentences.

> The Holy Scripture is intrinsically *perceived* as the word of the living God.[7]
>
> The essence of a faithful confession is nothing but the rendering of account concerning of the truth *perceived* through the Scriptures by its recipients.[8]
>
> [The Scripture is] *understood* as the word of the triune God who speaks and works through law and gospel.[9]

Briefly speaking, the Scripture is Word of God and its author is divine because its recipients perceived and understood it as such. Even, on matter of sacraments and justification and faith, experience plays a major role. Dr. Wenz says that "this existential breach is experienced in baptism and in every divine service. And this is

---

[4] Robert Kolb and Timothy J. Wengert (eds.), *The Book of Concord: The Confessions of the Evangelical Lutheran Church* (Minneapolis: Fortress Press, 2000), 526, 1.

[5] *Ibid.*, 527, 3.

[6] Wenz, 71.

[7] Wenz, 71. Emphasis here and in the following quotations mine.

[8] Wenz, 71.

[9] Wenz, 76.

the reason why baptism and the divine service including communion is the normal and original setting or context not only of justification and also of that confession which results from justification as an expression of that faith which receives justification".[10] I think that it may happen that the contextual and historical existence of the recipients may distort the meaning of the Scripture. For example, the framework of the law and gospel may be reduced to that of ethics. However, Dr. Wenz connects that existential frame with the catholicity of the teaching of the Early Church[11] and that of the biblical canon to control any possible deviation.[12]

The authority of the Scriptures relies on proclamation and teaching but not on itself as Word of God. Dr. Wenz says that "the Holy Scripture—intrinsically *perceived* as the Word of God—is the very authority, which empowers and obliges its readers and hearers to join in the confession of its very contents".[13] This authority is strengthened by the unity between the New Testament and the Old Testament. Despite the conflict above mentioned cited between both testaments, their unity resides in the revelation of the Father by His presentation of Himself (Exod 20:2–3; Deut 6:4) and the revelation of the Son through the Father (Matt 16:16). This faith in Christ is affected by the Holy Spirit. Christology and eschatology have "made the canon of the Old testament and of the New Testament writings mandatory for the church".[14] Conflicts concerning Christological formulas have established the biblical canon as historical biblical dogma for a dogmatic church.[15] Historically speaking, the biblical canon is now accepted "as a distinct, objective rule for her doctrine and practice".[16] Moreover, Christological dogma is just the result of "a history of decision making".[17] That is an Elertian perspective about the history of dogma. We can summarize that Scripture has the foundation of its authority and of its unity made out of the Christological and historical content. Again, we agree with Dr. Wenz that the Bible is the Word of the living God. But how textually divine is it for him? That is, whether *Sola Scriptura* is adequate, is a question to be addressed to this paper if we do not want to classify the Bible just as one more tradition handed down (*tradere*) to our generation.

---

[10] Wenz, 75.
[11] Wenz, 78.
[12] Wenz, 78.
[13] Wenz, 71.
[14] Wenz, 73.
[15] Wenz, 78.
[16] Wenz, 78.
[17] Wenz, 77.

Perhaps we have spent too much time on the nature of the Holy Scripture. However, we had to do it because anything else like hermeneutics, doctrine, confessions and church practices, derives from our foundation *vis-à-vis* the *Sola Scriptura*. The nature of the *Sola Scriptura* defines that of the confession. Our respective choice to *quia* or *quatenus* concerning Scripture and Confession depends much more on our stand before the *Sola Scriptura* than our stand before Confession from the simple reason that church teaching is drawn together from God's Word (*Sola Scriptura*) as "the pure, clear fountain of Israel, which alone is the one true guiding principle, according to which all teachers and teaching are to be judged and evaluated".[18]

Our summary has shown that for Dr. Wenz, *Sola Scriptura* does not textually stand by itself. The authority and unity of the Holy Scripture are not found in the scriptural text itself but behind it. Historical contents and the unifying and authoritative figure of Jesus as the crucified and the risen one who will come again to judge the living and the dead bind the Old Testament and the New Testament together in one authoritative unit. This theological posture forces us to ask the question of the authorship of the Holy Scripture.

We agree with Dr. Preus who stresses that the divine authorship of the Scripture is the fundamental principle for approaching it. The Scripture's author is divine not only because of its content but much more because of its textual origin.[19] He emphasizes that "the divine origin of the Scripture, its authority, its sufficiency, its Christological and doctrinal unity, its clarity and inerrancy, also its power and ability to authenticate itself"[20] are of primary importance about the nature of the Scripture. Everything else about the Scripture and the articles of faith from it hang on the divine origin of the Scripture.[21] *Deus est autor primarius.* Consequently, the Holy Spirit and Christ are not merely mediated by the Scriptures. The Holy Spirit is in the Word of God. Christ is the Word made flesh. And that is the incarnation of the Son of the God, the Father. Externality and internality of the scriptural texts do not contain conflicts. These seemingly conflicting units in divine institutions are

---

[18] FC SD, Rule and Norm, 3.

[19] Robert David Preus, 1973 'Reformation Lectures', *Lutheran Synod Quaterly* Vol. XIV No. 1 (Special Fall, 1973), 1–15. See also Robert David Preus, 'Biblical Authority in the Lutheran Confessions', *Concordia Journal*, January (1978), 16–24; Robert David Preus, 'Luther: Word, Doctrine and Confession', in theLutheran Confessional Web Page at http://www.confessionallutherans.org/papers/drpreus. htm, (1993) (accessed on 10 July 2012).

[20] Robert David Preus, 'The Interpretation of Scripture', http://heartoftn.net/users/gary27/Preus-th. htm.

[21] Robert David Preus, 'Luther and Biblical Infallibility', in John D. Hannah, Edit., *Inerrancy and the Church*, (Chicago: Moody Press, 1984), 99-142.

just *opera Dei*, for example, the *opus alienum et opus proprium* in Law and Gospel, in God's wrath and God's grace. Scripture interprets Scripture.

We have already touched upon hermeneutics in our discussion about the nature of the Holy Scripture. However, we shall make a short incursus into the matter for the sake of more clarity.

3 Scripture, Hermeneutics and Confession

Dr. Wenz gives a general guideline for doing hermeneutics in a confessional setting. He rightfully underscores the role of *Sola Scriptura* in hermeneutics. This has been the main reason why we have insisted on the divine origin, divine authorship and divine unity of the Scriptures. It is true that Scripture is the Word of the living God. But the Word is God and from God. In and through the Word, God speaks to us (*Deus loquens*). The Christological link between the Old Testament and the New Testament does not only consist in the explanatory locus of Christ about the Trinity but about Christ being the Word made flesh. The Old Testament anticipates the New Testament and the New Testament realizes and fulfils the Old Testament.

Unfortunately, he remains on this level of general guideline. He says that "the confessors emphasize over and over again that they do not want to confess anything substantially new that would go beyond what has been confessed before".[22] He continues that "the Lutheran Church also in this respect holds the middle line, taking seriously both the existential and the catholic dimensions of the true biblical confession".[23] By talking exclusively about the creeds, the catechism, Law and Gospel, salvation and eschatology, he confines Scripture and hermeneutics to the question of salvation. Many burning issues of today are left out.

Indeed, Law and Gospel and justification by faith alone constitute the core of the Scripture. The confessors reiterate it over and over. We join Dr. Wenz by adding our voice to the chorus. But Scripture embraces more than that issue alone. Gender issues concerning ordination, homosexual marriage and the like may profit of the occasion to take into account Scripture and Confession because they are all starting from hermeneutical presuppositions and prejudices.[24] Moreover, these issues were not of the theological preoccupations of the confessors. We have to tackle them in

---

[22]Wenz, 80.

[23]Wenz, 80.

[24]See Matthew C. Harrison and Joh T. Pless, eds, *Women Pastors? The Ordination of Women in Biblical Lutheran Perspective* (Saint Louis: Concordia publishing House, 2008); Elisabeth Schüssler Fiorenza, *In Memory of Her: A Feminist Reconstruction of Christian Origins* (New York: Crossroad, 1983).

our days if we want to be strongly anchored in our confessional faith instead of hav‑ing our boat floating free according the waves of history and cultures. Therefore, we need to transparently talk about methodology in doing hermeneutics which bears on our exegesis. Hermeneutics and exegesis generate doctrine. Doctrine leads to confession. Confession requires subscription.

Here, if we want to stand on our unequivocal *quia*, we again stress that "the several rules that govern Lutheran exegesis are certainly dependent on the divine origin of Scripture, its infallibility and clarity, and on the 'Scripture alone' principle; but it is nevertheless the hermeneutical rules that govern exegesis".[25] If we let the outside historical and cultural context get into the text and change the meaning of the text, then, we have a diluted *quia*, not to say a genuine *quatenus*. As we may have noticed that we have inadvertently moved from hermeneutics to the relation of our Confession to today's issues. The relation between Scripture, hermeneutics and confession has logically driven us so far.

4   Scripture, Confession and Contextualization

At the beginning of his paper, Dr. Wenz points his finger at the heart of the prob‑lems about being a confessional Lutheran today. He cites the problems of "connect‑ing the faith of our time with the Scripture of the past" and "the factual connection between Scripture, as it is interpreted and proclaimed, and faith which lives from the world, within the historically contingent fellowship of church".[26] He delimits "the dynamic connection of Scripture, proclamation, faith, and ecclesial fellowship" as a referential framework.[27] In that section, he rightfully and strongly underlines the seriousness of many challenges that one who wants to be confessional has to face. His position is to keep the substance which is in concord with what has been con‑fessed before and to walk in the middle line between the Reformed and the Roman Catholic understandings of dogma. We can define that this is his standing *quia*. All his confessional obligations concerning ecclesial life and practices support it.

To some extent, even though in a limited way, there is a parallelism between Dr. Wenz and a paper by Robert Bertram, entitled ' "Scripture and Tradition" in the Lutheran Confessions'.[28] We shall only mention some elements of some main‑line points of his argument in this paper. Robert Bertram also chooses to stand

---

[25] Robert David Preus, 'The Interpretation of Scripture', 4–14.
[26] Wenz, 69.
[27] Wenz, 70.
[28] Robert Bertram, ' "Scripture and Tradition" in the Lutheran Confessions', *Pro Ecclesia* Vol. X.2 (Spring 2001), 179–194

on the *quia* side. He believes that the Scripture is the biblical Word of God. He stresses a much more internal connection between the biblical Word and confession. He defines Scripture "as an independent criterion obliging the confessors to adjust to its hard data, its original intentions, its over- and-done events". He describes the Scripture as "the judge, the only judge" and the confessions as the judge's "witnesses". Then, he sets a scene of trial and conflicts between confessions and its accusers ("the papacy and other sects"). Indeed, he affirms that confessions "are reiterations of one and the same source, the biblical Word. Church's creedal and confessional decisions are compelling for posterity not only in what they affirm but also in what they reject". Focusing on salvation, he classifies law and Gospel as the hermeneutical red thread throughout the Scriptures and, consequently, everything else may be considered adiaphora. He puts confession in the stream of history. And streams are fluid.

However, "the confessional metaphor", used by the confessors, according to him, is "hazardous" because "it is God who is made ultimately responsible for the confessions" (which are "admittedly human confessions") and he qualifies this situation as a "blasphemy". He says that "the concordists and even their most 'confessional' descendants did not regard their confession as in principle beyond criticism or irreformable" *coram hominibus*. In addition, from an Elertian point of view, "confession, as dogma, does contain an obligation to teach but it does not contain an obligation to believe". Teaching takes place in a historical and contextual public square. It involves critics, adaptation and evolution. For Bertram, the *quia* issue finds its resolution in the coupling of confession with eschatology finality.

By starting with confession as tradition, he logically ends up with qualifying the Word as *traditioned Word*. Obviously, what happens to confession as tradition will happen with the Word as tradition. *Coram hominibus*, both confession and Scripture share authority but also vulnerability to critical scrutiny by the contextual public. Even though Bertram has taken another parallel street from that of Dr. Wenz, the arrival goal is the same. In both cases, the nature of Scripture is not treated at all. The voice is that of *quatenus* but the hand is that of *quia*.

5   Conclusion

I intentionally close this response to Dr. Wenz's paper by affirming that staying faithful to *quia* in the Scripture-Confession relationship involves a steadfast stand on the divine nature of the Scripture. Premises of that faithfulness are the divine authorship, divine authority and divine unity of the Scripture which result in the infallibility of the Scripture. To doubt its truthfulness and its clarity puts into question the attributes of God.[29] Confession is drawn from that divine Scripture.

---

[29] Joseph Randrianasolo, 'A Hermeneutical Challenge: The Context Contesting the Text', *Lutheran Theological Journal* 46:1 (May 2012), 59–72.

Part IV

God has spoken through the prophets … and by the Son: Word of God in Islam and Christianity

Chapter 7

God has spoken through the prophets … and by the Son: Word of God in Islam and Christianity

Dr. Adam Francisco

Western philosophy, particularly in the realm of epistemology, has in many ways maintained that to have certain knowledge about metaphysical things such information would have to come from outside human experience and originate with God. This was expressed as far back as the time of Plato when he took up the issue of the nature and destiny of the human soul. In *Phaedo* he suggested that the only way to obtain certainty on such a matter was if there was a word from God (*logou theou*).[1] He assumed there wasn't one and so explained that man is left on his own to come up with the most plausible theory about the way things are. Some 2400 years later Ludwig Wittgenstein expressed a similar position in his celebrated *Tractatus Logico-Philosophicus*. The perceived world is, as far as we know, all that is. Metaphysical propositions on the value and essence of things, if there are any, must come from outside of the world. But because "God does not reveal himself *in* the world" one "must pass over in silence" such matters.[2] In many ways, Wittgenstein set the tone for English and American philosophy for much of the 20th century. Metaphysics and

---

[1] See Plato, *Phaedo*, 85d.

[2] From D.F. Pears and B.F. McGuiness's translation of Ludwig Wittgenstein's *Tractatus Logico-Philosophicus* (Routledge, 1961), 73–74.

God-talk was considered, as A.J. Ayer put it, nonsensical and fictitious, for, while there may be various claims that God had revealed information about the world and the way things really are, no religion offered any sort of verifiable evidence for it.[3]

This critique of religion and its theological claims largely holds true for most of the world's religions.[4] Many such as Hinduism, Buddhism, and others don't even pretend to be based on a verifiable historical revelation from God. The only meaning they carry is that which the believer assigns to it. They certainly are not factual or truthful in an objective sense, even if whole civilizations value them. Christianity and Islam are different. Both assert God has *in fact* spoken in real human history. Accordingly, his revelation to man is at least in principle verifiable and therefore open to historical investigation. Christianity and Islam are in this sense very unique. For not only do they make certain claims about God, his disposition towards men and women, and so on, like other religions, but they do so in a way that is objectively meaningful. Ultimately they assert that God's word and the certainty that comes with it was and is in a factual sense available to human beings who, by virtue of their epistemic limits in reference to absolute truths, are stuck in a world of uncertainty. Both religions, then, must be taken seriously by anyone claiming to be interested in truth.

* * *

Both Christianity and Islam claim that God began to speak to man shortly after the creation of the first human. In Christianity, God's word to Adam began with almost unlimited blessings and a simple command not to eat the fruit of a certain tree in the midst of the garden. Then tragedy struck. Adam and Eve were seduced into disobeying God's command and through them "sin came into the world ... and death through sin" (Rom 5:12). This local sin had far-reaching consequences, Christianity claims, such that it affected the entire human race, condemning all as sinners before God in need of reconciliation but, due to this inherited sinful condition, without a way to achieve it on his own.

That is not the end of the story though. In fact, in many ways it is just the beginning in Christianity. Seeing what Adam and Eve had done, God spoke yet again. This time he condemned Adam and Eve for their sin all the while making a promise

---

[3] A.J. Ayer, *Language, Truth and Logic* (Dover Publications, 1946), 44–45, 115.

[4] One may try to get around verificationism and its criticism of religion by appealing to various streams of postmodern thought. Such manoeuvring, however, "places one in tension with the enterprise of serious inquiry." See C.J. Misak, *Verificationism: Its History and Prospects* (Routledge, 1995).

that one day sin, death, and the devil would be crushed by an offspring ascending from Eve. Christianity has historically asserted that this first annunciation of the good news was passed down through the patriarchs and continually revealed through the prophets of old. Those who looked forward to the coming of this chosen offspring, because they ultimately trusted in the redeeming work of this forthcoming prophet (Deut 18:15), priest (Gen. 14:18–20) and king (2 Sam 7:12–16) were, as Eusebius put it, "Christians in fact if not in name."[5]

The word of God revealed to and through the various prophets of old, Christianity teaches, found its historical terminus in the person of Jesus Christ. He came not only claiming to be of God but provided evidence of it such that when he, for example, fed the roughly five thousand men at Galilee they responded by proclaiming, "This is indeed the prophet who is to come into the world" (John 6:14). But Jesus isn't just seen as the last of a long series of prophets whose divinely-inspired utterances were eventually recorded and regarded as holy writ. He is seen as the fulfilment of historical prophetic message and, moreover, incarnation of the very substantial word of God.

The ancient pedigree and theological continuity of the good news first iterated in the garden and fulfilled in Jesus was the earliest apologetic for the Christian faith. You see it already in Luke's Acts of the Apostles where Peter and Paul attempted to prove and persuade (esp. 17:1–15; 26) those they spoke to from the Hebrew Bible that Jesus was the one whom God promised as "all the prophets" bore witness (10:43). It was developed by the early apologists (especially Justin Martyr) and became part of the classical Christian view of history (Eusebius and Augustine) particularly in its apologetic contest with Judaism.

* * *

But then came Islam, and it challenged all this by rewriting history. Its narrative of God's word transmitted in history begins in a similar manner. As in Christianity, Adam is regarded as the first human being as well as the first recipient of God's revelation. The circumstances in which God spoke to him are, however, very different. The Qur'an teaches that Adam and Eve were originally placed in a garden located in the heavens. They were commanded to refrain from eating the fruit from a particular tree within it but disobeyed. They were subsequently cast out and made to fall to the earth whereupon they were forgiven and Adam was made the first prophet of God when God, as Qur'an 2:37 puts it, "gave him words."

---

[5] Eusebius, *The History of the Church*, trans. G.A. Williamson (Penguin Books, 1965), I.4.6.

The words that were given to Adam were qualitatively different than what one finds in Genesis, and mark one of the significant theological differences between the two religions, for they were not words of promise but rather words of, what the Qur'an calls, guidance (*huda*). According to Islamic theology, God began with Adam to provide specific instructions on what to believe and how to live. So long as Adam and his descendants obeyed them their relationship with God and their fellow man would be one of peacefulness or *salam*, but God also tells Adam in Qur'an 2:38–39 that "those who disbelieve and deny our messages shall be the inhabitants of the fire, and there they will remain".

Here begins the lineage of the prophets in Islamic thought. Parallel yet contrary to Christianity's view of the continuity of the promise of God being delivered through prophets, Islam sees God's perpetually transmitted word as essentially ethical guidance. It begins with Adam and was continuously delivered by 124,000 prophets up to the time of Muhammad. Some of them—normally designated as messengers or apostles—even produced books—Moses, the Torah; David, the Psalms; and Jesus, the *Injil* or Gospel. Along with the 20 or more prophets named in the Qur'an and the 124,000 unnamed others, they all taught submission to and peace with God by following his guidance.

In other words, Adam, Noah, Abraham, Moses, David, Jesus, and countless others are seen by Muslims as prophets of Islam. And they all, beginning with Adam, saw the deliverance of the word of God as terminating with Muhammad. As one tradition reads,

> When Adam committed sin he said: "O Lord, I ask you by the right of Muhammad, will you forgive me?" God said: "How do you know about Muhammad, I have not yet created him?" Adam said: "Lord, because when you created me with your hand and breathed into me from your spirit, I raised my head and saw what was written on the foundations of your throne: There is no god but God and Muhammad is the Apostle of God. I knew that you would not place his name there unless he is the most beloved of creation to you." God said: "You are right, Adam. He is the most beloved of creation to me. When you ask me in the right of his name, I will forgive you. If only for Muhammad did I create you.[6]

---

[6] Brannon M. Wheeler, *Prophets in the Quran: An Introduction to the Quran and Muslim Exegesis* (Continuum Books, 2002), 30.

According the Qur'an (61:6) even Jesus looked forward to the coming of Muhammad when he announced the "good news" of a messenger coming after him named Ahmed (another name for Muhammad).

Islam sees Muhammad and, more importantly, the revelation delivered through him as the end of the prophetic lineage as well as the perfection of God's guidance. The famous Indian Islamic revivalist Abul A'la Mawdudi summarized this point well when he wrote, "God's true Prophets were raised in all countries: in every land and people. They all possessed one and the same religion—the religion of Islam. No doubt, the methods of teaching and the legal codes...were a little different in accordance with the needs of and the stage of culture of the people among whom they were raised."[7] God universalized his law, however, by the end of Muhammad's ministry when he declared through Muhammad the perfection of what he had progressively revealed through the ages (Qur'an 5:3). God's word to humankind was now a "complete and full-fledged system, covering all aspects of individual and material life of man. [Muhammad] was made a Prophet for the entire human race and was deputed to propagate his mission to the whole world."[8]

The conviction of the truthfulness of this alternative—Islamic—history of the transmission of God's word gave way to Muslim polemics and apologetics *vis-à-vis* Christianity. You see it already in the Qur'an at 3:64ff where Muhammad calls Christians to a common—presumably monotheistic—platform only to inform them that while they may claim to fall in line with the faith of Abraham (and Adam before him) the real faith passed down through the ages was Islam. In the light, or in anticipation, of counter-arguments based on the lack of textual support from Moses' Torah, David's Psalms, or the Gospel of Jesus that such a continuity exists, these assertions were backed up by Muslim apologists' claims that Christians misinterpreted earlier prophetic books, forcing its words into a procrustean bed of Christian theology. If only the right hermeneutic was employed—the quranic hermeneutic—then one would see the continuity between biblical and quranic teaching. Later, though, this morphed into the charge that the text itself had been altered by copyists to support a theology that developed out of the fusion of Græco-Roman ideas and the Jewish religion. This is the position most Muslim approaches to Christianity employ today, and they now take the work of text critics like Bart Ehrman as their ally asserting such things as the British Muslim Louay Fatoohi's claim that much of what one finds

---

[7] Abu'l-A'la Mawdudi, *Towards Understanding Islam*, 22nd edn. (Idara Tarjuman-ul-Quran, 1995), 43.

[8] *ibid.*, 48.

in the gospels, especially the high Christology of all of them, "were never part of the Injil [Gospel] and were added by their respective authors and editors."[9]

The conflicting and irreconcilable claims each tradition makes concerning the word of God did not keep Christians and Muslim from investigating the position of the other. There is, in fact, a long tradition of Christian theological discourse on Islam that began around the mid-eighth century, just a few generations after the conquest and subjugation of Byzantine Christian populations under Islamic rule. Much of it was comparative, for didactic purposes, but there was almost always an accompanying polemic or apologetic component. What is perhaps most interesting for our present topic is that rather than simply assuming the superiority of the Bible and Christian exegesis of it followed by the denouncement of Islam and limiting the discussion there, many early Christian authors on Islam went further and attempted to demonstrate the theological superiority of Christianity. Some even hoped to persuade Muslims to embrace Christianity. And they did so not so much by focusing on the inscripturation of the word of God, for they knew that the Muslim assumption that the Qur'an was God's word was—as basic presuppositions are—practically impenetrable. So they sought to demonstrate the truthfulness of the incarnation of the word of God, and they did so, in part, on the basis of the Qur'an.

It began with John of Damascus (c. 676–749).[10] In his work *On Heresies* (part two of a larger work entitled *Fountain of Knowledge*) he provided a brief explanation of the Qur'an's origins and outline of Islamic theology. Almost immediately he drew attention to the Qur'an's reference to Christ as the "word of God" (4:171) but, at the same time, its insistence that he was also a creature of God created by God's command in the womb of Mary (3:47). He sheds more light on the issue in his "manual of guidance for Christians who find themselves entering into theological discussions with Muslims" entitled *The Discussion of a Christian and a Saracen (that is, a Muslim)*.[11] "If you are asked by a Saracen: 'What do you call Christ?'" John wrote, "say to him, 'The Word of God.'"[12] And be confident, for this is what the scriptures call him. Moreover, this—the *kalimatullah*—is what the Qur'an calls him.

John also knew that the Muslim theological tradition had developed a theology of the word of God being eternal or, more appropriately, uncreated. It, however,

---

[9] Louay Fatoohi, *Mystery of the Historical Jesus* (Luna Plena, 2007), 37–38.

[10] See Daniel J. Sahas, *John of Damascus on Islam* (E.J. Brill, 1972).

[11] Hugh Goddard, *A History of Christian-Muslim Relations* (New Amsterdam Books, 2000), 40–41.

[12] John of Damascus, 'The Discussion of a Christian and a Saracen', in *The Early Christian-Muslim Dialogue: A Collection of Documents from the First Three Centuries (632–900 A.D.)*, ed. N.A. Newman (Interdisciplinary Biblical Research Institute, 1993), 144–147.

limited the temporal manifestation of God's word to the text of the Qur'an. In doing so, though, it limited God—mutilated him, as he put it in *On Heresies*—from manifesting himself differently in, for example, a person like Jesus Christ. In other words, while Islam permitted the inscripturation of God's word it arbitrarily precluded an incarnation even though at least in one place, in the Qur'an, it acknowledges it, at least according to John's exegesis. This should come as no surprise though, for Islam and the Qur'an was, according to John of Damascus, an incoherent assimilation of Christian scriptural traditions (and others) under the influence of an Arian monk.[13]

Unlike their eastern counterparts Christians in the west were mostly isolated from Islam for most of its early medieval development (except those in Spain). At the beginning of the high middle ages they, too, began to develop polemics against Islam. It started with Abbot Peter of Cluny (c. 1092–1156), or Peter the Venerable (though he was never canonized), when he began thinking about the opportunity of evangelistic work amidst Muslims during the early crusades in the Levant.[14] And in many ways he set in motion the mediæval European dream of converting Muslims to Christianity by sponsoring the translation of the Qur'an as well as other Muslim literature around the early 1140s so that the theological study of Islam could be facilitated. Not much more was accomplished, though, as the Muslim counter attack on the crusaders and their recently acquired kingdoms in the Near East beginning with Salah al-Din's conquest of Jerusalem began. The missionary vision to convert Muslims started to be realized again at the end of the thirteenth century, particularly with the establishment of the Franciscan and Dominican mendicant orders. But whereas the Franciscans focused on what might be described as works of mercy when living amongst Muslims, the Dominicans developed a theological approach.[15] Much of it was inspired in methodology by Thomas Aquinas' great *Summa contra Gentiles* but soon became much more specialized and directed not at some abstract gentile but at the Saracens.

The most influential among the Dominican Islamic specialists was the Italian missionary to Baghdad named Riccoldo da Monte di Croce (c. 1240–1320).[16] He had spent a number of years in the 1290s in and around Baghdad amidst Muslim

---

[13] John of Damascus, 'On Heresies', in *The Early Christian-Muslim Dialogue*, 139–141.
[14] See James Kritzeck, *Peter the Venerable and Islam* (Princeton University Press, 1964).
[15] See J. Hoeberichts, *Francis and Islam* (Franciscan Institute Publications, 1997) and John Victor Tolan, *Saracens: Islam in the Medieval Imagination* (Columbia University Press, 2002), 233–255.
[16] See L. Michael Spath, 'Riccoldo da Monte Croce: Medieval Pilgrim and Traveler to the Heart of Islam', *Bulletin of the Royal Institute for Inter-Faith Studies* 1:1 (1999): 55–102; 'De Lege Sarracenorum According to Riccoldo da Monte Croce', *Bulletin of the Royal Institute for Inter-Faith Studies* 2:2 (2000): 115–140.

scholars until he was recalled back to Italy at the turn of the century. It was here that he penned his famous and influential *Contra legem Saracenorum* wherein, after fourteen chapters of polemical tearing down of the Qur'an, he tried to demonstrate the truthfulness of Christianity from a critical reflection upon the Qur'an. His hope was that Muslims hearing such arguments would be compelled by force of reason to believe them. Riccoldo did so by drawing Christian doctrines out of the Qur'an. A good Dominican, he did not take the Qur'an to be authoritative *per se*. In fact, he saw the Qur'an as a devious book filled with ancient heresies and an infinite number of lies. But, as a missionary, he knew that amidst Muslims, who in his experience were eager to hear about the particularities of Christian doctrine, he had to start somewhere. And since Muhammad and the compilers of the Qur'an were not the most scrupulous of editors when they fabricated the quranic text from, among others, Christian texts they unwittingly left enough trace evidence of Christian doctrine in the Qur'an that could be used to persuade Muslims of the veracity of the God's triune nature, the deity of Christ, and the authority of the Bible.

His argument for Jesus as the word of God from all eternity is similar to that of John of Damascus. He starts with reference to Qur'an 3:45 and 4:171 and their "unequivocal" affirmation that "Christ is the word of God." This attribution is not used metaphorically nor is it a title for someone who speaks for God, he argued, for no other prophet—in the Qur'an—is referred to as the word of God. It is used in reference to Christ as a real and uniquely personal attribution. And, he continues,

> [I]f the Word is taken literally, it is clear that the Word of God would be everlasting and true God. For just as the word that proceeds from the mouth of a perishable man is necessarily perishable, so the word that proceeds from the everlasting mouth, through which He made the heaven and earth and the things that are in between (as the Koran likes to say) is necessarily everlasting and imperishable.
>
> Moreover, whatever proceeds from God is, essentially God, and in this way the Word of God is God....
>
> Therefore, Mohammed spoke the truth when he said that Jesus Christ the son of Mary is also the Word of God.[17]

He just didn't understand what he was doing. Interestingly, while Riccoldo suggests this was simply due to his ignorance of what he copied from Christian sources

---

[17] Riccoldo da Monte di Croce, *Refutation of the Koran*, trans. Londini Ensis (Charleston: Self-Published, 2010), 85–88.

Luther suggested in his German translation of Riccoldo's work that the Holy Spirit caused such things to be written in the Qur'an.[18]

These arguments, particularly in the initial stages of Christian and Muslim theological interaction, may have gained some traction in the Muslim world. For example, the first orthodox Christian that we know of to write primarily in Arabic, Theodor Abu Qurra (c. 750–829), is recorded in a few Christian and Muslim sources to have publicly debated Muslim scholars at the invitation of the caliph al-Ma'mun (813–833) in what seems to have been a remarkably liberal environment. And it was here that an agreement was reached between Christian and Muslim participants that Jesus was in fact "the word of God." This was followed by disagreement over whether he was the uncreated (i.e. divine) word of God or the word of God in the sense that he was created in the womb of Mary when God spoke him into existence by simply saying, "Be."[19]

This is the quranic position (3:47, 59). And Muslim responses to the particular argument for Christ as the "word of God" quickly developed in the light of it. In the ninth century, perhaps in response to the perceived headway or theological concessions Christian apologists achieved,[20] as Christians were reduced to the status of second class citizens by the caliph al-Mutawakkil (847–861) in 850, the orthodox Islamic position on the identity of the word of God was definitively established. Two major figures associated with this are Ahmad ibn Hanbal (d. 855) and Abu al-Hasan al-Ash'ari (d. 935). Both argued and established the position that while God's word was eternal and uncreated its temporal manifestation was only located in the text of the Qur'an.[21] The Qur'an is, in other words, God's word inscripurated. But it has not become incarnated.

* * *

Herein lays the essential theological divide between Christianity and Islam that has been debated for centuries since the initial medieval encounters between Christians and Muslims. And it is right that this issue has been front and centre in historical Christian-Muslim discourse. What's interesting, though, is the way the issue

---

[18]WA 53:366.31–33: "Also hat in der heilige Geist vermanet und getrieben, das er hat müßen mit worten unsers Glaubens hoechsten Artickel aussprechen."

[19]See Goddard, 53; Alfred Guillaume, 'Theodore Abu Qurra as Apologist', *Muslim World* 15 (1925):42–51. Cf. the critical commentary of John C. Lamoreaux, *Theodore Abu Qurrah* (Brigham Young University Press, 2005), xvii–xviii.

[20]Goddard, 41; Morris S. Seale, *Muslim Theology: A Study of Origins with Reference to the Church Fathers* (London: Luzac & Co., 1964).

[21]See http://www.yale.edu/faith/downloads/rp/WordGodIslamChristianity-English.pdf.

of the word of God in Islam and Christianity are being treated today. Muslim theologians for the most part have stuck with their classical position. The Qur'an is the
inscripturated word of God. It is therefore *al-Furqan* or the standard, which has been
"sent down" from God (Qur'an 25:1), and by which all things should be judged. And
so when they approach Christianity it is interpreted and addressed through the lens
of the Qur'an.

One of the more high profile examples of this is the common word movement.
It began in autumn of 2007, a year after the fallout from Pope Benedict's Regensburg
lecture, when 138 representatives from across Islamic civilization gathered together
and sent an open letter and call (*da'wa*) to the Pope and leaders of Christian churches
everywhere.[22] In short, it argued that because Christians and Muslims comprise
nearly half of the world's population it behoves both to work towards a peaceful reconciliation of the two faiths. And in fact both can be reconciled, for each share a
tremendous amount of common ground found in each tradition's sacred text. The
Christian response to this was rather predictable. Immediately hundreds of church-
men and scholars of every confession accepted the terms of what amounts to a veiled
call to Islam.[23] Such is the character of much Christian consideration of Islam. At
best, though, Christians nowadays tend to take the comparative approach—pitting
one text and its teachings against the other—assuming they have God's word while
Islam doesn't. And at worst they take the approach of the late Wilfred Cantwell
Smith and remain ambivalent to the whole question of epistemology and authority.[24]

There is a different approach, however. It has much in common with the initial
attempts of Christians such as John of Damascus and Riccoldo da Monte di Croce
in that it focuses on the issue of the word of God and Jesus. But its starting point is
not the Qur'an. It is with history.

Both Christianity and Islam claim that God has spoken his word through certain
prophets and in the texts that record their message throughout history. These texts
(the Bible and the Qur'an) are respectively regarded as the word of God by each
tradition. The texts and their teachings contradict each other on a number of points.
Where they do agree is in their identification of Jesus as a prophet. Christianity goes
further, of course, declaring Jesus was equally the incarnation of the prophetic word

---

[22] See http://www.acommonword.com.
[23] Sam Solomon and E. Al Maqdisi, *A Common Word: The Undermining of the Church* (Advancing
Native Missions, ANM, 2009).
[24] Wilfred Cantwell Smith, 'Is the Qur'an the Word of God?' in *On Understanding Islam* (Mouton
Publishers, 1981), 282–300.

of God. It does so not as the result of the process of theological development, as Muslims allege, but on the basis of Jesus' own testimony about himself.

The big question between Christians and Muslims in the realm of epistemology is whether or not there is sufficient evidence to make this claim. To make a long apologetic story short, yes. The gospels prove to be solid primary source material from which one can determine the nature of the life, work, and claims of Jesus (despite the claims of some of the higher critics masquerading as text critics and the enthusiasts of the non-canonical gospels). In them Jesus unmistakably associates himself with God yet also distinguishes himself from God the Father (John 20:17). John provides the explanation when he describes him as the *logos* of God. Jesus was (and is) the substantive word of God in time and space in a particular person.

Muslims claim essentially the same thing about the Qur'an. It is God's eternal speech inscribed in a text. When it is recited it is as if God is speaking from all eternity. The problem is that there is no evidence that can be adduced to support this assertion. So they argue that the Qur'an itself is evidence of its divine nature. It claims to be the word of God therefore it is the word of God. With Jesus the circumstances are different. Christianity does not demand circular, fideistic reasoning to establish its legitimacy, for according to the apologetic tradition up to and through John Warwick Montgomery there is ample evidence to trust Jesus was who he claimed to be. The resurrection is the best proof, so to speak, of it. It is even more far reaching than that, though, argues Montgomery, as it "constitutes an event subject to investigation: its synthetic character removes the central Christian claim that 'God was in Christ, reconciling the world unto himself' from the realm of technical meaninglessness into which ... so many religions fall."[25] This would, if no evidence can be adduced for its claims, include Islam. Montgomery goes further and argues that the resurrection not only validates Jesus' divinity but it also, through inductive processes, can lead to the conclusion that the Hebrew Bible and the apostolic writings are God's inspired written word.[26] This goes a long way in establishing the truthfulness of the claim that "God spoke to our fathers by the prophets, but in these last days he has spoken to us by his Son" (Heb 1:1–2) especially in a context where Islam and its claims to supremacy often escape the scrutiny of Christians. In a context such as our, then, in the midst of a global resurgence of Islam, it's time that the facts be restored to our thinking and in our persuasive discourse with Muslims concerning the *verbum* that *caro factum est*, for the incarnation of the word of God did not happen in an epistemological corner (Acts 26:26).

---

[25] John Warwick Montgomery, *Tractatus Logico-Theologicus* (Bonn: VKW, 2002), 97.
[26] *ibid.*, 129.

Chapter 8

Similarities and Differences between the Christian and the Islamic Views of Divine Revelation—Some Aspects And Questions: A Response to Adam Francisco

Rev. Dr. Martti Vaahtoranta

In August 2002 I was lecturing about the theological intentions of Johann Gerhard and of his view of Islam with a look to modern German Christian-Islamic dialogue at the NELA conference in Gothenburg. There was a short discussion after that. In this discussion Erik Okkels asked an important question. I couldn't give an answer to it, although I somehow intuitively knew it. I was not happy with some standard responses to the theological challenge of brother Erik, either.

Since then his question has been mine. If I were still a professional theologian with a task to research the relation of Islam and Christianity, I certainly would try to write something about it. But now I have my duties as parish pastor and no resources to write books or even articles. Therefore I can only "think" something "out loud" as a comment to the excellent lecture of Dr. Francisco and as a hypothetical answer to Rev. Okkels' question.

Unfortunately Dr. Francisco and I seem to be saying more or less the same thing. So it perhaps wouldn't be necessary at all to comment his lecture. But I'm going to do it anyway. Two witnesses is better than only one, and perhaps there are some new aspects to the topic in my commentary, too. Otherwise you must take it for a short summary of Dr. Francisco's lecture.

And now back to the question of Rev. Okkels. He was asking, what distinguishes the Christian view of God's revelation from the corresponding theological view of Muslims? For both of these "children of Abraham" believe in one God, who reveals Himself to human beings. They both believe that this Revelation is to be read in the Holy Book. They both believe in the divine inspiration and in the inerrancy of this Book.

* * *

However, and although the Muslims actually speak about only one Book of revelation, in reality there are two Books, the Bible and the Qur'an. For the Christians the Bible is the inspired, inerrant Word of God, and the Muslims say the same about there Qur'an.

Therefore we have to ask, what reasons we have to give to our belief that just *our* Book, not theirs, is the right one. How do we justify our faith? And how do the Muslims do it?

I think it's easy to find plenty of Christians and of course Muslims who say: "Our Book is the Holy one, inspired and inerrant, because it says so." This is probably more usual among Muslims, but it isn't unknown among Christians either. Especially we Lutherans are used to saying that every teaching should be proved by the written Word of God, and if someone asks us why we say so, we answer: "Because the Bible says so."

This argument, although it in itself begs the question, works among Christians, who all somehow believe that the Bible is the revelation of God and has therefore the ultimate authority in matters of religion. But it doesn't work in a discussion with the Muslims, who claim that not ours but their Book, the Qur'an, is the inerrant revelation of the only God. And why? Because the Qur'an says so!

There we are then: word against word - but who will judge between us? Or how do *we* justify our belief, our trust in the Bible, not in the Qur'an? Only because our Daddy is stronger than their Daddy?

Now, Muslims abhor calling God the "Father", because it seems to them a forbidden anthropomorphism. But surely they think to believe in the One and only almighty God, who is incomparable in his majesty and power and that our Christian faith on the Triune God is a corrupted form of the original Religion. Consequently they further think, that our Book is a corrupted version of the original one Book, given to the Jews and Christians, and which in Qur'an has been renewed in Arabic through the Seal of the Prophets, Muhammad. Therefore, the Muslims think, the Qu'ran reveals the original and rational truth about God and is the only uncorrupted written revelation and word of God.

* * *

Well, what shall we say to it? For there are a lot of similarities between the Bible and the Qur'an and generally between both of these religions "of the Book". Phenomenologically and historically we belong to the same family of religions.

Therefore it is of utmost importance to ask and think why Muslims still aren't our real brothers in the spiritual meaning of the word, why they are not children of the same Heavenly Father. What then is different between our faith and thinking and the Muslim's thinking and faith and how does the difference appear in our understanding about the theology of revelation?

Seeking answers to this question it is useful to compare the Qur'an with the Bible. It is quite a simple and more practical than a theoretical task. You just begin to read the Qur'an —and simultaneously You meditate on the Bible, just as it is.

For example, we are used to calling the written English or German or Finnish version of the Bible the "Word of God", and it doesn't only contain maybe totally inerrant "words *about* God", but it *is* the "Word" of God *Himself*.

If You then take a Qu'ran and read it in your own language, from the point of view of the Muslims you are not reading the real Word of God. Muslims believe that God speaks in the Qur'an only in Arabic. All translations of this Book are just commentaries on it. But we Christians assert that also the German or English or Finnish translation of the Bible really *is* the "Word of God". Actually we Lutherans say that even about the *preaching* of the Gospel.

Then you will perhaps read the Qu'ran from its beginning to its end. It's fascinating. You will, for example, find a lot of biblical reminiscences and stories from early Christian legends in it. But if you think about this book as a whole and about its particular chapters, do you really understand what the idea of this book is? What is its structure like and what is its goal?

Well, there are two topics, which occur often in Qur'an: the revelation of the *arithmetical Oneness* of the only God and his many *prophets*, who all are proclaiming this same message, like they prophecy the end of the world and the Last Judgement, too. This judgement will be hard for them who don't believe the message, for them who stay in their idolatry or polytheism and who live a selfish life in greed and with a hard, loveless heart. And, like Mohammed himself, all these prophets have been rejected by the majority of their own people.

On the other hand, it's difficult to find any structure in Qur'an at all. There is no systematic order, but there is no historical order either. Actually, the only structure in Qur'an as a whole is it's division to *Sures*, the chapters of it. And their order is purely technical. The *Sures* have been put in order according their length: the longest chapters are in the beginning of the book, the shortest and often oldest chapters in its end.

* * *

In the Bible you won't find a textbook of systematic theology, nor an encyclopedia of human history. Nevertheless, it is unlike the Qur'an in many ways. For example, it is much older than the Qur'an. Since the first beginning of writing the first texts of the Bible until its end and until the collection of the canonical books were more than thousand years gone by. The Qur'an on its part is some hundreds of years younger than the last books of the biblical canon, and it has been written in only about thirty years.

As the kind of really *historical* book that the Bible is, it tells a history, a *historical story*. It makes a majestic temporal arc from its beginning to its end. It begins with the beginning of everything through the Word of Creation in the Genesis, and it ends in the book of Apocalypse with the end of the time. This is what structures the Bible as a book, too, and not only its content. It is a *salvation historical* book.

That does not mean a strict chronology in the Bible. There is a great variety, too, a whole library with different kinds of books: there are chronicles, songs, preaching, reports, juridical books, poetry and proclaiming the Gospel by telling what God has done in His Son Jesus Christ and what He has preached —and this in four different books of Gospel, not, like the Muslims think, in only one "euangelion".

And of course there are in the Bible some books too, which seem to correspond with the view of revelation in Qur'an: the prophetic books, which tell about visions or auditions of God's message and how the prophets proclaim it as the word of God. But: this ecstatic speech is only a part of the Bible, which we call "the written Word of God" as a whole.

116

* * *

Now we are coming to the substance of my matter, while we are of thinking about the question of Erik Okkels in Gothenburg. To get a hypothetical answer to it I'll ask two further questions:

First, how is it possible that God as the absolutely transcendental Majesty in his total metaphysical otherness in Islam "speaks" in human words to people? — It is of course not a problem to think, that we can see God's great works in creation, in the wonders of the world and in us, human beings. But because God in His majesty and freedom is a diametrical "other" in his relation to the man, how could a human book with human words be "the word of God", even though we would presume that God has created these words as a part of his creation in the prophets. Therefore it's no wonder that the Muslims know a concept of an uncreated Qu'ran in heaven, too, although it brings them a new theological and philosophical problem to solve.

For the worst sin in Islam is the *shirk*, the *associating of anything with Him*. How can there, then, be an *uncreated Word* of God without destroying his arithmetical oneness and his metaphysical distance to the created man and his speech, words, language and thinking? Or otherwise: is it in Islamic theology possible at all to assume any ontological bridge, which could bring God near to man without destroying the diametrical otherness of God and without making him a part of the same ontological reality in which mankind lives in time and space?

Secondly, we Christians believe in a totally "other" God, too. The Lord is the Creator of everything, and the creature is only a creature. We human beings are not just a step in the "stairway to heaven". We are not able to come step by step to God like in the metaphysical system of neoplatonism. We do not belong to the same ontological system with God the Creator of heaven and earth. We have no direct way to the vision of God nor can we directly hear His voice with our human ears, only His *indirect speech* in the creature. God has no human voice. We have no divine ears.

But we believe in God's Word. We assert that we actually hear Him speaking in the Bible and in the biblical sermon. The text of the Bible is for us Christians God's word not only when we hear ecstatic words written by the prophets or according there preaching. We believe that the whole Bible in its immense variety is somehow "God's Word". It's not only—inspired or uninspired—speech *about* God, but the Word of God Himself. And that's what we say, although we quite clearly see that most of the Biblical texts are thoroughly human.

How is this possible? — I have no way to explain in a few sentences thoroughly and exactly what I mean. But the key to its understanding is written in Jesus' words in the Gospel according St. John in chapter 5:

> You examine the Scriptures carefully because you suppose that in them you have eternal life. Yet they testify about me. (John 5:39)

And the second biblical witness is the report about the discussion on the way from Emmaus in the Gospel according St. Luke in chapter 24:

> … beginning with Moses and all the Prophets, he explained to them all the passages of Scripture about himself. (Luke 24: 27)

* * *

I will make it short: *The Divine Word became Flesh.* The answer to Erik Okkels' question is deeply christological.

God himself became Flesh in His eternal and divine Word, which doesn't mean an uncreated book or eternal information in words and sentences and chapters, but the Son, the second Person of the Triune God. He became personally a part of our history, our material life in time and space.

Therefore in the whole Bible and in every biblical sermon the humanity of this *theanthroopos*, Christ, God in the flesh, resounds as the nucleus of the biblical canon in the human speech of the Bible.

This human resounding of the divine Word of God in the salvation history of the Bible corresponds with St. Paul's assertion in his first letter to the Corinthians in its first chapter:

> For Jews demand signs and Greeks seek wisdom, but we preach Christ crucified, a stumbling block to Jews and folly to Gentiles, but to those who are called, both Jews and Greeks, Christ the power of God and the wisdom of God. For the foolishness of God is wiser than men, and the weakness of God is stronger than men. (1. Cor. 1: 22-25)

We really seem to have a "weak God" if we compare Him with the view of the Muslims. But our God is the loving God. He is the Only but Triune God, who *is* Love. Just in His descending eternal love He shows us His real essence, *what* and *how* He really is. And just as the One who lets His only begotten Son die for the sinners, He really is the "stronger Father" whose word is true.

Then Muhammad didn't make any validation wonders as a Prophet, but Jesus did. He showed Himself as God's Son precisely where He was the Weakest one: in His resurrection from the death.

From my point of view it is just this most unbelievable resurrection of Jesus that is the fixed point of the lever outside the close world of the two competing books claiming their own authority: the resurrection has really happened. It is true.

Therefore we don't need to try to defend the uniqueness and grandiosity of the Bible with the same weapons the Muslims defend their own Book. For they have no other validation for it. They have only the Book itself.

But we do have it. We have the Lord who not only really died on the Cross but who was resurrected and who now lives and reigns for ever and ever and explains the Bible, filling it with His love, with His divinity and making the Bible totally divine, too—this totally human Book under the cross.

Part V

Letter or Spirit?

Chapter 9

Letter or Spirit? Modern Enthusiasms

Rev. Dr. Anssi Simojoki

1   Letter or Spirit—a misunderstanding

"He has made us competent as ministers of the New Testament, not of the letter, but of the Spirit; for the letter kills, but the Spirit gives life" (2 Cor 3:6). This sentence of St. Paul's has been a *locus classicus* in separating the text from the Spirit, in various attempts to overcome "dead biblical literalism" in favour of a "free spiritual understanding" of Scripture, in the spirit of Jesus and along the principles of love and freedom. Such an interpretation is a warning example of errors that arise when a single verse of Scripture is removed from its context. The apostle explains in this discourse in 2 Cor 3 the juxtaposition and opposition of Law and Gospel in terms of their respective glory, δόξα. The words γράμμα and περιτομή are signs of the fulfilment of the Torah, and yet they can neither contribute to it nor guarantee it. This antithesis "the letter—the Spirit" is related to St. Paul's discourse on the Law in Rom 7:9–13, which requires the theme verse in Rom 1:17: it is only through the Gospel that those who are being rightfully condemned by the letter of the Law, receive forgiveness, justification and the life in the Holy Spirit (Rom. 8), the new circumcision of man's heart in the Spirit of God. However, the antithesis of the letter and the

Spirit does not apply to γραμμά, Scripture, as such.[1] Unfortunately, the sentence in 2 Cor 3:6, out of its true context, has begun to live its own life as a misleading slogan. Extricated from the original context, the words of St. Paul have been, time and again, erroneously used as a general rule in questions concerning the inerrancy of the text of the Bible. Yet, "the letter that kills" in 2 Cor 3:6 does not refer to literal fidelity in the interpretation of Scripture, far from it. What St. Paul states here is the proper ministry of the Torah to accuse and condemn sinners unto the point of complete mortification. The vivification of sinners in the Spirit is the work of the Gospel. Passages that speak of the words and the text are found in profusion in the Bible. This verse, 2 Cor 3:6, is not one them. For this reason and for the sake of tex-tual clarity, let us salute the precious words of Apostle Paul in their genuine context of Law and Gospel and let them rest when we commence our study aiming to clarify the relationship between the text, context and the work of the Holy Spirit.

2   Looking for the roots of Enthusiasm

There are two different ways to study modern enthusiasm. One is to describe and classify the rich contemporary Pentecostal and Neo-Pentecostal or charismatic ve-getation in the world. A lecture of this kind could easily inundate the audience with a flood of personages and ministries that are busy all over the world proclaiming the other Gospel of miracles, health and wealth. Among this flora even new rites have been born that could be called kind of neo-sacraments or sacramental substitutes that have in importance replaced the baptism and the Eucharist. I mean particularly the Neo-Pentecostal version of the traditional altar-call practised by D.L.Moody (1837–1899) among others. The pristine revivalist type of making a public com-mitment to Jesus along the lines of Protestant decision theology, has evolved on its way from Billy Graham (1918–) via Kathryn Kuhlman (1907–1976) to Benny Hinn.[2] It means a predictable and controlled epiphany of the Spirit in which healings and blessings in the form of health and prosperity are regularly claimed. In the tele-vision programme "This Is Your Day" donations to Hinn's ministry are presented as the surest and speediest way of reaping spiritual-temporal blessings. The con-nection to the reputed words of John Tetzel (+ 1519) is not so far-fetched as one might be inclined to think: "As soon as a coin in the coffer rings etc." The veteran Korean health preacher David (Paul) Yongi Cho (1936–) has earlier on created a similar mega-church matrix based on the theology of three-fold blessings, namely

---

[1]H-J. Kraus, *Die biblische Theologie. Ihre Geschichte und Problematik* (Neukirchen-Vluyn: Neuk-irchener, 1970), 341–344. J. Mumme, 'Der Geist und die Geister.' *Lutherische Beiträge* 1/2012, 1–12.

[2]Toufik Benedictus Hinn, b. 1952 in Jaffa, moved to Toronto in 1968.

salvation for the soul, good health and prosperity leading to the fourth dimension of the Spirit "through the development of concentrated visions and dreams in imagination". They are fed with words. When we change our language taking our words from the Bible, the biblically charged tongue will take control of our personality. In the area of lush charismatic thickets, the boundary between the Holy Spirit as attested in the Bible and various other spirits finally disappears.[3] Yet, I want to stop here and change the course of my presentation. Instead of presenting a phenomenological study, an enterprise of all-embracing taxonomy in the fashion of the legendary Swedish botanist Carl von Linne (1707–1778), I have chosen a historical and systematic approach in the desire of not only knowing but rather of understanding the nature of religious enthusiasm in its relation to the Word of God. Such a systematic understanding can shed light on a number of hiding places in which enthusiasm might be unexpectedly discovered. The truth is that our present-day point of departure is very different from the situation that prevailed in the 16th century. The enthusiasts of various descriptions are everywhere, but shall we find the stable keel which Lutheranism, even Calvinism in its differing way, delivered with the doctrine of *Sola Scriptura* in the days of the Reformation? Learn to know the traditional Western mainline churches, how they fare today, and one scarcely can come across anything of its kind.

3   Luther's comtemporary "Schwärmer" and their posthumous reputation

"Enthusiasm" or "Schwärmerei" is well attested in the literature of the Lutheran Reformation. Historically, Martin Luther and his true heirs prosecuted their war concerning the truth of the Word of God and the life of the Christian Church on two fronts, namely against the Pope and the Pontifical Curia and the myriad of their theologians on one side, and against the tide of Protestants enthusiasts on the other side. Luther penned in the Smalcald Articles (1537) the pregnant Lutheran definition of Enthusiasm (III.VIII.3):

> In issues relating to the spoken, outward Word, we must firmly hold that God grants His Spirit or grace to no one except through or with the preceding outward Word (Galatians 3:2, 5). This protects us from the enthusiasts (i.e. souls who boast that they have the Spirit without and before the Word). They judge Scripture or the spoken Word and

---

[3] D.Y. Cho, *The Fourth Dimension* (Alachua, FL: Bridge-Logos, 1979), 40. J. Mumme,*ibid.*, 13–15.

explain and stretch it at their pleasure, as Münzer[4] did. Many still do this today, wanting to be sharp judges between the Spirit and the letter, and yet they do not know what they are saying (2 Corinthians 3:6).

When reading these lines of the Reformer, it is worth of observing that God's Word spoken in public sermons and God's Word written in Scripture are for Luther inseparably one. Similarly, doctrine is inseparably one with the word of the Bible. Therefore, Luther could speak of the Word of God and the catechism interchangeably as synonyms.[5] Enthusiasts are Christians who teach that the Holy Spirit works before and even without the Word. The Word, "the letter", is only a point of departure for *tours de force* of the Spirit. Christians who are in possession of the Spirit are competent to judge the text of the Holy Writ. The literal faith is inferior to the wisdom that emanates from the Spirit without the means of grace. Enthusiasm was sinking under the flood of human religiousness all that the Lutheran Reformation had discovered after the dark age of the tyranny of the Pope in Rome: the Bible, the distinction between Law and Gospel, the Keys, the sacraments and finally justification by faith alone.[6]

The reputation of the Enthusiasts of the 16th century evolved from bad to better. Where Immanuel Kant still termed the Enthusiasts as moral killers of all reason, the age of Romanticism gave some cautious credit to them. It was the prince of all Liberal theologians, namely Adolf von Harnack (1851–1930), who in his history of dogma compared the Enthusiast favourably with Martin Luther. It was the Enthusiasts that were bold enough to draw the radical conclusions from the Reformation by rejecting the Roman-Catholic scholasticism and sacramentalism, whereas Luther

---

[4] Thomas Müntzer (c. 1490–1525), since 1520 a pastor at Zwickau in Thuringia was under the influence of the three radical Zwickau prophets since 1522 and grew completely alienated from Luther. He sharply distinguished between the letter of Scripture and the Spirit. Although Luther met the "prophets" at several occasions, he did not mention them in his important 'Invocavit' sermons of 1522. When the three prophets claimed the authority of the Holy Spirit, Luther asked them to perform a miracle to authenticate their message, which they refused. Luther spared his polemical ammunition primarily against the leaders such as Thomas Münzer and Andreas Karlstadt. Münzer rejected church art in true iconoclastic fashion, as well as infant baptism, and understood the Sacrament of the Altar symbolically only. He interpreted the Magnificat in a political, revolutionary manner. When caught during the Peasants' War after the defeat Frankenhausen in 1525, he recanted his teachings in compliance with the Church of Rome prior to his execution.

[5] Large Catechism, Longer Preface 10: "Besides, catechism study is a most effective help against the devil, the world, the flesh, and all evil thoughts. It helps to be occupied with God's Word, to speak it, and meditate on it, just as the first Psalm declares people blessed who meditate on God's Law day and night (Psalm 1:2)."

[6] R. Hempelmann, 'Enthusiasmus', *RGG4*, Vol. 2, 1325–1327. Mumme, *ibid.*, 16–23.

stopped half-way, remaining a scholastic, biblicist man of the Middle Ages as much as he was the Reformer. Indeed, the Enthusiasts had a better understanding of the Gospel than did Dr. Luther. Adolf von Harnack was not at loss for acerbic words when it came to giving the Reformer a birching for his biblicism, his "legalistic adherence to the Bible", the dogma of the Early Church and the ensuing "sacramental superstition". Ernst Troeltsch (1865–1923) followed the same path of rehabilitating the Enthusiasts of the Age of the Reformation. He painted the Enthusiasts as harbingers of human rights and pioneers of our modern, tolerant society. They took seriously the human condition of life. Where Martin Luther concentrated all and everything on the Bible, it was the Enthusiasts that began to set individualistic Europeans free from the formal authority of the Holy Writ and the traditional ecclesial dogma. The enthusiasts though, being critics of contemporary faults, were not as productive in the field of constructing enduring orders and institutions for the future as were Luther and his legacy.[7] The famous Czech-German Marxist philosopher Karl Kautsky (1854–1938) wrote a book which was published in London in English in 1897: *Communism in Central Europe at the time of Reformation.* Kautsky defended John of Leiden and dismissed all his eccentric features as baseless rumour-mongering that had missed the point. Thomas Müntzer was also made a political icon in the former Communist East-Germany, GDR.[8] In the field of church history, Roland Bainton, Luther's masterly biographer, has distinguished himself also as a cautious revisionist concerning the legacy of the 16th century Enthusiast. Is such revisionism historically plausible? In my opinion, the revisionist views have had two weaknesses: First, they ignore the primary element of apocalyptic religiousness of the enthusiastic movements. Those movements were more religious, theocratic, apocalyptic, and less political than a revisionist scholar would like to admit. Second, they ignore the primary sources of the development of modern political thought

---

[7] A. von Harnack, *Dogmengeschichte, Vierte verbesserte und bereicherte Auflage* (Grundriss der Theologischen Wissenschaften IV, Dritter Band; Tübingen, 1905), 427–434: Luther confused the Gospel and doctrine, the evangelical faith and dogma. Harnack lamented the influence of Luther's "speculative" insistence on the Christological two-natures doctrine, what he called the confusion of God's Word and the Holy Writ, the confusion of grace and the means of grace, especially the sacraments inclusive of infant baptism, which to Harnack should not be considered a sacrament at all. Baptism was to him the sacrament of justification and not that of rebirth. K. Holl,.*Luther und Schwärmer. Gesammelte Aufsätze zur Kirchengeschichte I: Luther* (Sechste, neu durchgesehene Auflage; Tübingen, 1932), 420–467. F Enns and R. Stroh, 'Schwärmertum' *RGG4*, Vol. 7, 1047–1050.

[8] M. Bloch,.*Marxism and Anthropology: The History of a Relationship* (Marxist Introductions; Oxford-New York:OUP, 1983), 100–102. G. Brakelmann, 'Kautsky, Karl', *RGG4*, 913. Q. Skinner, *The Foundations of Modern Political Thought. Volume Two: The Age of Reformation* (Cambridge: CUP, 1978), 73–81.

which was brewing in the age of the Renaissance in Italy. The decisive political impulses permeated Central and Northern Europe from the far side of the Alps, not from peasants' rebellions and the like which for centuries were commonplace in Europe even before the turmoil of Reformation. 'La Jacquerie', peasants' revolts, occurred frequently in France after the 'Grande Jacquerie' of 1358.[9] In the age of the Reformation, religious themes were intertwined with socio-political discontent. Still, this kind of dissenterism did not *alone* contribute much to the desired changes in the world under the leadership of visionaries, seers and prophets. Only in co-operation with institutions of learning and politics, new ideas were forged to a form in which they could reach out and successfully begin to conquer the world. This was the case with the Huguenots and the scholarly discussion they provoked concerning absolutism, constitutionalism, submission, and self-defence.[10] On the platforms of political institutions, dissenters in England and in America were successful in their anti-slavery campaigns of the 18th and 19th century, from William Wilberforce (1759–1833) via David Livingstone (1813–1873) up to the North-American Civil War (1861–1865). The virtues of the Enlightenment should be, therefore, sought elsewhere where modern political philosophies were in formation and dissemination, the ideal of liberty, the republican values and the Macchiavellian—although he was only one of many—gilding of the absolute powers of kings and princes because the harsh realities seemed to override their initial republican ideals. In the absence of republican virtues, enlightened absolutism seemed to be the lesser evil. Thus, Martin Luther was not alone with the princes as if pocketed by them, contrary to the accusation that is oftentimes being hurled at him. Neither for Niccolo Macchiavelli (1469–1527) in Italy, nor for Martin Luther in Saxony, were there other options at hand than the national monarchies or regional princedoms. Nor should we forget Erasmus of Rotterdam (1466–1536) who was most ardently pressing for royal favours and a solid income in England at the courts of Henry VII (+ 1509) and Henry VIII (+ 1547).[11]

4 Pontifical Enthusiasm

Dr. Luther did not have only the Zwickau prophets, Thomas Münzer and other Protestant "celestial" prophets[12] such as the religious rebel leader John of Leiden[13] of

---

[9] 1381–1384, 1492, 1520–1550, 1570–1590, 1590–1600, etc.

[10] Skinner,*ibid.*, 239–301.

[11] Q. Skinner, *The Foundations of Modern Political Thought. Volume One: The Renaissance.* (Cambridge: CUP, 1978). T. Penn, *Winter King: The Dawn of Tudor England* (London: Allen Lane, 2011), 106–111, 235–240, 246–248, 255–257, 354–360.

[12] *Wider die himmlischen Propheten, von den Bildern und Sakrament*, 1525.

Münster (c. 1509–1536), Westphalia, in mind. To the Reformer, the entire awe-inspiring pontifical power-structure was a product of sheer enthusiasm. In terms of its origin, growth, and maintenance, it was not built the way Jesus Christ, the true head of the church, builds up God's temple in this world: "… built on the foundation of the apostles and prophets, with Christ Jesus himself as the chief cornerstone. In him the whole building is joined together and rises to become a holy temple in the Lord" (Eph. 2:20–21). This Christological reality motivated the Reformer to reject all pontifical claims of supremacy and the title of 'the Supreme Head of all Christendom' in the Smalcald Articles. The true Head of the Church is constantly present as he clearly promises in the New Testament, e.g. in Matt 28:20.[14] This true Head also actively governs his church with the word (doctrine) and the sacraments. In opposition to this governance of the Word of God, the Pope exalts himself as Antichrist with his claims to be equal or even superior to Christ. The pontifical claims concerning power and supremacy in Christendom were laid on similar shaky foundations as the Spirit-rap of the Zwickau prophets, the enthusiastic, triumphal but finally disastrous "rainbow assurance" of Thomas Münzer at Frankenhausen only moments prior to the massacre of the rebellious peasant army on May 15, 1525 and the short-lived Kingdom of Zion in Münster, Westphalia, in 1534–1536 established by John of Leiden who claimed to act with God's power.[15] What was miserably lacking in all those well attested instances of Protestant or Pontifical enthusiasm, was the fundamental justification of all genuine *Kirchenrecht*, namely divine right (*ius divinum*), which is the Bible. Luther makes his argument concise and clear in the Smalcald Articles:

> The pope is not *according to divine law or God's Word*, the head of all Christendom. This name belongs to One only, whose name is Jesus Christ (Colossians 1:18). The pope is only the bishop and the pastor of the Church at Rome and of those who have attached themselves to him voluntarily or through a human agency (such as a political ruler). Christians are not under him as a lord. They are with him as brethren,

---

[13] Jan Beukelsz, Jan Beukelszoon, John Bockold or John Bockelson.

[14] Special attention to the centrality of Matt 28:20 for the Christological realism and the Christological continuity of the Church: W. Höhne, *Luther Anschauungen über die Kontinuität der Kirche: Arbeiten zur Geschichte und Theologie des Luthertums, Band XII* (Hamburg:, 1963).

[15] J. Lortz, *Die Reformation in Deutschland I–II*, Zweiter Band (Unveränderte Neuausgabe; Mit einem Nachwort von Peter Manns; Sechste Auflage; Freiburg/Basel/Wien: Herder, 1982), 74–81. A parallel but a less conspicuous revolution occurred also in Lübeck led by Jürgen Wullenweber in 1535–1536.This religious and political revolution was crushed by the Holstein nobility and the King of Sweden, Gustavus Wasa, leading to the demise of Wullenweber.

colleagues, and companions, as the ancient councils and the age of St. Cyprian show. (SA II, IV, 1.)

Thus, the Lutheran Reformation was not somewhere in the middle of a linear religious spectrum as is conventionally presented in a myriad of text-books. In the place of a straight line one should think of a horseshoe. Indeed, the Lutheran Reformation was embraced and surrounded by what was called enthusiasm, i.e. by forms of religious life and structures that were designed solely by human spirit and man's profundity. They were not created and legitimised by the Word of God. They could never display the hallmark of *creatura verbi*. How should we then consider this radical divide between the letter and the Spirit, between revelation and Scripture, between *ius divinum* and *conditio humana*?

The rise and existence of the papacy was based on historical conditions and developments. It is neither written in the Word of God nor postulated by this word in any manner. Exegetically, the scriptural arguments for the papacy do not hold water. Christendom still suffers from the obstinacy of the Roman Curia when it arrogantly refused to enter into a fair dialogue with the Lutheran reformers and their confessions.[16] What remained belongs rather to historical positivism than to scriptural ecclesiology: the very development record of a structure is treated as a valid kind of justification of the same: something must be justified since it has happened; the acquired power positions speak by their mere existence. Theology and dogma have followed in an eclectic manner those turns of history pursuing expedient causes to increase the pontifical powers and to cement them in ecclesial jurisprudence. Curialism won the struggle against conciliarism, which prevailed in the Early Church and flourished, again, in the 15th century. Luther stated in the Smalcald Articles: "It is clear that the holy Church has been without the pope for over five hundred years. ... the papacy is a human invention that is not commanded and is not necessary but useless. The papacy is also of no use in the Church, because it exercises no Christian office" (SA II, IV, 4–5). The source of all this gigantic, historical and interpretative construction of the papacy, never accepted by the historical conciliarist party of theologians, was the claim that all ecclesiastical power and jurisprudence

---

[16] The Catholic Catechism of the Roman Catholic Church (1992 Latin, English translation (Nairobi: Pauline Press, 1994), 874–896. 236–241. The apparatus of the catechism makes references primarily to the dogmatic constitution "Lumen Gentium" of the Second Vatican Council 1962–1965. K Rahner and H. Vorgrimler, *Kleines Konzilskompendium: Alle Konstitutionen, Dekrete und Erklärungen des Zweiten Vaticanums in der bischöflich beauftragten Übersetzung* (Allgemeine Einleitung—16 spezielle Einführungen; 2., ergänzte Auflage; Herder-Bücherei Band 270/71/72/73; Freiburg/Basel/Wien: Herder, 1966), 105–200.

has its source within the heart of the pope, *scrinium pectoris*, of the beleaguered
Pope Boniface VIII (1294–1303) when he confronted the French King Filip IV the
Fair (1268–1314). Boniface VIII held that the pope exercises the power of the two
swords and that he has all the laws in the shrine of his heart: *Romanus pontifex iura
omnia in scrinio pectoris censetur habere*— "the Roman Pontiff is considered to have
all laws in the shrine of his heart." The hapless pope wrote his words in categories of ecclesial jurisprudence and canon law, not expounding the Holy Scriptures.
Therefore the verb *censetur*—"is considered"—refers to scholars of canon law, not
to scriptural exegesis. Luther wrote in his *Address to the Christian Nobility of the
German Nation Respecting the Reformation of the Christian Estate* in 1520: "At the
present time the canon law is not to be found in the books, but in the whims of the
Pope and his sycophants. You may have settled a matter in the best possible way
according to the canon law, but the Pope has his *scrinium pectoris*, to which all law
must bow in all the world. Now this *scrinium* is oftentimes directed by some knave
and the devil himself, whilst it boasts that it is directed by the Holy Ghost."[17] Closing with another quotation the Smalcald Articles: "When we distinguish the pope's
teaching from, or compare it to, Holy Scripture, it is clear that the pope's teaching
at its best has been taken from the imperial[18] and heathen law. … But in all of this,
nothing at all is taught about Christ, and God's commandments" (SA II, IV, 14).

5   The text and the human spirit

On our way from the Reformation up to modern enthusiasms we face the influence
of the 18th century Enlightenment and the legacy of European idealism. The foundations of modern critical scholarship of the Bible were laid in the 18th century. Suffice
it to mention names like H.S. Reimarus (1694–1768), J.S. Semler (1725–1791), G.E.
Lessing (1729–1781), J.P. Gabler (1753–1826) and J.G. Eichhorn (1752–1827). In
the 19th century F.C. Baur (1792–1860) and his critical Tübingen School built on
these foundations. The text of the Bible was placed under the scrutiny and judgement of human reason. All that did not meet the reasonable expectations and standards of the age was dismissed. Philosophical axioms and Western cultural imperat-
ives were not paid the attention they would have needed. The question concerning
the relationship between the Word and the spirit emerged in a mundane form: how

---

[17] M. Luther, 'Address to the Christian Nobility of the German Nation Respecting the Reformation
of the Christian Estate' in C.W. Eliot (ed.), *The prince / by Niccolo Machiavelli. Utopia / by Sir Thomas
More. Ninety-five theses; Address to the German nobility ; Concerning Christian liberty / by Martin
Luther ; with introductions and notes* (Harvard classics 36; New York: P.F. Collier, 1910), 81.

[18] This is a reference to the ancient, heathen Roman Empire, not to the contemporary Holy Roman
Empire of the German Nation.

could the ancient Biblical texts be compatible with the philosophically enlightened human reason and the facts of the fast-growing natural sciences? The idealistic groundswell postulated eternal principles not contingent scriptural truths.[19] Those principles were seen as the enduring message of Scripture. Ethos, *Sittlichkeit*, was of primary importance, not the salvation of man. It was a new kind of spirit claiming authority. This time, however, it was the human spirit, the "Zeitgeist". A solitary, critical voice against this *Zeitgeist* concerning the letter and the text of the Bible came from an eccentric, profound outsider, the "Magus of the North" from the East-Prussian city of Königsberg, namely J.G. Hamann (1730–1788). He despised the much-acclaimed, fashionable "eternal truths" of the Bible and, instead, focused on the words and Scripture in which God had condescended into our humanity just as his Son had done in the incarnation. Hamann was critical of Immanuel Kant, preferring Hume. He had a lasting influence on many luminaries of his time and even posterity.[20]

The Copernican turn in European philosophy concerning epistemological theories was caused by Immanuel Kant's (1724–1804) criticism of human reason. Kant's point of departure was the thesis that human knowledge is not caused by outward objects. Instead, it is created by forms of experience in the person seeking true knowledge. Thus, knowledge is primarily produced in the realm of human reason rather than in a process of interaction with the world of various objects and their impulses. Kant's teachings were diametrically opposed to David Hume's (1711–1776) empiricism. Jumping over large swathes of preliminaries of philosophy, I switch in to modern semiotics, especially the system of the semiotician C.S. Peirce (1839–1914) and his triadic semiotics. It links the process of understanding with reality in the semiotic process which works with sign systems. Against René Descartes (1596–1650) and his rationalistic intuitionism, Peirce holds that man has no introspective or intuitive powers, but he derives all knowledge by hypothetical reasoning from the knowledge of external facts and previous knowledge. So, there prevails a constant interplay between the subjective mind and the objective world. The contribution of the triadic type of semiotics—in opposition to the French dyadic version—is to make the laws of this interplay understandable. Dyadic semiotics limit the semiotic process to an axis between the subject and the object only. It is the subject that

---

[19] G. Lessing, *Lessing's Theological Writings*; Selected and Translated by H. Chadwick (A Library of Modern Religious Thought; Stanford:Stanford University Press, 1992). It was Lessing who criticized the Christian religion for the usage of contingent historical truths to prove metaphysical truths.

[20] F. Arnold, 'Hamann, Johann Georg', *RE 3* vol. 7, 370–375. H-J. Kraus, *op.cit.*, 201–203. U. Moustakas, 'Hamann, Johann Georg', *RGG 4* 3, 1396–1397.

produces the interpretation without interplay with and the control of the objective world. This necessary interplay and control has its place in the triadic kind of semiotics. Shortly: at the beginning of all understanding is the human process of handling signs and sign system which is called 'semiosis'. Concepts of intellect need sensible intuition and also concepts of objects to which they may be applied. An empirical concept derives from the sensations, through comparison with the objects of experience. Any empirical concept requires a perceptual judgement, and a judgement is always a mediated knowledge of the object.[21]

What has this to do with our study on the letter and the spirit? The great Swedish Lutheran theologian Bengt Hägglund (1920–) published a study on pre-Kantian hermeneutics in 2006.[22] Hägglund maintains that after the Reformation and its new principles for the interpretation of the Bible, questions of hermeneutics were dealt with thoroughly under new conditions. Matthias Flacius (1520–1575) pioneered a new path of Biblical interpretation with his work *Clavis Scripturae Sacrae* in 1567. Wilhelm Dilthey (1833–1911) and Hans-Georg Gadamer (1900–2002) have surprisingly appreciated Flacius as an innovative pioneer in the field of hermeneutics. Flacius and those scholars of Lutheran Orthodoxy who followed his path, namely John Gerhard (1582–1637), Wolfgang Franz (1564–1628) and Salomon Glassius (1593–1656) exercised exemplary grammatical, linguistic, rhetorical, and historical study of the text, always examining the textual passages in their history and the relevant context. There are no short-cuts for reaching a desired result. The stringent taskmaster of *Sola Scriptura* simply could not allow any liberties from the demanding method of biblical scholarship. Thus, it is untrue to coin the biblical interpretation of these men of Lutheran Orthodoxy as mere *dicta probantia/classica*, i.e. resorting to Bible verses out of their context to prove a dogmatic locus.[23] Critical scholars, past and present, have time and again hurled this baseless accusation at Biblical scholars who are not willing to sing in unison with them. In the company of the *dicta probantia* critics, albeit with a different agenda, stood also the great Pietist scholar J.A. Bengel (1687–1752) with his popular *Gnomon Novi Testamenti* in 1742.[24] Such an accusation is blind to the wider context of the concise mode of sentence-like ar-

[21] U. Eco, *Kant and the Platypus. Essays on Language and Cognition*, translated from the Italian by A. McEwen (London: Vintage, 1999), 57–122.

[22] B. Hägglund, 'Vorkantianische Hermeneutik', *Kerygma und Dogma* 52:2 (2006), 165–181.

[23] H. Räisänen, *Beyond New Testament Theology: A Story and a Programme* (London/Philadelphia: SCM, 1990), 3–5. Räisänen builds on J.P. Gabler's (1753–1826) separation of Biblical theology from dogmatic theology in his inaugural lecture of 1787.

[24] G. Sentzke, *Die Theologie Johann Tobias Becks und ihr Einfluss in Finnland, Band I.* (Schriften der Luther-Agricola Gesellschaft 8; Helsinki: Luther-Agricola-seura; 1949), 7–10.

gument in the traditional catechetical and dogmatic presentation. The concise sentence does not speak alone but it speaks on behalf of its wider, relevant context. One must presume that the ease with which these accusations have been hurled is too often based on *sola ignorantia* concerning the methods of Lutheran Orthodoxy. A couple of hours alone spent with Flacius or Gerhard, would have dispelled this illusion of *dicta probantia*. Even in theology, so much has been said by so many with so little knowledge about the sources, if I am permitted to hijack a famous Churchillian statement.

The Orthodox Lutheran tradition which flourished for two centuries ended up in absolute oblivion during the 19th century. The monumental *Clavis* with its 1100 double folio pages was published for the last time in 1719. Between 1567 and 1719 seven reprints of *Clavis* had been published, after 1719 none.[25] John Gerhard's *Loci theologici* (1610–1622) were last reprinted in Berlin 1863–1869 (Ed. Preuss) before the English translation of the third millennium which is presently in the process of being published by Concordia Publishing House, St. Louis, MI. The new dawn for hermeneutics in the 19th century was Friedrich Schleiermacher (1768–1834). There is no continuity between the earlier hermeneutics of Flacius and Gerhard and the new hermeneutics born in the aurora of the Enlightenment and Romanticism. Indeed, Schleiermacher has been seen in the history of hermeneutics as a completely new beginning. He changed the Biblical interpretation to "a general art of understanding" ("Kunstlehre des Verstehens"). This change, which was praised and further developed by Wilhelm Dilthey turned its attention from the textual handicraft of the Lutheran Orthodoxy to the psychological prerequisites of understanding. Hägglund's critique of Schleiermacher lies in the fact that a general art of understanding is impotent in opening the particular biblical language. Yet, every area of human science and art has its own language that must be known and properly interpreted: jurisprudence, various branches of literature, and the arts. Worse was still to come: Schleiermacher lived in the heyday of Romanticism. He himself vastly contributed to the romantic genius cult in the age of J.W. von Goethe (1749–1832), F. Schiller (1759–180) and others. A genius is a mediator between common life and the divine realm of spirit:

> Wherefore Deity sends at all times some here and there, who in a fruitful manner are imbued with both impulses, either as a direct gift from

---

[25] R. Keller, *Der Schlüssel zur Schrift: Die Lehre vom Wort Gottes bei Matthias Flacius Illyricus* (Arbeiten zur Geschichte und Theologie des Luthertums, n.F. Vol. 5; Hannover: Lutherisches Verlagshaus, 1984), 187ff.

above, or as the result of a severe and complete self-training. They are equipped with wonderful gifts, their way is made even by an almighty indwelling word. They are interpreters of the Deity and His works, and reconcilers of things that otherwise would be eternally divided. ... By their very existence they prove themselves ambassadors of God, and mediators between limited man and infinite humanity. ... They interpret to him the misunderstood voice of God, and reconcile him to the earth and to his place thereon. ... This is the true priest of the highest, for he brings it nearer those who are only accustomed to lay hold of the finite and the trivial. ... This is the higher priesthood that announces the inner meaning of all spiritual secrets, and speaks from the Kingdom of God.[26]

As an interpreter a genius leaves the guild of professional craftsmen and is transformed to a virtuoso in possession of divinatory skills that can even surpass the original author of a text. A diving virtuoso-interpreter understands the content of a text even better than its author. A decisive watershed is thus crossed. The hermeneutics under the auspices of Schleiermacher have left the letter and the text and resorted to the spirit whereas in the Lutheran Orthodoxy it was the word and the language that brought the creativity of understanding to life. In comparison with this potential of the word, the human intellect is blind or, at the most, screwing up its eyes like a bat. The unconditional goal of interpretation is the literal sense of the text growing up from the language in question, and not only through the mediation of a creative expounder. In his criticism of Jacques Derrida's (1930–2004) deconstructionism and the misinterpreted Peircean term of "unlimited semiosis", Umberto Eco (1932–) argues for three intentions: *intentio auctoris, intentio operis* and *intentio lectoris*. The very term 'text' includes the idea of the limits of its interpretation. In many cases, the intentions of the author may be sheer guesses of a reader of posterity. The intention of the reader is the horizon from which a researcher approaches the text. Central is the intention of the text with its vast potential of meanings, polysemy.[27] Hägglund concludes with a serious question: in the light of what various interpretative "virtuosos" in Schleiermacher's posterity have created, is it not true

---

[26] F. Schleiermacher, *On Religion: Speeches to Its Cultured Despisers*, translated by John Oman (Louisville:Westminster/John Knox, 1994), 6–7.

[27] U. Eco, *Die Grenzen der Interpretation* (München: 1992), 43–49, 54–55, 139–168 (English edition: *The Limits of Interpretation* [Bloomington: Indiana University Press, 1991]). A. Simojoki, *Apocalypse Interpreted: The Types of Interpretation of the Book of Revelation in Finland 1944-1995, from the Second World War to the post-Cold War World* (Åbo: Åbo Academi Press, 1997), 20–22, 27–28.

that something essential has been lost when the older Lutheran hermeneutics was left in oblivion? In his study of the Tübingen School, Horton Harris has come to an unconventional but persuasive conclusion. The Archimedean point of F.C. Baur's (1792–1860) critical study of the New Testament was not the Hegelian dialectics but Baur's inherent atheism which gave no space, no opportunity, for God's actions in history, if he existed at all. The entire text of the New Testament points to the bodily resurrection of Christ. Yet, in Baur's case, the spirit of an exegete-cum-atheist imposed a diametrically opposite hypothesis on the text. Since Baur, there have been so many other "spirits" of so many academic theological schools to impose on the text ideas that are absolutely opposite or unknown to the text. Rudolf Bultmann (1884–1976) with his modernistic demythologizing programme of 1941 is a towering figure amongst these academic enthusiasts.[28] Indeed, speculation may be called enthusiasm when the human mind departs from the text and replaces its contingencies with general, anachronistic abstractions. This abstract, ethereal, gas-like space of the Western mind too often overlooks the original attire of the Biblical message and cuts off any meaningful communication with the text. At this point a reference is to be made to one side of Karl Jaspers's (1883–1969) criticism of Bultmann's demythologizing programme: the form is part of the message. Ignoring the form, one may end up posing inadequate questions to the material.[29]

A similar incongruity occurs in defending the Word of God when the spirit is given a dominant role over the text and its history. Karl Barth is an example of this with his abstract distinctions between revelation, the word of the Bible and proclamation of Church:

> And we have said the same of the Bible: it must continually become
> God's Word. … The reference is to the freedom of God's Word. *Ubi
> et quando visum est Deo*, not intrinsically but in virtue of the divine
> decision taken ever and anon in the Bible and proclamation as the free
> God uses them. … When we speak about revelation we are confronted
> by the divine act itself and as such, which we have already had to bear

---

[28] H. Harris, *The Tübingen School: A Historical and Theological Investigation of the School of F.C. Baur*, with a new preface by the author and a foreword by E.E. Ellis (Leicester: IVP, 1990), 249–259.

[29] J. Macquarrie, *The Scope of Demythologizing* (The Library of Philosophy and Theology, ed. by J. Mcintyre and I.T. Ramsey; London: SCM, 1960), 154–185. Stanford Encyclopedia of Philosophy: Karl Jaspers.

in mind as the basis and boundary, the presupposition and proviso, of what had to be said about the Bible and proclamation.[30]

What Hägglund called "something essential (which) has been lost" is the capacity for combining scientific demands of hermeneutics with adequate theological understanding.[31] In the absence of it, critical scholarly enthusiasm has permeated and continues permeating the traditional academies and churches of the West apart from biblical-theological pockets here and there.

6   The Letter and the Spirit

Academic theology divided in the 19th century the old discipline of Scripture into two, namely to Old Testament theology and New Testament theology. The epochal Old Testament scholar at Heidelberg, the late Gerhard von Rad (1901–1971), concludes his classic *Theology of the Old Testament* (1960) with reflections concerning the subject. Against the presuppositions of critical scholars in the 18th and 19th century, the Old Testament is not a text-book of religion. The watch-word of theology was in those days "religion". Christianity was considered merely as the ethically supreme sub-species of "religion". The nature of the Old Testament, however, is completely different from a handbook of religion and morality. Neither is it a wrinkled carbon copy of ancient Babylonian religion as the influential school of the history of religions had taught, omitting the complexities of ancient Egyptian and Babylonian religions.[32] The Norwegian Gunkel-disciple Sigmund Mowinckel (1884–1965) had attempted to forge a universal key to the religion of Old Israel constructing the influential hypothesis that the texts are primarily liturgical reflecting the supposed New Year's festival of YHWH's ascending his throne. Gerhard von Rad's view was different: the Old Testament bears witness to a process in which the faith of YHWH, step by step, conquers various areas of life on its way towards the Father of the Christ. The history of this faith is accompanied and borne by the mediators of this revelation. When writing his scholarly envoy, Gerhard von Rad employed, time and again, the

---

[30] K. Barth, *Church Dogmatics*, Volume I: The Doctrine of the Word of God, Part One (eds. G.W. Bromiley and T.F. Torrance; Edinburgh: T&T Clark, 1975), 111–120. Cit. p.117.
[31] Hägglund, *op.cit.*, especially pp. 178–180.
[32] H. Frankfort, *Kingship and the Gods: A Study of Ancient Near Eastern Religion as the Integration of Society and Nature*, with a new preface by S.N. Kramer (Oriental Institute Essays; Chicago: Oriental Institute of the University of Chicago, 1978) focused on the deep difference between the aggressively ascending (chosen servant) Mesopotamian and the harmoniously descending (God incarnate) Egyptian concept of divine kingship and stressed the unique historicity of the Hebrew religion and the secular nature of its kingship.

word "confession" ("Bekenntnis") to characterize the text of the Old Testament. The Old Israel faced the deeds, the challenges, promises, reproaches, and punishments of YHWH in history and reacted to them. It was characteristic of the faith in YHWH that historical events and codes were repeatedly brought to the fore in a typological manner. This reality was the surprising yield of textual exegesis. In the light of what I have said above, it was the surprising corrective on the part of the biblical texts. Even New Testament scholarship is employed with typological re-espousing of the entire Old Testament. Therefore, Gerhard von Rad closes his impressive present-ation with a question whether, with boldness to think together, the new advent of Biblical theology combined would be coming closer.[33] The faith and the history in Old Israel were dominated by YHWH. Instead of sifting through material in pursuit of objective facts that could be verified, all historical events in the life of Old Israel came from and through YHWH. Therefore, this personal centre of history postulates a historical concept that is vastly different from Western academic works of history. Being historically true is formed differently in the presence of YHWH. It is the task of textual exegesis to understand this difference.[34] Thus, exegesis is a craftsmen's trade that also demands a craftsman's work ethic with the letter of Scripture.

Apart from a number of names and institutions, not forgetting Hermann Sasse (1895–1976), I have particularly in mind the New Testament scholar Anton Frid-richsen (1888–1953), who was professor at the University of Uppsala from 1928. He combined a strong Christian, Lutheran spirituality with strict scientific meth-ods and created a large school of Biblical scholars, the Uppsala School that was dis-tinguished by its Biblical realism.[35] The Swedish Lutheran systematician Hjalmar Lindroth (1893–1979) worked in the principles of his three-volume dogmatics on those methodological rules of academic science that are to protect the text from any kind of arbitrary enthusiasm of scholars. Scientific dogmatic work is a question of a sound method: 1. The possibility of objective argumentation; 2. Objectivity; 3. In the framework of pure objectivity, to present and understand the object of inquiry; 4. All scientific presentation must be logical and respect the very logic of the language. Therefore, it is important to distinguish between knowledge and science. Scientific methods contribute to the widening of the area of personal knowledge. Lindroth's

---

[33] G. von Rad, *Theologie des Alten Testaments. Band 2: Die Theologie der prophetischen Überliefer-ungen Israels.* (9. Auflage. München: Gütersloher Verlagshaus, 1987), 446–447. (English translation: *Old Testament Theology, Vol. 2: The Theology of Israel's Prophetic Traditions* [London: SCM, 1998]) R. Smend, *Bibel und Wissenschaft: Historische Aufsätze* (Tübingen: Mohr Siebeck, 2004), 191–195.

[34] von Rad, *op.cit.*, 442–445.

[35] W. Bauer, 'Zur Erinnerung an Anton Fridrichsen', *Zeitschrift für die Neutestamentlich Wissenschaft und die Kunde der Älteren Kirche*, Vol. 45:1 (1954), 123ff.

clear methodological requirements protect theological work against a philosophically unacceptable confusion of knowledge and science, against any loose talk of
"reality", which can never be canned, and to prohibit any all too hasty resorting to
spiritual short-cuts in order to achieve a desired result. "Reality" cannot be defined
since it is an absolute position which precedes any definition. When this truth is not
respected, the biblical Christian concept of reality has been attacked from corners
of metaphysical, uncritical and non-scientific concepts of reality as if those certain
concepts were a certain quantity. The Biblical Christian concept of reality is based
on statements of faith in Scripture that make the claim that they express and formu-
late reality and truth. We are back with Gerhard von Rad: "The faith and the history
in Old Israel were dominated by YHWH. Instead of sifting through material in pursuit of objective facts that could be verified, all historical events in the life of Old
Israel came from and through YHWH." This Biblical reality was different from the
ideas of Western historicist schools and yet, no less real.[36] The late Albrecht Peters
of Heidelberg (+ 1987) applied his scholarship in exegesis to cast the foundations
of his commentary on Luther's catechisms.[37] This serious work with biblical scholarship is remarkable, bearing in mind how the towering Lutheran scholars prior to
Peters, such as P. Althaus (1888–1966), W. Elert (1885–1954) , W. Maurer (1900–
1982) and others could in a masterly manner work on the enormous material from
Luther and church history but avoid questions of biblical theology as such. Dietrich
Bonhoeffer (1906–1945) pioneered in the world of post-idealistic and post-liberal
theology a true Biblical theology. This Biblical theology connected the Word and
the Spirit. The Church as *sanctorum communio* is established in and through Jesus Christ. The Church is the communion in the Holy Spirit. The Church bears
the Word. The Church lives on the Word which is its absolute authority. Bonhoeffer returned back to Biblical ontology, back to Lutheran theology from fashionable
contemporary speculations and from Karl Barth's pure actualism.[38] This difference

---

[36] von Rad, *op.cit.*, 9. Lindroth, Hj., *Kyrklig Dogmatik 1: Den kristna trosåskådningen med särskild
hänsyn till det eskatologiska motivet och den frälsningshistoriska grundsynen* (Acta Universitatis Upsa-
liensis; Studia Doctrinae Christianae Upsaliensia 12; Uppsala: Uppsala University Press, 1975) 198–
209, 210–222. Lindroth's criticism hits hard at Bultmann's Demythologizing programme which is
born out of an uncritical, metaphysical concept of one certain reality which does not necessarily exist.
Eco 2000, 9–56. "Therefore there is being because we can pose the question of being, and this being
comes before every question, and therefore before every answer and every definition." Eco 2000, 19.
[37] A. Peters, *Kommentar zu Luthers Katechismen 1–5*, herausgegeben von G. Seebass (Göttingen:
Vandenhoeck & Ruprecht, 1990–1994 (English Translation: *Commentary on Luther's Catechisms 1–5*
(St. Louis: Concordia, 2009–2013).
[38] D. Bonhoeffer, *Sanctorum Communio: Eine dogmatische Untersuchung zur Soziologie der Kirche*,
Herausgegeben von J. von Soosten (Dietrich Bonhoeffer Werke 1; München: Gütersloher Verlag-

can be illuminated by contrasting the purely Barthian watchword of WCC III Assembly in New Delhi 1961 "Witness, Service, Unity" and Martin Luther's teaching of the seven marks of the Church in his book *On the Councils and the Church* (1539). The Barthian New Delhi watchword is completely actualistic ("Akt"), devoid of ontology ("Sein"). Luther's seven marks of the Church are not abstract symbols but concrete marks of identification ("Kennzeichen") of which the One Holy Catholic and Apostolic Church can be recognised like we can identify living and acting animals on an African safari by their specific marks.

Such toil with the text of Scripture is, according to the text itself, spiritual. The prophetic and apostolic writings of the Bible are being inspired and produced by God the Holy Spirit. This has been the firm conviction of the Early Church from the beginning. This knowledge and conviction was given by Christ and his apostles. It was not born only in the 17th century or what is called Fundamentalism of the 20th century. God has spoken through the prophets and in his Son (Heb 1:1). As J.G. Hamann formulated it, God condescending in the world of men became author. This was the work of the Holy Spirit (Mark 12:36; John 6:63; Acts 1:16; Eph 6:17; 2 Tim 3: 16; Heb 3:7; 1 Pet 1:11; 2 Pet 1:21). We have a witness amongst many witnesses of the Early Church, namely the *Ecclesiastical History* of Eusebius. In connection with the heresy of Artemon, Eusebius (c. 263-339) concludes his charge against heretics with the following words: "But how daring this offense is, it is not likely that they themselves are ignorant. For either they do not believe that the Divine Scriptures were spoken by the Holy Spirit, and thus are unbelievers, or else they think themselves wiser than the Holy Spirit, and in that case what else are they than demoniacs?" (HE V, 28, 18). Oftentimes, the discussion concerning the divine inspiration of the Holy Writ, which resembles Adam's creation in Genesis 2:7 (Vulgata: *inspirare, spiraculum*), stops at the canonical text of the Bible and ends

---

shaus, 1986), 79–87, 126–128: the Church is neither a religious community nor the Kingdom of God; it is a unique sociological reality of God's revelation. It is Christ existing as the Church. The Church is not a bearer of values but of God's concrete revelation, i.e. the Word. 172–173. Bonhoeffer's point is different from Barth's idea of the Bible, proclamation and revelation (English translation: *Sanctorum Communio: A Theological Study of the Sociology of the Church* [Dietrich Bonhoeffer Works 1; Philadelphia: Augsburg Fortress, 1998]). D. Bonhoeffer, *Akt und Sein: Transzendentalphilosophie und Ontologie in der systematischen Theologie* (Dietrich Bonhoeffer Werke 2; München: Gütersloher Verlagshaus, 1988), 53–74: "Alles Denken ist immer nur eine Seinsbestimmtheit des Daseins. So erzeugt sich auch das Denken nicht seine Welt, sondern es find et sich als Dasein in einer Welt vor, es ist je schon in einer Welt, wie es je schon es selbst ist" (against Cartesius and his followers); pp. 64, 107–112. This statement comes close to Eco's "being" (English translation: *Act and Being* [Dietrich Bonhoeffer Works 2; Philadelphia: Augsburg Fortress, 1996]).

up in a tug-of-war concerning the details of inerrancy. It is as if the Holy Spirit had accomplished his work with the text of Scripture and had undertaken something else when the text has been finally chiselled or petrified. The doctrine that the Word of God is θεόπνευστος, entails, however, the continuous work of *Spiritus Creator* in and through the text. The Spirit should not be expected only to visit the text and the living voice that proclaims this word in the Barthian manner in discontinued impulses *ubi et quando visum est Deo*, as he misuses the words of the Augsburg Confession. No, the text as *creatura Spiritus* is logically all the time also the holy ground of the constant work of the Holy Spirit. This is the ground also for the Lutheran doctrine concerning the Word of God that creates the sacraments and gives life without further presuppositions, conditions and auxiliary arrangements. This teaching combined with an explicit Trinitarian motivation permeats e.g. John 14: "I will ask the Father and he will give you another Counsellor to be with you for ever—the Spirit of truth. ... I will come to you ... Because I live, you also will live. On that day you will realize that I am in my Father, and you are in me, and I am in you" (John 14:17, 18, 20). This Trinitarian presence in the Holy Spirit is created by the words of Jesus: "If you love me, you will obey what I command. ... Whoever has my commands and obeys them, he is the one who loves me" (John 14:15, 21).[39] The word of Jesus is Christological, containing him in person, and, at the same time, Trinitarian, creating the inseparable union with the Father and the Holy Spirit.

Having come thus far, conclusions are to be drawn from what has been said afore. YHWH is the Christ, "the Lord", κύριος. It is **Christology** that defines the question of the **context** in Scripture. If the Bible is considered only as a library of historical religious documents devoid of Christology, even the translation of the Good Book can take a different direction. As a prime example, we can look at רוח אלהים (Gen 1:2). Is it "wind" or "Spirit"? If it is determined by history of religions alone, one might feel it to be only natural to jump to the Mesopotamian creation myth "Enuma Elish" with its primordial hurricane and vote for "wind" of which this fragment might speak about. In the Christological and Trinitarian context of Scripture, such a turn would be a monstrous anachronism, to say the least. Gen. 1:2 is not an isolated fragment without connection to the entire Bible. Think only of the Prologue of John (John 1:1–18). Already in Old Israel, Genesis 1 had a differ-

---

[39] G. Schrenk, ἐντολή *TDNew Testament* II, 553–554. The Christian message encapsulated in ἐντολή, as opposed to Gnosticism and Libertinism, has nothing to do with Pharisaic legalism in the Johannine context. The love of the Father and the revelation of the Son find a response in the inner life of disciples, who truly possess (ἔχειν) this love through the revelation of Jesus and stay faithful to it (τηρεῖν).

ent meaning in connection with YHWH-ELOHIM than ever in the Mesopotamian myth.

Christology also determines the boundary between the Lutheran method of **"Sola Scriptura"** on one side, and Fundamentalism and Biblicism on the other. Fundamentalism/Biblicism primarily operates with principles.[40] Yet, we stand in the Spirit with the present Lord. Therefore, the text must be examined and expounded properly avoiding any kind of textual arbitrariness. One form of arbitrariness is to flee from Christology and treat the Bible as an heap of antiquarian religious fragments. Another form of arbitrariness is too often being witnessed in enthusiastic charismatic mega-meetings where a verse or two are being read completely out of the canonical context and applied to the situation without any true connection with the Biblical text. Such a token text serves only as a whimsical oracle, a take-off platform for wildest flights in spirit/spirits. They have nothing to do with Christology. And, as we all should always remember, fundamentally, all theology is Christology: *Ubi Christus, ibi Spiritus—ubi Christus ibi ecclesia.*[41]

---

[40] I have chosen J.T. Beck as my paramount example of Bibicism since he followed in many respects the tradition line of another prominent biblicist J.A. Bengel. R. Kübel, (A. Hauck), 'Beck, Johann Tobias', *RE3* 2, 500–506. S. Raedler, 'Beck, Johann Tobias', *RGG8*, 1194–1195: There prevails in Beck's theology a general opposition between literal doctrines and mystical, ethical "life". Beck rejected the concept of the literal inspiration of Scripture. There is a wedge between the letter and the divine content. The interpreter of Scripture must be a person who is led by the Spirit. The Kingdom of God and its morality bestowed on a believer in the act justification remarkably override Christology to the extent that the classic Trinitarian dogma is in jeopardy. The characteristic Beckian *quatenus* condition ("insofar as") concerns also the Son and the Holy Spirit: they are God insofar as they participate in the godhead of the Father (subordinationism).

[41] H. Sasse, 'Jesus Christus der Herr: Das Urbekenntnis der Kirche', in *Gesammelte Aufsätze und Kleine Schriften von Hermann Sasse*, Herausgegeben von F-W Hopf (In Statu Confessionis 2; Berlin-Schleswig-Holstein 1976), 36–42. Ignatius, Epistle to the Smyrnaeans 8, 2: ὥσπερ ὅπου ἂν ᾖ Χριστὸς Ἰησοῦς, ἐκεῖ ἡ καθολικὴ ἐκκλησία.

RE3   *Realenzyklopädie für protestantische Theologie und Kirche.*
        Begr. von J.J. Herzog. In dritter verbesserter und ver-
        mehrter Auflage unter Mitwirkung vieler Theologen und an-
        dere Gelehrten herausgegeben von A. Hauck . Bd. 1–22.
        Leipzig: J. C. Hinrichs'sche Buchhandlung, 1896–1909. Ergän-
        zungsbände 23 und 24, 1913.
RGG4   Die Religion in Geschichte und Gegenwart. Vierte, völlig neu
        bearbeitete Auflage herausgegeben von H.D. Betz, D. S. Brown-
        ing, B. Janowski, E. Jüngel. Tübingen: Mohr Siebeck, 1998–
        2005, 2007
TDNT   Theological Dictionary of the New Testament Edited by Ger-
        hard Kittel. Reprinted. Translator and Editor W. Bromiley.
        Grand Rapids: Eerdmans, 1983–1985.

Chapter 10

A Response to Anssi Simojoki

Rev. Drs. Jonathan Mumme

Taking a "historical and systematic approach" to addressing the "nature of [modern] religious enthusiasm" as it relates to "the Word of God"[1] Anssi Simojoki has delivered a valuable account of enthusiasm and its developments from the Reformation to the present day. Tracing its movement out from the two fronts of the Lutheran Reformation he argues that said enthusiasm is not a strictly religious trend, but rather a phenomenon that has progressed along with political and academic developments of the intervening eras. As the counterpoint to his critical diagnosis he suggests an approach to the text of Scripture with similarities to triadic semiotics that would rediscover a lost element of older Lutheran hermeneutics, namely an honest and scholarly struggle with the text on all levels[2] that is guided by the text's christological *context* and understands itself as a Spiritual exercise in a text through which the Holy Spirit remains constantly at work. This response will not contest his constructive conclusion, but will, rather, seek to add a few notes to the historical diagnostic work so as to nuance our understanding of a non-enthusiast interaction with the Scriptures in our day.

Encouraged to heed context, 2 Cor 3:6[3] begs our attention again. Though I do not disagree that this passage pertains to the difference between the Law and the

---

[1] Simojoki, Section 2 (p. 125).

[2] Simojoki, Section 5 (p. 133)): "grammatical, linguistic, rhetorical, and historical".

[3] "[God] has made us competent to be ministers of a new covenant, not of the letter but of the Spirit. For the letter kills, but the Spirit gives life."

Gospel, the *context* is nothing other than an *apologia* for the apostolic ministers. Here we are not simply dealing with a word that kills and a word that makes alive, but with an *office* that kills and makes alive,[4] with ministers[5] bold[6] to address their readers in a we/you-*Gegenüber*, with ambassadors of Christ[7] in whose very bodies[8] he himself is present.

The paper tracks the radical enthusiasm of the Reformation through the Enlightenment and Romanticism and then goes on to identify the legacy of an *academic* enthusiasm alive still today. Against this tendency engaging the text in its christologically defined context has been recommended. 2 Cor 3:6 was our point of departure, but it was departed without noting that the apostolic ministry and the apostolic ministers are of an indivisible piece with the christology defining the context of this text. The suggestion that I would like to add is that if we miss the fact that God dealing with us through his Word means him dealing with us through a particular office to which he has entrusted the authoritative preaching and teaching of that Word, then we perpetuate *an ecclesiological and finally an ecclesial enthusiasm*.

'The Word of God'—*was ist das*? What is that? Already at this very symposium we have had occasion to note that, at least for Luther, 'the Word' may refer to Christ himself, the Holy Scriptures, or the *mundliches Wort*—found in someone's mouth. But, it seems to me, we have yet actually to wrestle with the implications of such a notion, namely that Jesus Christ, the Holy Scriptures, and the *Predigtamt* form an insoluble union.[9] The Reformation was, by definition, an unstable period. 500 years later it remains a challenging task for Lutherans to look back and identify stabilizing factors in what was a maelstrom of history. The preeminence of Holy Scripture's authority in Martin Luther's theology is clear, but to say that *sola Scriptura* was "the stable keel"[10] of the Lutheran Reformation stops short of the historical reality. The enthusiasm or fanaticism that confronted Luther is a case in point. The challenge

---

[4] 2 Cor 2:15f.

[5] 2 Cor 3:6. The "we" of the *Gegenüber* includes Timothy, 2 Cor 1:1; cf. Silvanus in 1:19.

[6] 2 Cor 3:12.

[7] 2 Cor 5:20.

[8] 2 Cor 4:10.

[9] Luther can distinguish Scripture from the oral word, and at the same time, hold the two together (see for eample SA-III,VIII,3: 'Scripture or the oral Word', cited by Simojoki, Section 3 [p.2]).

It is noteworthy that the very title of the symposium, "'Built on the Foundation of the Apostles and Prophets": *Sola Scriptura* in Context', makes reference to Eph 2:20, and without further ado simply takes 'apostles and prophets' as a reference to the prophetic and apostolic scriptures, as if (1) this is what Paul (an apostle without a collection of apostolic scriptures!) were talking about or (2) this were the only appropriation of the reality here addressed that we have today.

[10] Simojoki, Section 2 (p. 125); emphasis JM.

146

that the *Schwärmer* posed was not simply hermeneutical, a question of proper use of the Bible based on a right understanding of the relationship between the Holy Scriptures, the Holy Spirit, and the human spirit. They also posed an ecclesial, social and political challenge, and all the facets of this multi-sided challenge were *theological*. The challenge was met not only by right teaching, but also by polemics, visitations, catechisms, enforcing of ecclesial jurisdiction, regulated theological education, central ordinations, the ordination of bishops,[11] enforceable church orders, and later on the office of Superintendent.[12]

Sola Scriptura, one of a varying number of convenient (and accurate) summaries affixed to the theology of the Lutheran Reformation by a subsequent generation, is not a Latin nominative, but an ablative. Scripture does not stand alone; rather, it is the lone norm *by which* teaching and practice are to be judged. We dare not take the view that Luther pitched the ecclesial structure (nor the whole ecclesiology!) of the late-medieval western church and replaced it with the Bible to govern it; he did not. By means of Holy Scripture one can establish what is happening *de iure divino* (by divine right) from that which is going on *de iure humano* (by human right).[13] Statements like, "the entire awe-inspiring pontifical power structure was a product of sheer enthusiasm"[14] are in need of attention and differentiation. The late-medieval papacy as such? Yes. The entire ecclesial authority structure associated with it, that it had, to a large degree, co-opted? No. The English translation of SA-II,IV,1, which we heard, is dubious. Not only is the pope *not* by divine right or according to the Word of God the head of all Christendom; he is by divine right the bishop and parson of Rome.[15] The Word of God does not govern the church according to Lutheran theology; the bishops, pastors, and parsons govern the church according to the word of God. Luther may have burned some canon law, but regions turning to the Lutheran reformation received Lutheran church orders.

---

[11] Augustinus Sander, *Ordinatio Apostolica: Studien zur Ordinationstheologie im Luthertum des 16. Jahrhunderts Band I: Georg III. von Anhalt (1507-1553)*, (Innsbruck-Wien: Tyrolia), 2004. Peter Brunner, *Nikolaus von Amsdorf als Bischof von Naumberg: Eine Untersuchung zur Gestalt des evangelischen Bischofsamtes in der Reformationszeit* (Gütersloh: Gütersloher Verlagshaus), 1961.

[12] Dorothea Wendebourg, 'Das Amt und die Ämter', *Zeitschrift für evangelisches Kirchenrecht* 45 (2000): 5-37. The more political end of the response could be as sharp as the swords that ended the Peasants' War in 1525.

[13] That which is going on *de iure humano* is not rejected as such, but is kept and maintained except in those instances where it can be shown in contradiction with Holy Scripture.

[14] Simojoki, Section 4 (p. 129).

[15] The point of comparison is the extent of his claim and his jurisdiction.

Between the commended age of Lutheran Orthodoxy and the Enlightenment followed by Romantism, whose receptions of enthusiasm have been noted, came Pietism, which could perpetuate a reception of Luther's theology not dissimilar to Pope Boniface VIII, who ascribed much to the shrine of the heart.[16] With Schleiermacher the heart, or at least a feeling of complete dependence, stands at point number one. Ecclesiologically this comes to mean that believers, as such, precede any mediation of the church.[17] In a later historical maelstrom, namely mid-nineteenth century Germany, Schleiermacher's ecclesiological conviction became the foundation for J. F. W. Höfling's understanding of the ministry as something *delegated* to the ministers by the gathering of Christian believers, to be carried out for them on their behalf.[18] This ecclesiologically significant understanding of the ministry came at a time when the world was being turned upside down; if Kant defines a "Copernican turn in European philosophy",[19] the age of European revolutions amounts to a Copernican turn for western civilization. The ordering of society (and much of the church!) had changed; authority no longer worked from top to bottom,[20] but from bottom to top.[21] Anything that could now be called the 'preached' or *mundliches* Word of God was preceded by the believers, as such, and their collective delegation. Belief before Word as a fundamental premise of the new ecclesiology is nothing less than *ecclesiological* and finally *ecclesial enthusiasm*.

This fact is not one with which modern Lutheranism (even much of the 'confessional' variety) can seem to come to terms. We need only change a word for it to be said of us that "theology and dogma have followed in an eclectic manner those turns of history pursuing expedient causes to increase [congregational / representative] powers and cement them in ecclesial jurisprudence".[22] In those swathes of Lutheranism governed by congregationalist and purely synodical polity, the office of the keys, the office of the ministry, sinks in a flood of individualism manifesting itself in consent to majority rule and a structuring of the church based on a false

---

[16]Cf. Simojoki, Section 4 (p. 131).

[17]F. D. E. Schleiermacher, *Der christliche Glaube nach den Grundsätzen der evangelischn Kirche im Zusammenhange dargestellt (1821/22)*, (Berlin: Walter de Gruyter, 1980), SS28. This is, in fact, the defining difference between the Protestant faith and Roman-Catholic faith, namely that of an immediate vs. a mediate relationship with God.

[18]J. W. F. Höfling, *Grundsätze evangelisch-lutherischer Kirchenverfassung* (Bläsing, 1850), 2ff. (SS3).

[19]Simojoki, Section 5 (p. 132): "The Copernican turn in European philosophy concerning epistemological theorie.s'.

[20]In the way of katabatic gifts.

[21]In the way of anabatic struggle.

[22]Cf. Simojoki, Section 4, (p. 130): "...increase the pontifical powers ...."

ecclesiological premise.[23] In 75 percent of the sermons I hear when visiting parishes of the Lutheran Church—Missouri Synod, for example, the letter of the Word is simply a point of departure; the text is a pretext. And if what follows is a *tour de force*, which it often is not, then it is because the man has a 'charismatic'[24] personality. The congregationalism is so pervasive that it is often only the charismatic force of the pastor as individual among individuals that keeps him from being dismissed by them; as according to Schleiermacher, men "equipped with wonderful gifts" must "prove themselves ambassadors of God".[25]

As we consider the challenge and danger of modern enthusiasm we cannot well afford to ignore its ecclesiological and ecclesial dimensions. Thus, in closing, I would like to pose a few questions. First, if an "inherent atheism" truly caused F. C. Baur to give "no space …to God's actions in history",[26] are Lutherans post-New Testament atheists? In other words, do we cease to see anything identifiable as God acting in history after the date of the last books of the New Testament canon? If not, can we then identify "forms of religious life and structures" not "designed solely by human spirit and man's profundity",[27] but identifiable as part of the Holy Trinity's ongoing work in history? Secondly, is it possible for ecclesiology, right down to its forms and structures to be intentionally theological, as opposed to being flippantly dismissed via the misunderstood Lutheran bench mark 'adiaphora', and so left to the judgement of human reason, popular pragmatism, and expediency? And finally, if it is possible with J. G. Hamann to articulate the condescention of God as Author,[28] is it possible to articulate with Luther Christ's continued condescension as minister?

---

[23] Cf. Simojoki, Section 3 (p. 126): "Enthusiams was sinking under the flood of human religiousness … the Keys … ."

[24] 'This appellation, at least among American Lutherans, is not a sign for caution, but a tag of praise.

[25] Cited by Simojoki, Section 5 (p. 135). Cf. 2 Cor 5:20 and n7 above.

[26] Simojoki, Section 5 (p. 136).

[27] Cf. Simojoki, Section 4 (p. 130).

[28] Cf. Simojoki, Section 6 (p. 132).

Part VI
Biblicism

Chapter 11

Biblicism and the Imminent Death of American Evangelicalism

Rev. Dr. John Bombaro

Biblicism seems alive and well in the United States. Virtually any survey of the top selling books among American Christian bookstores or online distributors will reveal not content-rich theological or exegetical tomes by credentialed peer-reviewed experts, but rather the blockbuster fare of theologically gaunt biblicist authors.[1] It is not just books either; biblicism dominates Christian radio programming, television broadcasting, the blogosphere and the megachurch movement, too.[2] But do not be deceived by the full parking lots at The Rock Church in San Diego or the national syndication of Harold Camping's "Family Radio" programming. The prognosis for evangelical biblicism is terminal.

Biblicism is a particular approach to reading, interpreting and using the Bible by the overwhelming majority of evangelical traditions, particularly within the United States. It is the same spectrum of evangelicals, who believe that the Bible is a divine word of truth that should function as an authority for Christian faith and practice,

[1] Consider, e.g., the monthly updates of the Best-Seller Lists (BSLs) on The Christian Booksellers Association (CBA) website: http://www.cbaonline.org/nm/BSLs.htm.

[2] Fully 48 of the 50 largest churches in America, in terms of weekly attendance, are biblicist congregations led by evangelical biblicist pastors (http://www.sermoncentral.com/articleb.asp?article= Top-100-Largest-Churches). For a delineation of top Christian radio programmes, see http://www. hearchristianradio.com/popular-radio-stations/; or for podcasts see, http://christianity.about.com/od/christianbooksmovies/tp/christpodcasts.htm.

and who want to espouse a coherent position that justifies and defends that belief, that are charting a course of imminent death for their own interpretative tradition, indeed, for evangelicalism itself. American "biblicism", I contend, is an indefensible position that has, in our present cultural climate, fatal implications for gospel presentation and the viability of evangelicalism's future. Biblicism spells death to contemporary gospel proclamation, while at the same time inducing its own death.

The death of biblicist evangelicalism, however, shall not come at its own hand; though there is an undeniable sense in which it is self asphyxiating. Instead, it shall be die by the hand of another—secular society. Consequently, "biblicism" should not be thought of as evangelical slouching towards suicide but rather the malfunctioning weapon with which American evangelicals have charged into battle against a superiorly armed and malcontent foe who is eager to slay them. Biblicism is not so much killing evangelicalism as the reason that it will be killed, and that perhaps within my lifetime and yours.

It is because of this imminent death of evangelicalism that a clarion call to our respective Lutheran bodies in general and all confessional Lutheran priests in particular must be issued. A summon to action needs to be made because a disconcerting representation of confessional Lutherans have been courting a date with the proverbial Grim Reaper. Within the Lutheran Church—Missouri Synod (LCMS) and the Wisconsin Evangelical Lutheran Synod (WELS), to say nothing of independent Lutheran churches, there persists a legion of ideological biblicists who, in certain circles, mandate functional allegiance to the principles and practices of evangelical biblicism. These same Lutheran must distance themselves from biblicist commitments and neo-evangelical tendencies that persist within our Lutheran communions lest our collective gospel witness suffer the same consequences as the inevitable trajectory of evangelical fundamentalism—death-like marginalization.

What this paper will not do is call into question the divine authority of Holy Scripture or the Bible as uniquely θεόπνευστος (2 Tim 3:16) or, indeed, its *sola Scriptura* standing within the Church catholic. These are non-negotiable articles for confessional Lutherans, substantiated by the facts of canonicity.[3] What this paper will do is identify biblicism as untenable and, increasingly to the mind of secular Americans and undoubtedly Europeans, dangerous. And as a dangerous proposition, its days are numbered. Thus, confessional Lutheranism has been issued notice: to the degree that those within her ranks tether themselves to biblicism is the degree to which Lutheranism courts ruination.

---

[3] The facts of canonicity are rehearsed and defended in Michael J. Kruger, *Canon Revisited: Establishing the Origins and Authority of the New Testament Books* (Wheaton: Crossway, 2012).

But do not think that the only viable alternative to biblicism necessitates embracing theological liberalism.[4] It does not. Circumstances are different today. The choice is not between Bultmann or Sasse, much less St. Louis or Seminex. Theological liberalism, ingesting its own course of hemlock, has proven itself to be terminally unfaithful and equally dangerous to the gospel as biblicism. Statistics evidencing the systemic, decades-long abandonment of liberal mainline Protestantism, including the Evangelical Lutheran Church of America (ELCA), are irrefutable. Attrition or, better, anorexia has set in. Mainline liberalism is withering to death. No, theological liberalism is not and cannot be an alternative much less the only one.[5]

Rather, a faithful and obedient tradition of interpretation is one that submits to the Scripture's in-built hermeneutical principles presented to us by none other than Christ himself,[6] such that are safeguarded and substantiated by multiple extra-biblical sources of corroborating authority (for example, the liturgy, creeds, and consensual patristic commentary on Scripture *and* the much-neglected oral tradition known as the "canon of truth" or the "rule of faith"). As the all-authoritative and regal Word of God, Jesus Christ invests the eventually inscripturated words of God— the message of the new covenant gospel itself—with an authority derived from himself because they immediately pertain to himself, recalling of course that "*all authority* in heaven and earth" had been given to him (Matt. 28:18). The King is the authority and we must leave the interpretive principles to be what he has disclosed.[7] And there begins the narrowing of the field of interpretation. Christ's divine authority establishes the authority of Scripture within its purposed domain. But there is more. Scripture's authority is corroborated, substantiated and buttressed by several other extra-biblical but by no means unbiblical sources of gospel authority. Together, Christ's in-built scriptural hermeneutics and Christianity's extrabiblical authorities comprise the classic consensual interpretation of Scripture that distinguishes orthodoxy from heterodoxy and heresy.

---

[4]Christian Smith, *The Bible Made Impossible: Why Biblicism Is Not a truly Evangelical Reading of Scripture* (Grand Rapids: Brazos Press, 2011), ix.

[5]To be sure, swathes of evangelicalism already have morphed into forms of theological liberalism. See, *e.g.*, Michael Horton, *Christless Christianity: The Alternative Gospel of the American Church* (Grand Rapids: Baker Books, 2008); Thomas Oden, *The Rebirth of Orthodoxy: Signs of New Life in Christianity* (New York: Harper San Francisco, 2003); and David F. Wells, *No Place For Truth: Or Whatever Happened to Evangelical Theology* (Grand Rapids: Eerdmans, 1993).

[6]See for example, Luke 24:44f, where Jesus sets himself as the reading horizon for the Hebrew Bible. The writers of the New Testament epistles consciously understood their work as expounders of the Jesus hermeneutic: Hence, the christocentric self-disclosed commitments found in, *e.g.*, Hebrews 1 and 2, Romans, 1 Peter, etc.

[7]Cf. Luther, *Luther's Works, Word and Sacrament* IV, 38:38.

This harnessed, orthodox, christocentric interpretation of Scripture and understanding of its authority *is* the inheritance of Lutheranism. Biblicism is out of bounds.
All things considered, the interpretative horizon is, as it were, already set for Lutherans in the classic consensual interpretation of Scripture according to the Christocentric tradition again, such that is found in the ancient λειτουργία, creeds, and
commentaries, but especially in the "rule of faith" or "canon of truth".[8] Lutherans understand this to be so and testify to the same with the Book of Concord.
To stray into theological liberalism (with its tenuous and selective commitment to
confessional standards) or biblicism prognosticates the same death for evangelical-
catholicism (*i.e.*, Lutheranism) as it does for American evangelicalism.

Historian Mark Noll once pleaded with Lutherans to rise up and forge the future (rescue) of evangelicalism.[9] That future begins with the abandonment and repudiation of biblicism, coupled with embracing the creedal, confessional, liturgical,
patristic and council authorities of the Church catholic. Only then can evangelicalism be authentically evangelical or, which is to say the same thing, at home in the
conservative, confessional Reformation. Until that happens, confessional Lutherans should heed to quarantine. Unfortunately, America's evangelical-catholics more
readily mimic the evangelical than underscore their catholicity.

1   Biblicism Defined

In *The Bible Made Impossible*, University of Notre Dame sociologist Christian Smith
defines biblicism as a theory about the Bible that "emphasizes together its exclusive
authority, infallibility, perspicuity, self-sufficiency, internal consistency, self-evident
meaning, and universal applicability".[10] Greater emphasis falls on differing vari-
ations of combinations of the aforementioned within various biblicist communities,
for not all manifestations of biblicism are equal. Nevertheless, all together they form
"a constellation of assumptions and beliefs", now entrenched as a subculture, that
define a particular theory and practice of Bible interpretation, use, and application.

American evangelicalism's plausibility structure may possess a motley of traits
ranging from rapturist theology to literal seven-day creation, but all such traits—
both uniting and dividing literally evangelical denominations and associations—

---

[8] *I.e.*, the oral tradition of the gospel that persisted as *the* authoritative word of Jesus the Christ
throughout the period that preceded New Testament composition and recognition of its canonicity.

[9] Noll, "The Lutheran Difference", *First Things* 20 (Feb 1992): 31-40.

[10] Smith, *The Bible Made Impossible: Why Biblicism Is Not a Truly Evangelical Reading of Scripture*
(Grand Rapids: Brazos Press, 2011), viii.

emerge directly from the categorical biblicism to which all evangelicals must adhere as the emblem of orthodoxy.

Smith does a service by articulating ten distinctive features of biblicism that are held as assumptions or beliefs about the Bible's nature, purpose, and function. Though some have demurred that some of these characteristics are debatable,[11] there seems to be a certain consensus even among Smith's detractors that he has rightly identified biblicism by the following ten features:

1. Divine Writing: The Bible, down to the details of its words, consists of and is identical with God's very own words written inerrantly in human language.

2. Total Representation: The Bible represents the totality of God's communication to and will for humanity, both in containing all that God has to say to humans and in being the exclusive mode of God's true communication.

3. Complete Coverage: The divine will about all of the issues relevant to Christian belief and life are contained in the Bible.

4. Democratic Perspicuity: Any reasonably intelligent person can read the Bible in his or her own language and correctly understand the plain meaning of the text.

5. Commonsense Hermeneutics: The best way to understand biblical texts is by reading them in their explicit, plain, most obvious, literal sense, as the author intended them at face value, which may or may not involve taking into account their literary, cultural, and historical contexts.

6. Solo Scripture: The significance of any given biblical text can be understood without reliance on creeds, confessions, historical church traditions, or other forms of larger theological hermeneutical frameworks, such that theological formulations can be built up directly out of the Bible from scratch.

7. Internal Harmony: All related passages of the Bible on any given subject fit together almost like puzzle pieces into single, unified, internally consistent bodies of instruction about right and wrong beliefs and behaviours.

---

[11] See the negative reviews of *The Bible Made Impossible* by Kevin DeYoung, http://thegospelcoalition.org/blogs/kevindeyoung/2011/09/01/those-tricksy-biblicists/; Peter J. Leithart, http://www.firstthings.com/onthesquare/2011/08/a-cheer-and-a-half-for-biblicism; and Robert Gundry, http://www.booksandculture.com/articles/2011/sepoct/smithreens.html.

8. Universal applicability: What the biblical authors taught God's people at any point in history remains universally valid for all Christians at every other time, unless explicitly revoked by subsequent Scriptural teaching.

9. Inductive Method: All matters of Christian belief and practice can be learned by sitting down with the Bible and piecing together through careful study the clear "biblical" truths that it teaches.

10. Handbook Model: The Bible teaches doctrine and morals with every affirmation that it makes, so that together those affirmations comprise something like a handbook or textbook for Christian belief and living, a compendium of divine and therefore inerrant teachings on a full array of subjects–including science, economics, health, politics, and romance.[12]

These distinctive features constitute the particular theory about and style of use of the Bible by biblicists, again with greater or lesser emphases falling on certain traits, which themselves may be more accurately honed by nuance. Still, it is the characteristics delineated above that render the Bible, in Smith's appraisement, "an impossible book", strangling and perverting the potency of its authority, and making it do too much in terms of over-application and at the same time not nearly enough when it comes to God's performative speech-acts and attestation to Christ himself. *That* assertion can hardly be denied.

Biblicism, as described above, is manifest at all levels of evangelical commitments to the same—popular, institutional, and scholarly. Despite the caveats of Smith's most vocal critics (incidentally, all evangelicals) biblicism pervades evangelicalism in such a way that can only be described as an entrenchment plausibility structure.

Popularly, one encounters cliché biblicism in bumper-sticker, window decal, and T-shirt aphorisms such as "God said it, I believe it, that settles it!" and "BIBLE— Basic Instruction Before Leaving Earth". It is the biblicist sort of pop-Christianity that is the object of pop cultural caricaturing and lampooning on *The Family Guy*, *The Simpsons*, *South Park*, *Futurama*, and YouTube. Good examples of pop-culture targeting biblicist subcultural holdings are found on the trendy website *thethinkingatheist.com*, particularly under the heading "Refuting the Bible", where biblicist doctrines are summarily stated then thoroughly decimated. The irony here is that The Thinking Atheist usually attacks the biblicist on biblicist grounds. The effect,

---

[12]Smith, *The Bible Made Impossible*, 4–5.

however, is the same. American biblicists are thought to be representative of all biblical traditions, including confessional Lutherans. How much more so when Lutherans parrot the same biblicist doctrines, including literal six-day creation, young earth geology, and the spontaneous generation of species, to say nothing of legislating evangelical morality and Republicanism? A "biblical" Christian has become in popular thought and depiction culturally synonymous with idiocy and fanaticism, retarding the intellectual and moral progress of humanity which, of course, is dangerous to an enlightened society.

Institutional biblicism may be found within the code of conduct communiques of evangelical institutions of higher education. One need only consider the student handbooks and pithy statements of faith (as opposed to a *confession* of faith) of learning centers such as Bob Jones University, Moody Bible Institute, Oral Roberts University, Columbia International University, Pensacola Christian College, Multnomah University, Liberty University, and Bethel College, to name just a few. These institutions represent communities that reinforce biblicist interpretative principles with biblicist interpretative consequences spilling into the realms of moral codification, vocational expectation, and even dating.

Scholarly representation reaches back to the Great Awakening and, more recently, the likes of Princeton Theological Seminary's Charles Hodge. The most comprehensive articulation and defense of biblicist holdings, of course, comes from the pen of Hodge's Princeton colleague, B.B. Warfield, within the pages of his treatise, *The Inspiration and Authority of the Bible.*[13] It would be Warfield, not Hodge, who contributed the volume concerning the nature, purpose and function of Holy Scripture in *The Fundamentals* series. These writings, which consolidated a whole course of biblicist convictions and gave intellectual expression in the fundamentalist/liberal controversy, formed a readily identifiable subculture that has persisted to this day in the works of J.I. Packer and John Stott and through the likes of such pop Christian icons as Billy Graham and Joel Osteen.

Biblicism also pervades the evangelical publishing industry under the imprints of Thomas Nelson, Harvest House, NavPress, InterVarsity Press, Crossway, Zondervan and others through publications frequently devoid of the Bible's self-disclosed authorial intention, viz. "These things were written so that you may believe that Jesus is the Christ, the Son of God" (John 20:31). Instead, many of their books posit divinely authoritative answers on any topic upon which the inspired, infallible and inerrant Bible touches, ranging from economics and medicine to the physical sci-

---

[13] Benjamin Breckenridge Warfield, *The Inspiration and Authority of the Bible*, ed. Samuel Craig (1894; repr., Philadelphia: P&R, 1948).

ences and politics. If the subjects of geography or geology or the antiquity of the earth and cosmos are broached, then God has spoken and that word is final, the findings of physicists, geologists, evolutionary geneticist, mathematicians, and scientists notwithstanding. If politics or economics are broached, then those eternal words from God are all-availing and always applicable, having been mined through the inductive Bible study method.

Outside of biblicist subcultures, such posturing of the Bible's ability to speak definitively on all subjects is viewed as absurd and patently false. In popular culture and academia, the wrongness of the Bible's statements on the age of Earth easily carry over to the wrongness of its statements on the fallenness of humanity and necessity of salvation, which repudiations themselves have a pedigree in the Enlightenment. A global deluge or a resurrected corpse are tantamount to the same thing—preposterous religious fabrications dogmatically asserted by religious fundamentalists. And, as everyone knows in today's post-9/11 milieu, fundamentalists are dangerous to normative (secular) society. Compounded by the scandal of Christian particularism and Augustinianism's pessimistic anthropology, the dictum of Frederick Nietzsche seems to obtain: "Convictions are more dangerous enemies of the truth than lies." Enemies of the populace, of course, must be sequestered if not eliminated, especially when such repellent and bigoted religious content indoctrinates otherwise innocent children.

2   Epistemological Foundationalism

Evangelical literalism is an interpretative tradition that is a species of belief tradition in relationship to a text, though not a tradition bound to any restraining source of authority other than that internal to and perpetuated by biblicist culture and the final arbiter of truthful interpretation—the individual.[14] In other words, biblicism is a habitualized subcultural mandate pertaining to a particular style of thinking and believing in relation to the Bible that precludes all sources of authority save for that of the individual-as-interpreter. The same individual-interpreter may, while speaking authoritatively over Scripture as to what is the truth of Scripture, claim the authority of the Bible's "say so". That very traceable pattern of habit, that relationship to the text (in whatever given biblicist community), has established a motley collection of sub-cultures which have entrenched how evangelicals as a whole "know what the Bible says" and therefore "how now we shall live". Knowing how the Bible is to be

---

[14]See Brain Malley, *How the Bible Works: An Anthropological Study of Evangelical Biblicism* (Walnut Creek, CA: Altamira Press, 2004).

read, knowing what the Bible says, and knowing the implications of that reading are issues the emerge directly from epistemological considerations.

When the Reformers trumped papal authority with the Bible as the final or ultimate rule on matters of Christian doctrine a new trajectory was set. Ongoing Protestant disputations with the Church of Rome forged a source of authority on an entirely different plane than papal supremacy or, later, infallible *ex cathedra* utterances. The doctrine of biblical inspiration was buttressed by characteristics that made the Bible "perfect as your heavenly Father is perfect" down to every jot and tittle. The result was a kind of divinization of the biblical texts, the ascription of attributes which nearly rivalled the attributes of the Almighty. If the pope or Fathers or councils or creeds spoke with authority, the Scriptures spoke with an authority that negated them to the point of irrelevance and, in many cases, made these previously established forms of authority the enemies of Bible-believing Christians.[15] Confessional American Lutherans, so far from recoiling from such a notion, historically aligned themselves with the Reformed on this point, lest they too be branded enemies of *sola Scriptura* or, virtually synonymously, of God.

This trajectory was undergirded by the Enlightenment quest for the foundation of knowing. Epistemological foundationalism is a conviction that, in the words of Christian Smith, "rational human beings can and must identify a common foundation of knowledge directly up from and upon which every reasonable thinker can and ought to build a body of completely reliable knowledge and understanding".[16] Once discovered (as opposed to achieved), it would naturally withstand all challenges by competing philosophies and, of course, would be ratified by legitimate science. Once secured, "the resultant knowledge that will be built from and upon it will be for all rational people absolutely certain, completely truthful, and universally binding".[17] Thus the modern epistemological foundationalist endeavour promised and pursued the kind of certainty, universality, and security long desired by humanity and such that was requisite for the ushering in of a utopian society.

Enlightenment philosophers pursued various streams of empiricism or rationalism in the hope of achieving the afore-mentioned goal. But both the Cartesian and the British empiricist schools failed. The entire epistemological foundationalist endeavour collapsed, in large part thanks to David Hume, and has been abandoned—except by one party. Evangelicalism appears to have bought the foundationalist

---

[15] Philip Jenkins, *The New Anti-Catholicism: The Last Acceptable Prejudice* (New York: Oxford University Press, 2003), 25–27.
[16] Smith, *The Bible Made Impossible*, 150.
[17] *Ibid.*

farm. Instead of pursing paths of Cartesian certainty or British *a posteriori*, much less Kantian intuitionism or any of the "neo" manifestations of post-Kantianism, evangelicalism opted for a divine epistemological foundation—the omnisapient, omniscient God's inscripturated word. Whether it was in hope of an American Christian utopia that would serve as "the light upon the hill" or not, *sola Scriptura* took on a startlingly new connotation. It was the *only* infallible, inerrant, self-sufficient, guaranteed, all authoritative source of knowledge. It was a matter of epistemological fact: eternal revelation trumps all other means of spatio-temporal knowing. It was the perfect word from the Perfect One: certain knowledge straight from the horse's mouth. And, as such, it was capable of withstanding any and all challenges based on its plenary inspiration and source of authority. Smith reflects upon this development:

> Without realizing it, evangelicals embraced as view of scripture that was more driven by Cartesian and generally modern preoccupations with epistemic certainty than by scripture itself and a long Christian tradition of Scriptural interpretation. A clearly modern standard that was derived independent of and indeed against scripture—the modern philosophy of epistemological foundation-alism—came to be the legitimizing basis upon which the authority of scripture was championed.[18]

Antedating the *Mediations* by just three years, the opening article in the 1638 *Westminster Confession of Faith*, "Of Holy Scripture", evidences incipient evangelical theologizing predicated upon the Bible's epistemic foundation. The final and comprehensive revelation of God was not Jesus Christ but the Old and New Testaments. Articles on God and Christ *followed* the article on Scripture. It was a new way of doing theology—the evangelical way—and it started with its epistemological foundation. The metanarrative, grounded in jurisprudence-like testimony and witness about real phenomenological events, became a secondary consideration. For the Calvinist, Westminster signalled an important advancement towards the development of biblicism and away from the theology of the 1576 *Heidelberg Catechism*. The Bible was the foundation and thus possessed all authority on matters of faith and life. The Bible was the way, the truth, and the life. The Bible brought salvation. The proceeding to God was through Scripture and Scripture alone because Christ

---

[18] *Ibid.*, 151.

could only be found and only spoke in Scripture. The "book of nature" was now understood to be mostly typological.[19] Plato would have been proud.

Salvation, however, was only the tip of the iceberg. The utilization of another Enlightenment method, the analytical method, by which biblicists atomized Scripture into proof-texts to substantiate a given topic and thus have God speak authoritatively and irrefutably on it, revolutionized biblical applicability. Now the antiquity of humanity, the age of the earth, calculations of the imminent return of Christ, political theory, and even business principles could be extrapolated from the pages of Scripture, thus revealing the Almighty's timeless, universal mind and will on such subjects. The narrative was lost to a topical reading of Scripture.[20] The Bible morphed into a tetragrammaton—the queen of the sciences—and would remain so within emergent biblicist communities, even in the face of scientific discovery from the Enlightenment through the present day.

Thus, the motive to use biblicism to domesticate and control Scripture to speak authoritatively on any and every given topic comes directly from a modern outlook, from modernity and the Enlightenment. Since then, post-modern thinkers have summarily critiqued and condemned modernity and the Enlightenment's epistemological foundationalist project as arrogant and naïve, but also culturally imperialistic and dogmatic or, which is to say the same thing, dangerous to society. Erstwhile, biblicists engage today's culture with a self-divinizing epistemological anachronism that *de facto* marginalizes, indeed, as an anachronism possessed of all the worst traits of modernity. Any group of Christians that hitch their missional wagon to the biblicist horse is not playing the part of the martyr in contemporary society but rather the moron.

In sum, biblicism has become a blight on the American intellectual scene through (1) its massive misapplication of Scripture to speak infallibly and with ultimate divine authority upon any topic found within its pages; (2) its flattening the topography of the Bible's self-disclosed authorial intention; (3) its brazen challenge to the established findings of science and astrophysics, to name but two disciplines; and (4) last but not least, its self-defeating presuppositional circular-reasoning of biblical inerrancy and infallibility. Fifty years ago, churches were bulging and springing up like

---

[19]See, *e.g.*, T. H. Davis, 'The Traditions of Puritan Typology', in S. Bercovitch (ed.),*Typology and Early American Literature*(Amherst: University of Massachusetts, 1972), 37f., and L. Knight, 'Learning the Language of God: Jonathan Edwards and the Typology of Nature,' *William & Mary Quarterly* 48 (1991): 531–51.

[20]N. T. Wright, *Scripture and the Authority of God: How to Read the Bible Today* (San Francisco: HarperOne, 2011), 23-24.

mushrooms throughout suburbia. Today, the situation is reversed. The American mood is quite different, especially among the generations that followed the baby-boomers. Few are listening. And when they do listen, the likes of Westboro Baptist Church show them where unchecked biblicism may lead and they are scandalized, not by the gospel but by biblicism itself. It is little wonder, then, that biblicism has become the twentieth-century's version of the Galileo affair.

Two other events are significant and can be mentioned only in passing. The first is the nineteenth century Vatican I pronouncement of papal infallibility. The evangelical tradition famously responded with fundamentalism. Warfield joined the fray and took the biblicist definition to a new level of fortification. However, thanks to the emergence of the German higher critical movement within the United States, the conversation quickly morphed into the "liberalism v. Orthodoxy" debate of J. Gresham Machen fame.[21] Conservatives now view Warfield–Machen–Packer as the lineage of evangelical orthodoxy concerning the doctrine of Scripture. To deviate either to the left or right equates with apostate liberalism or heretical Roman Catholicism.

The second event was the momentous new paradigm introduced by Darwinianism. Again, the answer to natural selection and a long, slow macroevolutionary process was clear and easy for the biblicist—literal 6 day creation. Worldviews were now set in perpetual conflict. The scientific community—armed with the empirical, analytical method and gravitating towards physicalism—confirmed the noumenal/phenomenal divide. Biblicists, despite archeological, geographical and historiographical confirmations, were being more and more marginalized as anti-intellectual, detached from the megashift in scientific and technological plausibility structures, and combatant. Academia discontinued the conversation, while secularization continued afoot. Biblicists, no longer invited or welcome to the table of discourse or, increasingly, the public marketplace of ideas, retreated into insular Bible conference and Bible college movements. The wider culture was forming a hermeneutic of suspicion. It would take another 75 years for evangelicals to be welcome back to the marketplace of ideas for discussion with contemporary culture but that invitation came with a price, namely giving consumerist culture what they want from religion with their own methods. When "the world sets the agenda for the church"[22] Lutherans can be confident the gospel mandate will be fatally compromised and with it the raison d'etre for Lutheranism.

---

[21] Machen, *Christianity & Liberalism* (Grand Rapids: Eerdmans, 1923).

[22] This was the official slogan of the 1968 World Council of Churches conference, Uppsala, Sweden.

3   Solo Scriptura

Luther taught *sola Scriptura*, meaning that the Bible, although not the only source of truth, is the final authority over the church's other sources of authority: tradition, councils, creeds, patristic writings, liturgy, reason and experience. Scripture is the ultimate authority where other acknowledged sources of authority must yield and, on occasion, be determined or corrected. But teaching about the Bible as the "sole source" and "sole rule" is a departure from the Lutheran principle *sola Scriptura*.

Calvin took a giant step towards biblicism with the "regulative principle": the Bible explicitly laying down the prescriptions and proscriptions of Christian worship. In liturgics as well as theology, *sola Scriptura* came to mean that true Christian doctrine contains nothing which is not grounded in the Bible and the Bible alone. Though not grammatically correct in Latin, the idea of *solo Scriptura* obtained. *Solo Scriptura* says there is no religious authority which men must obey but that of the biblical word. But the Scriptures understood this way would mean that modern understandings of cosmic origins, genetics, psychology, the physical sciences, medicine, history, etc., are overruled and deemed irrelevant to faith by the Bible's purported understanding of the aforementioned. Such a view essentially forecloses on all intelligent discussion on issues which are, or seem to be, treated in the Bible.

If the Reformation principle *sola Scriptura* was a steadfast anchor for the Reformers, then its misuse or rather purposed perversion through extreme expressions of fundamentalist loyalty to the text of the Bible, verbal plenary all-authoritative inspiration, and inerrancy, has become a crippling intellectual impediment to proclaiming the gospel, and it does so in this way: When the natural, historical and theologically legitimate boundary providing extra-biblical means of authority are eliminated and the Bible is touted and used as the *only* means of authority (true to foundationalist principles) and issues of geography, marriage, geology, economics, politics, and matters secular are elevated to the same level as that of the metanarrative of Scripture, as that of grace, faith and the gospel, then the material authority of the Word in the Bible is undermined. The gospel is relevantized and trivialized when set on equal authoritative footing as biblical business principles. The Good Book is just full of good advice, one bit of which is somehow the gospel and since everyone is entitled to offer their good advice and even conflate it with good news, it is no wonder that the United States alone has more than 33,850 denominations. Christianity in America has become synonymous with biblical relativism and therefore irrelevance. The gospel message has been embarrassingly squelched by ten of thousands of interpretations, all equally authoritative, all standing on equal authority.

It is beyond the purview of the gospel, let alone the Bible, that trusting Christ as the world's rightful king should entail equal faith in every single word in the Bible, including its statements about medicine, clothing, science and the calculated date of Christ's return. Biblicism's characteristics as all-authoritative, sufficient, infallible, inerrant and wholly inspired are a massive and unavoidable obstacle to the ability to proclaim the gospel today not just for American biblicists but for confessional Lutherans. With the death of the evangelicalism's gospel message comes the death of the evangelicalism's voice and the death of the evangelicalism itself. It is this spiral of death, I contend, that has enveloped no small portion of confessional American Lutheranism.

One need look no further than the landmark 1978 "Chicago Statement on Biblical Inerrancy", signed by more than three hundred notable evangelical scholars and diplomats, including leading Lutherans, for evidence of ideological commitments to biblicism within contemporary confessional Lutheranism. The Statement itself is categorically biblicist:

> Holy Scripture, being God's own Word, written by men prepared and superintended by His Spirit, is of infallible divine authority *in all matters upon which it touches* [1]: it is to be believed, as God's instruction, in all that it affirms [and] obeyed, as God's command, in all that it requires ... Being wholly and verbally God-given, Scripture is without error or fault in all its teachings, *no less in what it states about God's acts in creation, about the events of world history, and about its own literary origins under God, than in its witness to God's saving grace in individual lives.*[23]

This statement is not representative of historic Lutheran dogmatics on bibliology. It is out of bounds. When readers of the Bible have to navigate divine pronouncements on events of world history and matters secular, which are of much more interest in terms of entertainment value to unbelievers, to say nothing of creation science, evolution, egalitarianism and homosexuality, the path to the cross is lost and so too the point of the Church. Not only is the Lutheran distinction between law and gospel conflated within the articles of the Chicago Statement but so is the *theologia crucis* theological method. This is said mindful of the extraordinary circumstances that surrounded the 1970s controversy within the LCMS's St. Louis seminary; circumstances that seemed to necessitate the need for evangelical camaraderie.

---

[23]http://www.bible-researcher.com/chicago1.html. Italics added.

Presbyterians, Baptists, non-denominational types and other evangelicals applauded and welcomed the men who defending Christian orthodoxy within the ranks of the LCMS and invited their input for the crafting of the Chicago Statement. Robert D. Preus and David P. Scaer were two representatives of the Lutheran contingent at the meeting and affixed their signatures to the document. The situation was complicated. After the initial draft of the Statement, Scaer told Preus that he could not sign it without "the christological aspects that should be included in [the doctrine of] inspiration".[24] Preus lobbied for Scaer to draft that portion of the Statement, which he did. It included qualifying statements that put inspiration within the auspices of Christology and the filioque aspect of the Trinity. However, Scaer's christological insertion was omitted en route to the full assembly. Assuming it was there, Scaer did not give the final form of the Statement a close reading and signed the document. In retrospect, he would say, "I [recently] looked at the Chicago Statement and it was worse than I thought … We Should Not Have Signed It. The Chicago Statement appeared in 1978, four years after the Saint Louis situation came to a boil and we are caught in the loving and destructive embrace of Evangelicalism."[25]

But a precedence had been set. By all appearance, LCMS Lutherans took a major step into an evangelical camp that codified its identity with "destructive" biblicism. For a substantial number of Lutherans, who already held evangelical leanings and the Calvinist definition of sacrament (muting or even nullifying Holy Absolution as a sacrament, to say nothing of the Office of Holy Ministry), the Chicago Statement justified their employment of evangelical ministries, theology of worship, outreach methods, and more. Blame cannot be laid at the feet of either Preus or Scaer. Neither are at fault. The exigencies of their overwhelming circumstances indicated that participation in the International Council on Biblical Inerrancy was situationally important, perhaps even necessary. At the same time, it said to evangelicals and Lutherans that disagreement on the efficacy of the sacraments, theological method, and the priesthood were secondary considerations to agreement on the Bible—things that were paramount for the Reformation tradition. However perceived and however conceived, signing the Chicago Statement was a serious concession with far-reaching implications.

Today many Lutheran parishes are liturgically, theologically, and methodologically indistinguishable from evangelical biblicist churches. *Solo Scriptura* allows such parishes to think of all Lutheran distinctives as adiaphora, de-emphasizing all

---

[24] Email correspondence dated 23 August 2012. Reproduced with permission by David P. Scaer.
[25] Email correspondence "To: John Bombaro", dated 21 August 2012. Reproduced with permission by David P. Scaer.

that would tether Lutherans with Catholics and giving every appearance that they are themselves evangelicals.

Significantly, it is also David Scaer who sets the course for corrective Lutheran action: acknowledgement of the destructiveness of evangelical biblicism for Lutheranism and a reversal of any said commitments or concessions. Lutherans, as Professor Scaer teaches, are the Reformation's evangelicals and, so, we have a vested interest in the survival of evangelicalism, but an evangelicalism that is itself repentant of betraying it's first love—Jesus Christ—for an idolatrous affair with the Bible.

4   Problems with Biblicism

The problems with biblicism are legion. By holding that the Bible contains only the word of God (and is the only word of God) and does not possess (mingled with the divine Word) the wisdom, ignorance or prejudices of human authors, such a position requires believers to attribute solely to blessed Trinity, for example, an array or irrational acts, emotions states, prejudices, cruelty and senseless rape that is found in many texts, and to accept them as revelation of God's immutable will and character. Fundamentalism as the defender of supernaturalism has so supernaturalized the Scriptures through biblicist principles as to render them not in any way "of this world" and, consequently, the world does not and cannot relate. We have lost vital points of contact with an unbelieving world.

The authority the Scriptures possess in biblicist circles is of an authoritarian kind, commanding blind faith and obedience. This is so because it is affirmed that they are to be believed not because of what they say, but purely because they say it. The Scriptures are endowed in this view with causative authority, so that in the language of biblicism it is said that the Bible creates faith and obedience; the Scriptures create an assent to the truths believed. This type of language indicates that the distinction between the Holy Spirit, who alone according classic Christianity possesses such creative, regenerative, and illuminating power, and the Holy Scriptures has virtually collapsed.

But of all of biblicism's ills "pervasive plural interpretations"[26] is the most self-damaging. The very same Bible—which biblicists insist is perspicuous and harmonious —gives rise to divergent understandings among intelligent, sincere, committed readers about what it says about most topics of interest, if not all topics whatsoever.

In a crucial sense it simply does not matter, then, whether the Bible is everything that biblicists claim theoretically concerning its authority, infallibility, inner consistency, perspicuity and so on since, as Smith has noted, in actual functioning the

---

[26]Smith, *The Bible Made Impossible*, x.

Bible produces a pluralism of interpretations that fragment the church uncontrollably. This is what happens when the established, ancient extra-biblical sources of authority are precluded, save for one—the sovereign reader. All notions of obedience to creeds, councils, liturgy, and Patristic commentators are ignored so that the individual may interpret the Scripture with authority by appealing to the authority of the Scripture. In this way, biblicism is shorthand for evangelical gnosticism, that which provides epistemic warrant for Christian spirituality however one may define it. Robert K. Johnson succinctly states the issue: "To argue that the Bible is authoritative, but to be unable to come to anything like agreement on what it says (even with those who share an evangelical commitment) is self-defeating."[27] To paraphrase Kevin Vanhoozer: It is one thing to posit the Bible's truthfulness in all that it affirms, quite another thing to say what the truth of the Bible is. Pervasive interpretive pluralism kills the message of Scripture by burying it under innumerable competing messages.

This fact of innumerable irreconcilable interpretations is the stuff of pop cultural mockery and the cornerstone of contemporary indifference to the Bible, the Church, Jesus Christ. North Americans, and it might be safe to say Europeans, hold at the fore of their thought the fact that Christians are wildly and radically divided over what the Bible says and, in the end, are convinced that Christians hear only their own voice in Scripture, the authority of the ego. Bible interpretation is nothing more and nothing less than autobiography. It is an elastic text to them since it is an elastic text to the evangelical. Pervasive interpretive pluralism, the inevitable consequence of biblicism, is a colossal impediment to gospel proclamation because outsiders cannot discern whether there is a meaning to the text, to whom they should listen, and if it really matters. So much so that even evangelicals are no longer reading the Bible and feel they have no need to do so in order to have an authentic Christian spirituality. Consider the following antidote.

At Wheaton Colleen, the Bible and Theology Departments conducted a four-year study of the biblical and theological literacy of incoming freshmen, from 1996-1999. Wheaton, lauded as an "evangelical Harvard", receives perhaps the best of the evangelical world. Students are intellectually ambitious and spiritually passionate, representing nearly every Protestant denomination in America. Professor Gary M. Burge analyzed the findings. The results were antithetical to what one would expect to find within a culture that distinguishes itself from not only the world but even the

---

[27]Johnson, *Evangelicals at an Impasse: Biblical Authority in Practice*(Atlanta: John Knox, 1979), vii–viii.

greater portion of Christianity in its exclusive deference and adherence to biblical authority.

When asked to complete a test in which a series of biblical events must be placed in order, our students returned surprising results. One-third of the freshmen could not put in the following order: Abraham, the Old Testament prophets, the death of Christ, and Pentecost. Half could not sequence: Moses in Egypt, Isaac's birth, Saul's death, and Judah's exile. One-third could not identify Matthew as an apostle from a list of New Testament names. When asked to locate the biblical book supplying a given story, one-third could not find Paul's travels in Acts, half did not know the Christmas story was in Matthew or that the Passover story was in Exodus.[28]

Burge's analysis found that experience or, if you prefer, enthusiasm, was the determining component in their belief apparatus. N.T. Wright treats this subject with considerable attention in *Scripture and the Authority of God*, so I will forego further comment. Experience, one's impression of things spiritual, was sufficient to guide one's Christian life. Following one's heart where there was the "leading of the Spirit" displaced the Word where there already wasn't sacrament. In other words, biblicism negated the confidence of those growing up within the ranks of biblicism because it renders the Bible incoherent and antiquated in the light of modern criticisms. The alternative for these evangelicals was nothing other than subjectivism—personal spirituality defined by the self.

From 2007–2011, a five year period, I conducted the same survey in similar conditions at the University of San Diego, a Roman Catholic university with a greater than 50% representation of non-Church of Rome Christians. The USD results yielded a trajectory indicating that the problem was not confined to evangelicalism but that it had also grown worse.

Of the more than 500 students surveyed, only 19% could rightly order Abraham, the Old Testament prophets, the death of Christ, and Pentecost. Just 12% could sequence: Moses in Egypt, Isaac's birth, Saul's death, and Judah's exile. More than two-thirds could not identify Matthew as an apostle. Staggeringly a full 96% could not find Paul's travels in Acts, and only 10% knew the Christmas story was in Matthew or that the Passover story was in Exodus.

---

[28] Burge, 'The Greatest Story Never Read', *Christianity Today* (Aug 9, 1999), 45–46.

Disclosures from the students, however, indicated that the availing factor in their biblical illiteracy was not ideological but sociological. Students considered the reading of the Bible incompatible with twenty-first century intellectual aspirations. The Bible was associated with "religion" and religion was nothing more than an anthropological phenomenon. Spirituality could not be scrutinized like biblicist beliefs. And after all, both Bible interpretation and personal spirituality individuate. What is more, the final arbiter of truth is the same, too—the individual.

5   Death Blows

None of this has been lost on the new atheists and an ever-expanding agnostic population. Subjectivism in pervasive interpretative pluralism, radical denominational fragmentation, ideological biblicism, and its consequent doctrines about reality that produced the likes of abortion-clinic-bombers, Westboro Baptist Church, tele-evangelist scammers, cults of personality, the Moral Majority, and right wing evangelical political activists, signalled a new agenda. Whereas in the past evangelicals were marginalized as a cultural force and voice, and later treated with antipathy or a subcultural curiosity by gainsayers, mass media, and academia, now evangelicals could be attacked as dangerous to society.

Our hemisphere's prevailing secular culture is beginning to associate biblicist evangelicalism with violent Islamism. My students feel it. Your neighbours feel it. To be a people of the Book is no virtue today but a vice, and perhaps of the worst sort. Fundamentalism as biblicism is stifling authentic Christian witness because it is in fact intellectually untenable, ridiculous, and absurd. Though only at present on the lips of a few, such as Daniel Dennett and Richard Dawkins and Laurence Krauss, it will not be long before evangelical Christianity is widely or universally prohibited within public discourse due to the dangerous potential it carries especially, as these and other outspoken antitheists warn, because it corrupts children by forcing paralyzing and hate-mongering beliefs upon them. As society progresses in its evolutionary development biblicism cannot survive. It must not survive say the antitheists. Biblicists in Canada and the United States are already finding themselves under the sanctions and prohibitions of the state due to alleged hate-speech against protected groups such as homosexuals. This is only the beginning.

Harvard's Robert Putnam has linked the rapid decline of evangelicalism as a culture force to biblicism, asserting further in *American Grace*[29] that guilt by association has meant further decline for the Roman Catholic Church (which has its own set of

---

[29] Robert D. Putnam and David E. Campbell, *American Grace: How Religion Divides and Unites Us* (New York: Simon & Schuster, 2012).

problems) in its anti-homosexual pronouncements and lobbying for a US Constitu-
tional amendment on the definition of marriage, neither of which direct unbelievers
to gospel concerns but rather functions of the law. Both items are perceived to be
dictates emerging from biblicist principles of interpretation. Evangelicals and Roman Catholics have become familiar bed-fellows (no pun intended) with the likes
of Mormons on matters of morality, politics, legislation and economics. Biblicism
is a disease killing evangelicalism and infecting all that associate with it.

In *Bad Religion*,[30] Ross Douthat attributes the change to five major social cata-
lysts that have gained steam since the 1960s: First, the political polarization that has
occurred between the Left and Right drew many churches into it (mainline Protestants towards the Left, evangelicals towards the Right). This has greatly weakened
the church's credibility in the broader culture, with many viewing churches as mere
appendages and pawns of political parties. Secondly, the sexual revolution means
that the Biblical sex ethic now looks unreasonable and perverse to millions of people,
making Christianity appear implausible, unhealthy, and regressive. Thirdly, the era
of decolonization and Third World empowerment, together with the dawn of glob-
alization, has given the impression that Christianity was imperialistically "western"
and supportive of European civilization's record of racism, colonialism, and anti-
Semitism. The fourth factor has been the enormous growth in the kind of material prosperity and consumerism that always works against faith and undermines
Christian community. The fifth factor is that all the other four factors had their
greatest initial impact on the more educated and affluent classes, the gatekeepers
of the main culture-shaping institutions such as the media, the academy, the arts,
the main foundations, and much of the government and business world which is
now reacting against evangelicals by means of mockery, isolation, alienation, and
denunciations as dangerous, brainwashing and potentially violent.

Evangelicalism is dying because of biblicism. It has become terminal in terms
of intellectual respectability. It has become terminal in terms of a viable voice for
societal wisdom. It has lost its audience for the gospel. No one is listening. It has
lost back to back generations and is well on its way to losing any future whatsoever.
Dispensationalism has crumbled and become a byword in pop culture. And in very
short order to be an evangelical will be to be an extremist and there ends the vitality
of evangelicalism: strangled by cultural mandate.

---

[30] Ross Douthat, *Bad Religion: How We Became a Nation of Heretics* (The Free Press, 2012).

6 Lutheran Capitulation

In 1932, the Lutheran Church—Missouri Synod adopted "A Brief Statement of the Doctrinal Position of the Lutheran Church—Missouri Synod". In the section "Of Holy Scriptures"[31] the LCMS maintains the doctrinal position regarding the Bible under four headings:

1. Holds to the verbal plenary inspiration of the Bible;
2. Teaches the inerrancy and infallibility of the Bible;
3. Believes the Bible is the sole source from which and sole rule by which all teachers and doctrines are evaluated;
4. Rejects the idea that the Bible contains "the word of man" which (might contain error) in addition to the word of God.

We cite but just a few lines from this document. The opening lines state, "We teach that the Holy Scriptures differ from all other books in the world in that they are the Word of God. They are the Word of God because holy men of God who wrote only that which the Holy Ghost communicated to them by inspiration ... Since the Holy Scriptures are the Word of God, it goes without saying that they contain no errors or contradictions, but they are in all their parts and words the infallible truth, also in those parts which treat of historical, geographical, and other secular matters."[32]

The comprehensive scope of statements such as these offer little to no distinction from the first article of the Calvinist *Westminster Statement of Faith.* Note that the first article of Westminster does not concern itself with who God is in relation to creation, much less Jesus Christ as the supreme revelation and authority of God, but rather a ponderous seven-section long overstatement on Scripture. For Lutherans to echo the same, asserting that the Bible also contains divine instruction, facts, and wisdom about matters secular including presumably economics, politics, and dating is entirely biblicist and betrays our inherited Christocentric hermeneutic fortified by multiple means of corroborating authorities that substantiate the Bible's authority in witnessing to the truth about God in Christ reconciling Himself to the world. That the proceeding decades of the LCMS were enculturated in evangelical fundamentalism, if not epistemological foundationalism, is betrayed by the assumption that

[31] See http://www.lcms.org/pages/internal.asp?NavID=523.
[32] *Ibid.*

these pronouncements concerning inerrancy and infallibility on any subject upon which the Bible touches "goes without saying".

When the mechanisms of divine speech preserved in the curacy of the divine liturgy, creeds, and so on, are abandoned and exchanged for "just so" biblicist pronouncements and presuppositionalism, then a cultural of evangelicalism is established and with it evangelical commitments to biblicism, and with that the consequences of biblicism.

7   The Lutheran Distinction

In the theology of the Reformation we are faced with two doctrines of the authority of Scripture. For Luther and Melanchthon and their closest pupils the authority of Scripture is grounded in its witness to Christ. The Scripture is to be believed on account of Christ, its essential content and interpretative determiner. The other doctrine of biblicism holds that Scripture is trustworthy because of the philosophical commitments that supposedly prove its divine origin by means of inspiration. Our heritage, our responsibility and accountability is to the former not the latter.

Lutherans both need to distance themselves from all forms of biblicism and, indeed, all forms of bibliolatry less we too suffer the loss of witness due to guilt by association. The traditional Christian view that the basis of Christianity is not a book but the person of Jesus.[33] The important distinction must always be maintained. We bring people to Christ, not to a book. The Bible as the Word of God will always lead us to Christ Jesus as the all-authoritative One, the comprehensive revelation of God, the One who is God with us, the One who is the Lord our Righteousness, our salvation.

8   Conclusion

It is ironic, if not tragic, that such a strong and unwavering view about the Bible itself, which claims to reconcile all possible discrepancies, errors or contradictions in the Bible, in fact leads to a position that cannot reconcile with other Christians, let alone facilitate reconciliation among unbelievers.

The challenges of gospel witness today are exceedingly challenging. Biblicism, however, is about to make it near impossible. Its death is coming. It will either kill itself or be rendered moot by secular society. Either way, this is the day for evangelical catholicism, otherwise known as Lutheranism, to distinguish itself in its gospel witness by a *solus Christus* handling of the word of truth which may, with the help of God, save evangelicalism from itself and itself from evangelicalism.

---

[33] Mark A. Noll, *Scandal of the Evangelical Mind* (Grand Rapids: Eerdmans, 1994), 133.